CALIFORNIA

First Edition
1991

TABLE OF CONTENTS

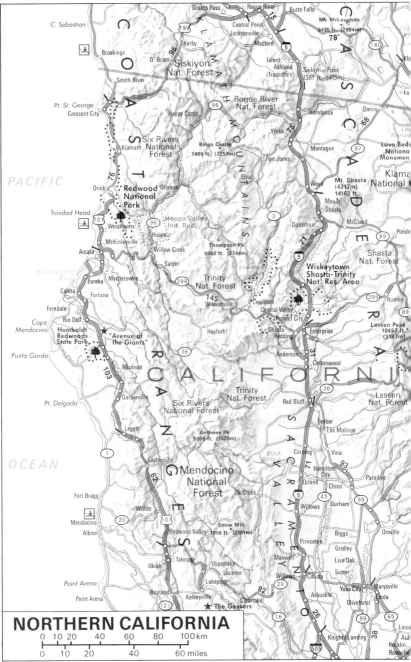

NORTHERN CALIFORNIA

0	10	20	40	60	80	100 km
0		10	20	40		60 miles

LIST OF MAPS

Please note: in some cases the spelling of the place names on the maps is not the same as in the text, because the spelling on the maps is according to UN guidelines, whereas the usual English spelling is used in the text.

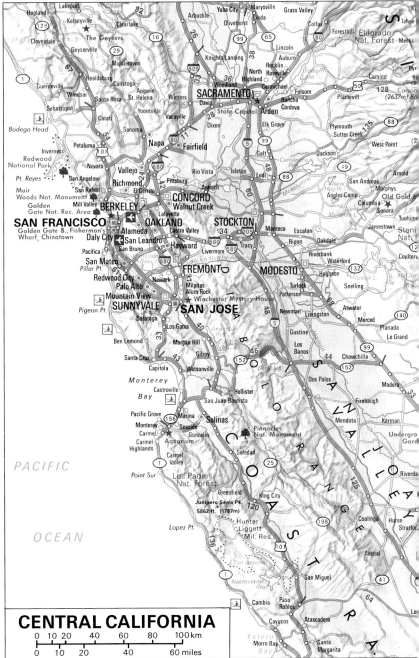

CENTRAL CALIFORNIA

0 10 20   40   60   80   100 km

0   10   20   40   60 miles

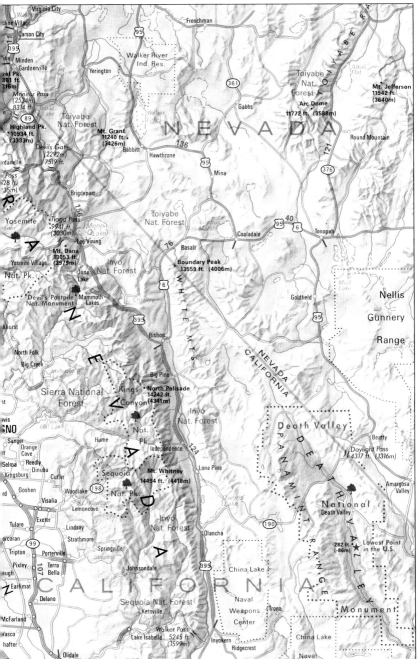

Virginia City

Frenchman

cline Village

Carson City

95

Minden
Gardnerville

Yerington

Walker River
Ind. Res.

Toiyabe
Nat.
Forest

Mt. Jefferson
11942 ft.
(3640m)

el Pk.
88 ft.
316m)

Monitor Pass
(2534m)
8314 ft.

89

Topaz
Lake

361

Gabbs

Arc Dome
11772 ft. (3588m)

Highland Pk.
10934 ft.
(3333m)

Toiyabe
Nat. Forest

Mt. Grant
11240 ft.
(3426m)

N E V A D A

Round Mountain

Devils Gate
(2292m)
7519 ft.

Babbitt

121

ardanelle

Hawthrone

Brigdeport

Pass
28 ft
35m)

Walker
Lake

Mina

95

136

376

R
A

Yosemite

Tioga Pass
9941 ft.
(3030m)

Mono
Lake

Toiyabe
Nat. Forest

Columbus
Salt Marsh

40

95

6

Tonopah

Lee Vining

Basalt

76

Coaladale

Mt. Dana
13053 ft.
(3979m)

Yosemite Village

Inyo
Nat. Forest

June
Lake

Boundary Peak
13559 ft. (4006m)

Nat. Pk.

N

Devil's Postpile
Nat. Monument

Mammoth
Lakes

Crowley

6

Goldfield

Nellis

Mud
Lake

95

khurst

Bishop

W
H
I
T
E

M
T
S

Gunnery

North Folk
Big Creek

E

395

N E V A D A
C A L I F O R N I A

Range

Sierra National
Forest

Big Pine

Kings
Canyon

North Palisade
14242 ft.
(4341m)

V

Death Valley

Beatty

avis

NO

Sanger
Orange
Cove

Hume

Nat.
Pk.

Inyo
Nat. Forest

A

Daylight Pass
4317 ft. (1316m)

Independence

124

Selma Reedly

Dinuba

Cutler

Sequoia

Mt. Whitney
14494 ft. (4418m)

Lone Pine

Amargosa
Valley

Kingsburg

D

P
A
N
A
M
I
N
T

Goshen

Woodlake

198

Nat. Pk.

Owens
Lake

National

Visalia
Lemoncove

Kaweah

A

Death Valley

Tulare

Exeter

Inyo
Nat. Forest

190

orcoran

99

Lindsay

Strathmore

Olancha

-282 ft.
(-86m)

Lowest Point
in the U.S.

Tripton

Porterville

Springville

Success

R
A
N
G
E

Pixley
Terra
Bella

107

China Lake

augh

Earlmat

Delano

Johnsondale

395

Naval
Weapons
Center

Trona

M o n u m e n t

C A L I F O R N I A

McFarland

Sequoia Nat. Forest

Kernville

China Lake

lasco

hafter

Walker Pass
5245 ft
(1599m)

Lake Isabella

Inyokern

Naval

Olidale

Ridgecrest

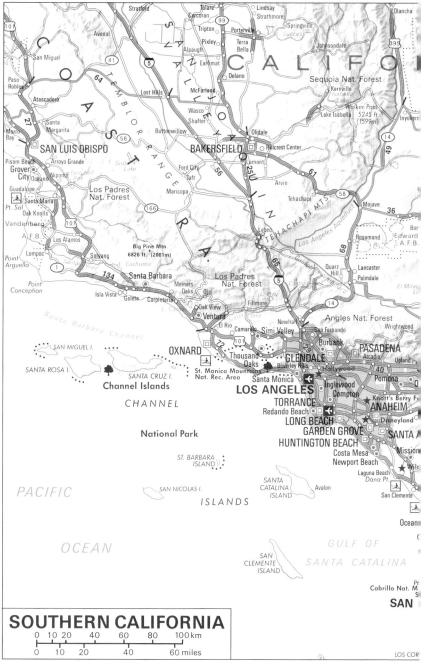

SOUTHERN CALIFORNIA

0 10 20   40   60   80   100km

0   10   20   40   60 miles

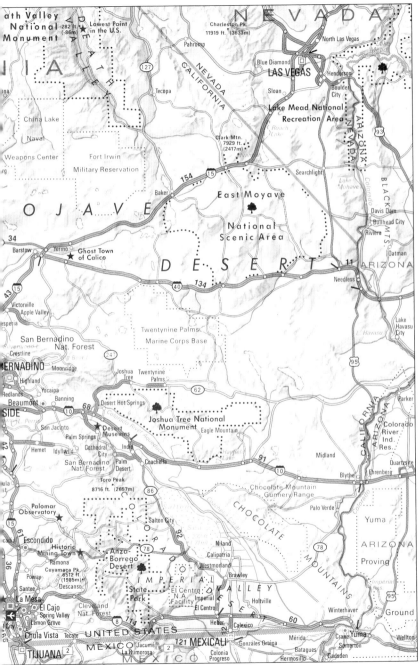

ath Valley
National 282 ft. Lowest Point
(-86m) in the U.S.
Monument

Charleston Pk.
11919 ft. (3633m)

N E V A D A

North Las Vegas

Pahrump

(127)

Blue Diamond

LAS VEGAS

Henderson

Tecopa

Sloan

Boulder
City

Lake Mead National
Recreation Area

China Lake

Naval

Clark Mtn.
7929 ft.
(2417m)

Davis Dam

Weapons Center

Fort Irwin

Military Reservation

Searchlight

Bullhead City

Riviera

154 (15)

Baker

East Moyave

Oatman

O J A V E

National
Scenic Area

A R I Z O N A

34

Barstow Yermo Ghost Town
of Calico

D E S E R T

11

Needless

43 (15)

(40) 134

Victorville
Apple Valley

Lake
Havasu
City

esperia

Twentynine Palms
Marine Corps Base

San Bernadino
Nat. Forest

Crestline

(247)

ERNADINO Moonridge

Highland

Joshua Twentynine
Tree Palms

Yucaipa

(95)

Redlands

Beaumont Banning

Desert Hot Springs

Parker

SIDE (10) 68

Joshua Tree National
Monument

San Jacinto Desert
Museums

Palm Springs

Eagle Mountain

Colorado
River
Ind.
Res.

Hemet Idyllwild Cathedral
City

Indio

San Bernadino
Nat. Forest

Palm
Desert

Coachella

91 (10)

Midland

Quartzsite

Toro Peak
8716 ft. (2657m)

(86)

Blythe Ehrenberg

Palomar
Observatory

Chocolate Mountain
Gunnery Range

Salton City

Palo Verde

Yuma

cadia

(15)

Escondido

Historic
Mining Town

92

Niland

A R I Z O N A

36

Ramona

Cuyamaca Pk.
6512 ft.
(1985m)

Poway

Descanso

Anza-
Borrego
Desert

(78)

Calipatria

Westmorland

Proving

Santee

I M P E R I A L

Brawley

(78)

La Mesa

El Cajo Spring Valley

Cleveland
Nat. Forest

State
Park

El Centro
N.A.
Facility

V A L L E Y

(95)

Lemon Grove

El Centro

Holtville

Winterhaven

Ground

Chula Vista Tecate (8) 174

Heber

Calexico

60

Crane Yuma

TIJUANA 2

Jacume
La Rumorosa

121 MEXICALI

MEXICO 2

Colonia
Progreso

Gonzáles Ortega

Mérida

Bataques

Somerton

Wellton

UNITED STATES

M E X I C O

Hermosillo

Gadsden

11

CALIFORNIA IN MYTH AND HISTORY

California is as much a state of mind as place, as a Missouri newspaper editor noted in the last century. A sense of destiny, of boldly leading the way into the future is as much a part of how the world sees California as of how California sees itself.

And California is a notoriously extravagant place. Reality has never tarnished the legendary luster. The state's population has doubled every 20 years since at least 1848, fueled by the voluntary exodus of Europeans to the United States between 1814 and 1915. A tradition of mobility and opportunity endures today.

California's myth begins with gold – a gift, Americans believed, intended by God for them alone. Spain and Mexico, two of the preeminent mining countries in the world, ruled California for nearly 80 years without finding significant amounts of the precious material. That discovery was made by an American. Their race, their religion, and their superior personal virtues made Americans special – or so the immigrants of 1849 boasted to each other and to the world.

Even the timing of the discovery seemed special. John Marshall stumbled across the precious metal in 1849 just days before Mexico ceded California to the United States. The U.S. paid $18.25 million for California, Nevada, Utah, Arizona, New Mexico, and parts of Texas and Colorado. Within a decade, miners had pulled 30 times that amount from the goldfields of California alone.

Preceding pages: Footsteps to the sun. Training for the Guinness Book of Records. San Francisco, the twinkling city. Yosemite National Park, from the gates of the valley. Left: Gold country church in Angel's Camp.

It did not hurt that as gold yields sagged, silver was discovered just across the border in Nevada, so tightly controlled by San Francisco that California was said to be the only state with four senators. No wonder that California seemed special!

Even climate joined the conspiracy. As gold and silver lost their luster, farmers realized that California is the only part of North America where the rains fall only in the winter. With the help of irrigation, the unique pattern of winter wet and summer drought made California an agricultural powerhouse. Climate was just as important in luring modern industry, including movie and aircraft production.

California has long led the way, in automobiles, in college students, and in tax revolts. It is both the leading agricultural and industrial state, outproducing the rest of the nation in almost every manufacturing category and dozens of agricultural crops from lettuce to marijuana. If California had remained a separate republic, it would rank sixth or seventh in the world in gross national product – not a bad record for a state that was founded on myth, built on fraud, fueled by luck, and tempered by cupidity.

Climate and Geography

The California myth begins with physical features. The state covers 780 miles (1,255 km) north to south, 10 degrees of latitude, nearly the distance from Cape Cod, Massachusetts, to Savannah, Georgia. The corrugated coastline stretches 1,264 miles (2,034 km), much of it scoured by swift cold currents flowing south from Alaska. The broad sandy beaches of popular image are part of Southern California, where golden sands meet indigo seas under dazzling blue skies.

California contains both the highest and the lowest points in the continental United States. Like so much of the state, the two extremes are within driving dis-

tance. Death Valley, 282 feet (86 m) below sea level, is a scant 90 miles (145 km) from Mount Whitney, 14,494 feet (4,418 m) tall.

Boosters call the climate Mediterranean, though the pattern of winter rain and summer drought is more like North Africa than Italy or Greece. Rain, when it comes, falls in torrents, from more than 100 annual inches (254 cm) in the northwest corner to less than 2 inches 50 mm in the southeastern deserts. Redwood forests along the north coast are shrouded in perpetual mists. The shimmering sands between the Imperial Valley and the Colorado River boast some of the highest temperatures ever recorded on earth.

The Coast Range flanks the coastline, cloaked with heavy forests in the north and explosively flammable brush in the south. The Sierra Nevada form the eastern border, rising gently on the western

slopes and dropping precipitously into stark eastern deserts. Between the mountains lies the Central Valley, an oval 400 miles (640 km) long and 50 miles (80 km) wide. North of the Valley is a jumble of peaks fanning out from the Coast Range, south a series of east-west mountains called the Transverse Ranges, linking the Coast Range with the Sierra. The Sierra are blanketed with up to 50 feet (15 m) of winter snow. The melt roars down to the Valley through canyons 2,000 to 5,000 feet (600 m to 1,500 m) deep every spring. Watered by winter rains and spring runoff, the Valley floor becomes a lush green carpet. Under the searing summer sun, it withers to a parched, dusty brown that early real-estate hucksters called golden. But tame the spring runoff for summer irrigation, and the Central Valley bursts with crops.

In the north, the runoff flows through the Sacramento River, in the south through the San Joaquin River. These two streams meet and flow westward, through 1,200 square miles (3,100 square km) of

Above: The Pacific ocean meets the Big Sur coastline. Right: A vigorous climate has etched Central California.

wandering waterways called the Delta, into San Francisco Bay, the only major break in the Coast Range.

California is earthquake country. More than 5,000 seismic shocks ripple from a statewide network of fault lines every year. Californians tend to ignore the daily shaking, for most earthquakes are too small to be felt. But not all. The $10 billion Las Pritchard quake that rattled San Francisco in 1989 was neither the first nor the last trembler to shake lives as it tumbled buildings, bridges, and freeways. In California, earthquakes are simply one more reason the state is like no other. They are part of the myth.

Spanish Discovery and Settlement

The Spanish who settled California soon realized that it was special. But unlike today's residents, the Spanish were disappointed in their northwestern colony. It was not the most remote of their holdings around the world, but it was one of the least successful. Hernan Cortez,

conqueror of the Aztec empire in central Mexico, was responsible for the discovery of what the Spanish came to call "The Californias". He lusted after the seven fabled Cities of Gold and El Dorado, "The Gilded One". Instead of El Dorado, Cortez' expeditions discovered the peninsula of Baja, or lower, California. The Indians were hostile, there was no gold to be seen, the landscape was barren, and navigation was treacherous. Maybe it was derision that led explorers to give the desolate new land the name California. Maybe it was hope. "On the right hand of the Indies ... very near to the terrestrial paradise" was where Garci Ordonez de Montalvo placed the island of California in a romantic novel (1510).

Montalvo filled his mythical land with black Amazons, ruled by Queen Calafia. Into battle they rode griffins, half eagle and half lion. Weapons were of gold, "for in all the island there is no other metal." Not too accurate, in a land where romantic legend and history are almost inseparable, but hardly inappropriate.

The coast of Alta, or upper, California was first sighted in 1542 by Portuguese adventurer Juan Rodriguez Cabrillo. It created not the slightest ripple of interest. Cabrillo left the West Coast of Mexico with two leaky ships, a convict crew, and an impossible assignment. He was looking for a land rich in spices, as much gold as the Aztecs had owned, and the Strait of Anian, a saltwater shortcut between Europe and Asia. All he saw was a harbor he called San Miguel, now San Diego. Cabrillo died on the voyage. The rest of the expedition beat as far north as Oregon, then ran home from what Spanish authorities called a useless adventure.

Manila galleons were next to visit the California coast. Spanish traders laden with silver from the mines of Mexico sailed from Acapulco to the Philippines, bought silks, spices, ceramics, and other exotic goods, then sailed north to catch the westerly winds. The winds carried the

Above: A view of San Francisco when it was still Yerba Buena.

lumbering traders to landfall along California. Half starved on maggoty food and suffering from scurvy, the sailors turned south toward Acapulco and profits.

The voyage was hard enough without pirates. The as yet unknighted Francis Drake, "master thief of the unknown world", rounded Cape Horn in 1578 to plunder Spanish ships. He did so well that he had to land his *Golden Hind* for repairs when hull seams gaped open from the sheer weight of Spanish silver. He probably landed at Drake's Bay, just north of modern San Francisco. A brass plaque found at the bay in 1937 claimed Nova Albion for "Her Majesty, Queen Elizabeth of England". The plaque is probably a forgery, but Drake's descriptions of the bay and the local Indians match the area.

Drake earned a knighthood for his exploits. Spain decided to find a port of refuge in California. The job fell to Sebastian Vizcaino, who was promised his own Manila galleon in return for success. He hoped to amass a fortune in true California style, by cutting corners. He began by "discovering" the great bay of San Miguel and calling it San Diego. He also renamed other landmarks as far as Monterey. The bay had been described by another explorer seven years earlier, but Vizcaino claimed it as his own in 1602, naming it for his viceroy and patron, the Conte de Monterey. Vizcaino described it as a safe harbor, "well protected from all winds. ... There is much wood and water in it, and an immense number of great pine trees, smooth and straight, suitable for masts ... (and) good meadows for cattle, and fertile fields for growing crops." It was an outright lie, for Monterey Bay has almost no naturally protected anchorage.

For the Spanish, California was everything it should not have been. It should have had gold, and did not. It should have held agricultural riches, and did not. It should have held a sea route to Europe, and did not. Mexico was the edge of the world during three centuries of Spanish empire; California was over the edge. Spain established her first Pacific Coast settlement in 1519, at Panama City. It took more than two and a half centuries to settle California. Once Vizcaino's exaggerated reports of Monterey had been filed and forgotten, Spain ignored California for 167 years.

The California Indians

Spain's neglect was a new lease on life for California Indians, who had lived in limited contact because of the rugged landscape. Life in California had remained physically and culturally undisturbed for thousands of years. Rain patterns precluded agriculture except along a few stretches of the Colorado River where the Yuma Indians planted corn, pumpkin, squash, and beans after the annual flood. Other groups lived by hunting and gathering. There were no fierce braves in war bonnets clinging bareback

to war ponies, no established warrior class and no horses before the Spanish arrived in 1769. There were no massive buffalo hunts, for there were no buffalo in California during historic times. Even the prehistoric mammoths had vanished before the first Indians migrated from Asia during the last Ice Age. Food was plentiful. Acorns were the staple, usually ground and made into porridge or bread. Deer and small game were abundant. Rivers and ocean were so rich that coastal groups left piles of discarded shells 30 feet (9 m) high. Early American arrivals called the Indians "diggers" after seeing women digging for roots. But the roots were prized for fiber, not food. The Indians developed basket weaving instead of pottery, turning out woven baskets as sturdy and as watertight as any clay pot.

Pre-Spanish Indian population estimates run from 150,000 to 300,000. It was the largest, densest human population north of central Mexico, four times the population of any other comparable area in pre-European America. Diversity and isolation ensured their survival. California Indians spoke about 135 different dialects from 21 major language groups, barely more than 2,000 people per language. The Indians of San Diego, for example, could not talk to their neighbors in San Luis Rey, a few miles north. The Diegueno spoke a dialect of the Yuma family while the Luiseno spoke a dialect of Shoshone.

Diversity kept the level of political organization local. Elsewhere in North America, the tribe was composed of several thousand people with a strong group identity. In California, the village was the largest political unit. Warfare was also rare. Rugged terrain made travel and conquest impractical. So did the climate.

Before the Spanish and Americans arrived, California Indians had never had to adapt to change. Once their world did begin to change in 1769, they never had the chance to learn how to adapt.

Spanish Settlements

The Spanish did not set out to exterminate the Indians; they lacked the manpower. When the northern frontier was finally settled, there were seldom as many as 100 soldiers in all of California. Instead, colonial authorities planned to turn the Indians into colonists. Life in the frontier colonies was highly unattractive to Spanish women and families. Men either took local wives or did without, encouraged by official policy.

The English generally treated Indians as savages and impediments to civilization. The Spanish, on the other hand, regarded Indians as legal subjects with specific rights and responsibilities. Indians were also seen as human beings with souls to be saved. And they were a valuable economic resource. In return for legal protection and the salvation of their

Above: Mission Dolores in San Francisco.
Right: Father Junipero Serra, who worked at the Carmel Mission.

souls, Indians were required to contribute the labor of their bodies. The Indians of California were to be made Spanish – in language, religion, and culture, through education and intermarriage.

The Spanish plan had three parts: the mission, the *presidio*, and the *pueblo*. The mission brought the Roman Catholic word of God to the Indians and taught them to farm. When the Word alone was not enough, the soldiers of the army garrison, or presidio, provided physical encouragement. As the Indians became "civilized", they were expected to form a pueblo, or town, a seed of New Spain that would eventually grow to cover the colonial world. It did not work. Missionaries and soldiers seldom trusted each other, and with good reason. The missionaries depended upon a handful of ragtag soldiers for protection. The soldiers, then, undisciplined and unmarried, ran roughshod over the neophytes, as the new Christians were called.

The Indians received little education and training in selfgovernment. The missionaries treated them like unteachable children. Instead of helping them to cope with the new world, the missionaries turned them into dependents. Every aspect of daily life was controlled: work, play, clothing, even the choice of mates and all contact with other Europeans. When the missions dissolved, so did Indian communities.

José de Galvez got the job of revitalizing Mexico in 1765. All it would take, he decided, was a colony in Alta California, a plan abandoned 160 years earlier.

Galvez fanned old fears that another European power might take possession of California unless Spain beat them to it. The Dutch were active in the Pacific. The British had just won control of the Mississippi Valley. They were also expanding across Canada, as trappers and explorers from the Hudson's Bay Company moved westward in search of furs. When they reached the Pacific, they might turn south. The Russians, pursuing the rich sea otter fur trade in Alaska, were already looking toward California.

Galvez built a new supply port at San Blas, north of modern Puerto Vallarta. In 1768, he sailed to Baja California to complete plans for the "sacred expedition" to colonize Alta California the next year. The goal was a small presidio at San Diego and a larger fort on the shores of Vizcaino's fine bay at Monterey. He planned to send two overland columns from mainland Mexico and three sea approaches from Baja California. The land routes were blocked by Indian rebellions in Sonora. The revolt was an old one, but Galvez thought he could settle the problem. His unsuccessful efforts drove him mad, proclaiming that he was God. The solution to the revolt, he declared, was to import 600 monkeys from Guatemala as soldiers.

The "sacred expedition", led by Gaspar de Portola and a Franciscan, Father Junipero Serra, headed for San Diego from Baja California. Two land parties

marched north from Baja. Three leaky ships sailed for San Diego; only two arrived. Of the 300 or so men who began the expedition, fewer than half survived to reach San Diego between April 11 and July 1, 1769. Fewer than half of those were well enough to travel on. Death and sickness did not stop Portola. Leaving Serra to tend the sick in San Diego, Portola and a small party headed north. Their route would eventually become El Camino Real, "The King's Highway", almost identical to the present Highway 101.

When the group finally reached Monterey, they kept right on going – Portola saw nothing that looked like Vizcaino's fine, protected harbor, just an exposed anchorage offering only little protection. Worse still, a party of advance scouts climbed a ridge between the present cities of Pacifica and Millbrae and found the way blocked by a huge bay. Only a monk, Father Crespi, seemed to recognize the potential importance of what would someday be called San Francisco Bay. "It is a very large and fine harbor", Crespi wrote in his diary, "such that not only all the navy of our Most Catholic Majesty but those of all Europe could take shelter in it." It would be years until the Spanish even sailed into San Francisco Bay. Unable to find a way around the spreading body of water, Portola headed back to San Diego. Not much had happened during his absence. Serra had founded the mission of San Diego de Alcala on July 16, and had failed to win a single convert. An expected supply ship had not yet arrived, leaving the group to face starvation. Portola finally set a deadline. If relief did not arrive by March 19, the Feast of St. Joseph, the entire party would return to Baja on March 20. Serra and Crespi began praying. Nine days later, on the afternoon of March 19, a supply ship sailed into San Diego. California would not be abandoned.

Portola sent the ship north to Monterey and set out overland himself. This time, he realized that he had already seen all there was of Monterey, an open anchorage with no protection from the prevailing north wind. But ever the good soldier, he followed orders and built a crude fort while Serra built a mission nearby. Both were dedicated on June 3, 1770, and Portola sailed for Mexico.

There was great rejoicing over the new province of Alta California, a rejoicing that Portola failed to share. If the Russians really wanted California, he told the viceroy, they deserved it as punishment. The presidio at Monterey would never stop anyone from settling California. It would be impossible, he wrote, "to send aid to Monterey by sea, and still more so by land, unless it was proposed to sacrifice thousands of men and huge sums of money." Portola was right, but neither the viceroy nor Visitor-General Galvez were prepared to admit defeat. San Diego and

Monterey were to remain, the mission system was to be expanded, and California would prosper.

Early Adventurers

The Spanish presence in California had gone from nothing to pinpoints at San Diego and Monterey, 450 miles (720 km) apart. It took the Pacific voyages of Captain James Cook to prod Spain into expanding settlement.

Missions were founded at San Antonio, San Gabriel, and San Luis Obispo. In 1774, Captain Juan Bautista de Anza suggested a new land route from Sonora, in northern Mexico, to Monterey. Mining discoveries in Sonora and a population boom had finally quelled Indian unrest. A new viceroy in Mexico City, Antonio de Bucareli, with eager encouragement from Serra, decided to open the land route and settle strategic San Francisco. De Anza crossed the Yuma River from Arizona into California, traversed the Anza Desert and the Borrego Valley, visited Mission San Gabriel, and continued on to Monterey. He earned a promotion, and a chance to lead settlers north in 1775. In the same year, a small launch built at Monterey sailed north and became the first Spanish vessel to enter San Francisco Bay.

De Anza brought 30 soldier-colonists with their families and four civilian families north from Mexico. They were California's first pioneers – 196 people and 1,000 head of livestock. The need for married soldiers was obvious. Spain needed women in California to increase the number of solid Catholic families. More importantly for immediate survival, sexstarved soldiers stationed far from family and home were creating problems with the Indians.

On April 26, 1776, de Anza planted a cross near the end of a windswept peninsula now called Fort Point. Most of the San Francisco peninsula was covered

Right: Juan Batista de Anza. Far Right: George Vancouver in 1793.

with barren sand dunes, but de Anza found a small creek and oasis about three miles from the presidio. He planted a second cross on Laguna de Nuestra Senora de los Dolores, Our Lady of the Sorrows. The Mission of San Francisco de Asis is still called Mission Delores. The 23 missions founded between 1769 and 1823 were placed for agriculture. The four presidios, San Diego, Monterey, San Francisco, and in 1782, Santa Barbara, were in more exposed positions overlooking important ocean passages. But even the strategically placed San Francisco presidio was more symbolic than defensive.

Crops planted by retired soldiers failed to thrive in the salty ocean air. Cattle and horses had to be moved to sunny inland valleys to graze. Supply ships were few and far between. The missions were barely self-supporting and could not spare supplies for the garrisons.

The answer, in 1777, was to start agricultural pueblos on prime farming land. But almost no one, not even the poorest, was willing to leave the grim but familiar poverty of Mexico for an unknown future in California. Fourteen families, 68 people in all, settled San José, California's first civil community. Only one head of family could read and write.

El Pueblo de Nuestra Senora la Reina de los Angeles del Rio de Porciunculla, the Town of Our Lady the Queen of the Angels by the River of Porciunculla, got an even worse start in 1781. With no harbor or navigable river, only 44 people were willing to chance life in the new village they began calling Los Angeles.

They were the last settlers on the Anza Trail before Yuma Indians cut the lifeline to Mexico at the Colorado River. The Indians had been cheated of promised payments. Soldiers molested their women. Livestock raided their Yuma fields. Outrage finally flamed into attack, and the trail was closed for half a century. California was on its own.

The mission system continued to expand, but it never turned the Indians into colonists. There were about 600 non-Indians in California in 1781, perhaps

3,000 when Mexico declared independence from Spain in 1821. The increase was only due to new births.

The late 18th century was the beginning of the end for Spain. The empire drifted from humiliation in Canada to disaster and dissolution in South America. In 1789, Spain sent Esteban José Martinez to take possession of Vancouver Island and the sea otter fur trade. When he arrived, he found American, Portuguese, and British ships already riding at anchor. Martinez seized two English ships and England threatened war. Spain backed down and gave up all claims north of California. England sent Captain George Vancouver to work out details of the Nootka Sound Treaty. In 1793, he visited California. Spanish defenses were laughable. The two cannons at San Francisco could not be fired. The three cannons at San Diego had never even been mounted.

Above: The old Mission of Carmel. Right: The rancho became the center of economic and social life for the 19th century.

Santa Barbara had two serviceable cannons, Monterey eight.

Spain decided to build a new agricultural pueblo that would also strengthen coastal defenses. Branciforte, on the north shore of Monterey Bay, was to be colonized by retired soldiers who would farm and fight the English. In Mexico, there were no volunteers. The colonists who finally arrived in 1797 were nearly all petty criminals. The community struggled along, but disappeared around 1810. Except for scattered cattle ranches granted to retired soldiers, it was Spain's last attempt to colonize California.

Missions and Rancheros

The missions were finally beginning to prosper. By 1800, they housed 13,000 neophytes. Vineyards, orchards, herds, and wheatfields flourished. Buildings began to assume a familiar appearance: white-washed stone churches topped by red clay tiles, bordered by arched colonnades surrounding lush central gardens

cooled by fountains. Indian artisans covered every available wall with lively paintings. Indian musicians played for daily church services and regular civil celebrations. Indian craftsmen worked metal, tanned hides, made bricks and tiles, wove blankets, and worked leather.

Material success could not have come at a better time. The Yuma uprising had already cut land routes to Mexico. From 1810 until 1821, the Mexican War of Independence cut sea lanes. The presidios levied the missions for food and supplies. As the number of missions and neophytes increased, so did the amount of work required by both church and state. A bloody Indian revolt shook three Santa Barbara missions in 1824. Stunned padres blamed military demands. The Franciscans shared the blame. They were, very quickly, killing the Indians. From 1769 through the end of the mission period in 1833, they took in 82,100 Indians. Statistically, there should have been about 40,000 deaths during those 64 years. The missions recorded 62,000 deaths.

They housed the Indians in permanent dormitories where epidemics of measles, cholera, and common colds raged. The infant mortality was 50 per cent in 1810. By 1820, it was 86 per cent. No one knows how many Indians fled the missions, nor how many were hunted down and returned by soldiers. The Franciscans were charged with wanton abuse of Indians by a newly independent Mexico, charges the friars angrily denied. After all, they pointed out, there were never more than three dozen missionaries in California and fewer than 100 ragged soldiers. It would be impossible for so few to enslave 20,000 Indians. Mexicans pointed out that the soldiers had guns, which the Indians did not.

Secularizing the missions was an easy way to meet the demand for private land. Some of the livestock and pasturage could be divided among the Indians; the rest could be opened to ranching.

The first ten missions were placed under secularized control in 1834, the last five in 1836. The Indians were expected

27

The Indian population dwindled, but non-Indians increased from 3,700 to 8,000, including 700 non-Hispanic foreigners. With the mission system in ruins, the ranchos became the basic social, cultural, and economic unit. It was the time that gave California its hazy, rose-tinted heritage of dashing *caballeros* and swirling *senoritas*. It was one of the largest non-nomadic pastoral societies the world has ever seen. The Mexican elite called themselves Californios. Mestizos, the offspring of Mexican and Indian parentage, were down the social ladder. Indians were at the bottom.

Californio living standards were poor. Few ranch houses had wooden floors or glass windows. None had running water. El Camino Real was a horse track with public schools non-existent; illiteracy remained the rule until the Gold Rush.

Hides and Tallow

The easing of trade restrictions after Mexican independence coincided with the growth of industry and trade in New England. American whalers also plied the coast, reaping a rich harvest from whales migrating between Alaska and Baja California. Cattle were exported to Tahiti. Cattle, horses, and *vaqueros*, or cowboys, from California started Hawaii's ranching industry. But hides and tallow were the primary products. The United States needed hides for shoes and tallow for soap and candles. It also needed new markets for manufactured goods. California met both needs.

America's first good look at California was Richard Henry Dana's *Two Years Before the Mast*, an account of beating up and down the coast in the hide and tallow trade. Ship owners and captains soon developed a better system to collect a full cargo of 40,000 hides. Resident merchants, most of them Americans, purchased whole cargoes of imported goods and accepted delivery of hides all year.

to settle near their former mission homes while the white administrators managed what remained of their estates. It did not work. A succession of governors handed out land as though there were no tomorrow. Nearly 750 grants (12 million acres) were made between 1834 and the middle of 1846. Unschooled in government, commerce, or law, the Indians were cast adrift. Most were cheated out of their shares by incompetent or corrupt administrators. With no idea of how to survive in a modern society, they slipped into poverty and underpaid work in the overnight ranchos. With free land, endless supplies of cattle, and cheap labor, the new *rancheros* prospered and developed a culture that looked richly idyllic to the urbanites who came later.

The Mexican years, 1822 to 1846, were the closest California had ever seen to a population explosion at that time.

Above: This señorita, a californio, belonged to the state's Mexican elite. Right: Riding the range in the Eastern Sierra.

Their system of credit helped expand the *ranchero* system and formed the basis of California's first banking system.

Californios sold upwards of 75,000 hides a year for $2 each. There were no public works or taxes to speak of, so the income went into luxuries. With no local industry beyond simple handicrafts, California depending upon traders for everything from spurs to needles. Importers provided tea, spices, cocoa, cutlery, tools, cloth, even brooms and table service. Hides that went to Boston came back as fancy boots and ornate slippers. Women slipped into rustling petticoats and dresses of Chinese silk.

The Californios live on, of all places, in the world of high finance. Crusading newspaper editor Horace Greeley is supposed to have been a guest at a fight between bears and bulls. When he returned to New York, he gave the names of California's favorite fighters to the more familiar antagonists of Wall Street.

The Adventurers

Government remained weak throughout the decades of Hispanic California. Any group could, and often did, defy authority with impunity. Residents revolted against governors. Foreign commercial adventurers traded where and when they pleased, bribing officials at every port. The first commercial invaders arrived during the 1790s, when sea otters flourished from Alaska to Baja California. A single adult pelt, five feet (1.5 m) long and two feet (0.6 m) wide, was worth $300 in Canton. Fur traders were scouring the coast for pelts to trade for Asian goods in demand in New York and Boston. The Yankees developed a global route. They sold New England-manufactured goods for otter pelts collected by the Indians of the Pacific Northwest. Then they sailed to Hawaii, trading their remaining goods for food, water, and sandalwood. In Canton, they traded pelts

and sandalwood for tea, silks, spices, and ceramics, which they carried across the Indian Ocean, around the Cape of Good Hope, and home to New England.

As the otters became scarce in northern waters, traders turned their attentions to California. Spanish law forbade foreign trade, but the imported goods were irresistible. Protected coves became as popular for those early smugglers as they were nearly two centuries later during Prohibition. More knowledgeable *contrabandistas* simply sailed into harbors to trade beneath tiny cannon that could not be fired. The only problem, from the smugglers' point of view, was the low rate of return. It took too long to collect enough pelts to make the voyage worthwhile. Indians were the primary hunters, and the California Indians lacked good hunting boats. Joseph O'Cain, a New England captain, proposed that Alexander Baranov, head of the Russian-American Fur Company of Sitka, Alaska, provide 20 Aleut hunters. O'Cain would transport the hunters and their skin boats.

VIEW of FORT ROSS, near BODEGAS, former RUSSIAN SETTLEMENT. by C.J. DENNY

The Russian and the American shared the pelts. It was profitable for everyone except the sea otters. In five months, the Aleuts collected nearly 1,800 pelts. As word of their success spread, other American ships joined the hunt.

The Russians soon followed. There was a shortage of Russian ships in the North Pacific, so they erected a base at Fort Ross, 80 miles (129 km) north of San Francisco. It was a trespass, but the Russians had other problems to worry about. Crops failed regularly in cold, foggy Sitka. When supply ships failed to arrive on time, as they usually did, the Russians faced starvation. They hoped to farm at Fort Ross and trade for food.

California officials protested with no visible effect. The commander at Fort Ross ignored messages demanding that he leave, knowing that there was no force in California to push him back to Alaska.

Above: Fort Ross, a Russian supply station. Right: "Kit" Carson. Far right: Jedediah Smith in the Sierra Nevada, 1827.

In 1830, the Mexican governor of California acknowledged the obvious and ordered small settlements to be established in the sunny valleys north of San Francisco Bay. He hoped that obvious occupation would discourage the Russians, as well as the Hudson's Bay Company beaver trappers who were moving south from the Columbia River. Californians had no intention of giving up their illegal trade. It was the only source of luxuries as well as essential supplies. When the Russians abandoned Fort Ross in 1841, American hide ships had already taken over the import trade.

The Original Western

Furs also brought the first American visitors by land. In November 1826, Jedediah Smith led a party of trappers to San Gabriel Mission. But Governor Echeandia in San Diego suspected a trick or a spy mission that would reveal California's weakness and had Smith put into the city jail. After American ship

captains had interceded for Smith he was allowed to leave, headed through the San Joaquin Valley and found a trapper's paradise for furs. After several more trips – and more nights in jail – Smith was killed by Comanches on the Santa Fé Trail.

James Ohio Pattie entered California from New Mexico with his father, Sylvester. Echeandia put the pair in jail, where Sylvester died. James was released after his medical skills stemmed an epidemic of smallpox – or so he claimed in *The Personal Narrative of James O. Pattie, of Kentucky*. The epidemic was measles, not smallpox, and Pattie's vaccination story one of many tall tales. The *Personal Narrative*, first published in 1831, was written by Timothy Flint, an author of many works about the West which mix fact and fiction. The pair created the original Western, the prototype for thousands of stories that still feed the world's appetite for vicarious thrills in the Wild West.

Even true tales of death and disaster did little to stem the tide of trappers who

were probing California in increasing numbers. A trapper named Ewing Young gave the first lessons in wilderness survival to a young runaway named Christopher "Kit" Carson. The trail they traced from Santa Fé to Los Angeles around 1832 became one of the main overland routes during the Gold Rush. The next year, Joseph Reddeford Walker made the first westward crossing of the central Sierra along the Humboldt River, a trail that was to become the busiest route during and after the Gold Rush. Walker was working with Captain Benjamin Bonneville, who was exploring the West during a two-year furlough from the U.S. Army. His ostensible purpose was trapping, but it seems now his travels may have been the first official U.S. interest in California.

Americans were not alone in their interest. The Hudson's Bay Company had been sending trapping expeditions from the Columbia River into the Sacramento Valley since 1829. The Americans knew what their rivals had found. As one

Above: The birth of a cinemathique myth, settlers heading west.

American trapper joked, the initials H.B.C. stood for "Here Before Christ."

Early Settlers

Most of the foreigners who came to California before the 1840s were adventurers, not immigrants. They came to turn a quick profit, legally or not, then left. Immigrants were no less interested in profits, but they planned to make their fortunes in the new land and stay.

The first foreigner to settle permanently in California was a reluctant immigrant. An English captain left Scotsman John Gilroy at Monterey in 1814 because of illness. Gilroy recovered, married into the powerful Ortega family, and turned the family rancho into a flourishing town that still bears his name.

The first American settler was only slightly more willing. Joseph Chapman was captured in Monterey in 1818, but claimed that he had been kidnapped in Hawaii and forced to sail to California. It may have been a convenient story, but his skills as a millwright and boatbuilder made him a welcome resident.

Chapman was the first of a string of Americans who came to trade or smuggle but remained to found economic and political dynasties. William Goodwin Dana and Alfred Robinson in Santa Barbara, and Abel Stearns in Los Angeles, became major landowners as well as leading merchants. Thomas Larkin became the most important merchant in Monterey.

California was an attractive place to settle. Land was cheap and property taxes were unknown. Californio society emphasized family and fun, yet business was an acceptable road to social and financial advancement. Californios preferred ranching, but they recognized the role the new residents played in importing the manufactured goods. And in a society that was based on European heritage, white Americans were welcome.

William Dana was one of the first Americans to willingly settle in California. He arrived in Santa Barbara from Boston in 1826 and quickly espoused Mexican citizenship, the Roman Catholic faith, and 14-year-old Josefa Carrillo. Following the marriage he still had to wait two years for naturalization, but Dana used the time profitably. When the more conventional Richard Henry Dana visited Santa Barbara a few years later, he reportedly refused to see relative William, who had renounced family, country, and religion. Richard may have had William in mind when he wrote that certain Americans in California "had left their consciences at Cape Horn".

In theory, all foreign residents had to become naturalized Mexican citizens and Roman Catholics. An unofficial third requirement was marriage to a Californio. Thomas Larkin, another Massachusetts Yankee, was one of the few foreigners who succeeded without embracing the Mexican nationality, the Roman Catholic church, or a native daughter.

On the long voyage out from Boston, Larkin met Rachel Hobson Holmes, on her way to join her husband in Hilo, Hawaii. The husband had died by the time she reached Hilo, and Larkin proposed by mail a few months later. The two were married aboard a ship off Santa Barbara to avoid any entanglements with Mexican law, and Mrs. Larkin became the first American woman in California.

Larkin opened a general store in Monterey and set himself up as an agent for ranchers and traders. He had, a later historian noted, "no inconvenient veneration for the revenue laws", and built a flourishing charge-account business – with the chief officials of California heavily in debt to him.

Another Massachusetts man, "Dr." John Marsh, was the first American settler to arrive overland. Marsh graduated from Harvard University in 1823 and began to study medicine with a surgeon, but the surgeon died before Marsh completed his studies. His next activity was illegal arms sales to the Sioux Indians and a hasty retreat to Mexican Los Angeles to avoid arrest by federal agents. Marsh's chief asset was a smooth tongue. He used his Harvard Bachelor of Arts diploma as a medical degree, correctly guessing that he was the only person in Los Angeles who could read Latin. Cash was in short supply, so Marsh accepted payment in hides. A few months later, he sold out for $500, converted to Roman Catholicism and Mexican citizenship, and bought an immense rancho near Mount Diablo on the Sacramento San Joaquin delta. He built a successful rancho by accepting payment for medical services in cattle: 50 head per treatment.

Sutter's Fort

John Sutter came to California in 1839 from Hawaii, and played a shadowy role in the Santa Fé trade. Rumor suggested that he was less than honest with funds entrusted to him by Swiss friends for investment in the U. S. History reports that he fled Switzerland, a wife, five children, and a failed business to avoid debtor's prison. By the time he arrived in California, Sutter had promoted himself to Captain Sutter of the Royal Swiss Guard of France. His self-proclaimed military background was enough to win over the governor of California. Sutter got official backing to erect a fort in the Sacramento Valley to counter potential expansion by the Russians at Fort Ross. The governor also saw Sutter's Fort as a counter to the growing power of rival Mariano Vallejo north of San Francisco Bay.

After one year, the minimum period of legal residence, Sutter got not only citizenship but 11 square leagues of land (nearly 50,000 acres, or around 20,000 hectares) and appointment as a regional official. He was authorized "to represent in the Establishment of New Helvetia all

the laws of the country, to function as political authority and dispenser of justice, in order to prevent the robberies committed by adventurers from the United States, to stop the invasion of savage Indians and the hunting and trapping by companies from the Columbia."

Sutter started with beaver pelts and brandy distilled from wild grapes, then built a cattle ranch, a farm, and a wooden fort. When Fort Ross was abandoned in 1841, he bought the implements and livestock for $30,000. The $2,000 down payment was the only cash the departing Russians ever received, though their cannon strengthened Sutter's fort and their cattle helped build his herds. Sutter's Fort became a beacon for early American overland immigration. The first party of overland immigrants, pioneers as later generations would call them, left Missouri in the spring of 1841. Lured by let-

Above: The "Bear Flag" flies during the 1846 revolt. Right: John Charles Fremont, who ended Mexican domination of California.

ters from John Marsh, the Bidwell-Bartleson Party had to abandon their wagons on the eastern side of the Sierra and walk across the mountains.

The first wagon train to make the crossing did not arrive until 1844. Four wagons were hoisted up and over a sheer granite face. Another 13 wagons were left on the east side of the pass in the care of a teenager. His crude cabin sheltered a later party that would give its name to Donner Pass. The Donner Party was the worst single disaster in the history of California immigration. Following a guidebook written by a man who had never been to California, they were delayed in Utah. By the time they reached the eastern Sierra on November 2, 1846, an early winter had descended. The main group was snowbound until February. Of 87 in the original party, cannibalism helped 40 to survive the winter.

Under the best conditions, Donner Pass is a steep obstacle to wagons and livestock. The Donner tragedy gave the pass a killer reputation. The main gold rush trails crossed the Sierra at Johnson Pass, near modern Highway 50, and Henness Pass, just north of Interstate 80.

American immigration to California hit 250 in 1845 and more than 500 in 1846. But most Americans moving west between 1840 and 1847 were headed for Oregon which was a disputed territory under joint occupation with Great Britain. Protestant missionaries had been promoting the virtues of Oregon for years, virtues that included bringing the light of God to heathen Indians and expanding American territory. Americans felt an unspoken duty to keep "perfidious Albion" (England) out of Western lands which belonged to the United States by divine right. California was up for grabs.

The Bear Flag Revolt

California languished under a succession of governors appointed from Mexico City, nine of them from 1831 to 1836 alone. North-south rivalries had already begun. Monterey, capital of California, had the Customs House and the only substantial tax revenues. Los Angeles was a ranch town that wanted a share of government power. The growing numbers of foreigners were a wild card.

An official French observer assured Paris that Sutter, with one of the strongest military positions in the state, would support a French takeover. The British minister to Mexico City pushed for annexation in lieu of repayment of $50 million in worthless Mexican bonds. But the hardest push came from Americans.

The expansionist zeal of Manifest Destiny that was focused on Oregon spilled over to California. If the United States took over the territory, the great American whaling fleets would gain a valuable base in San Francisco. American merchants along the coast would be able to expand trade with Asia, while the interior, inhabited only by Indians, filled with American pioneers. Californios would

reap the benefits of American culture and Protestantism, whether they wanted them or not. Besides, the argument usually concluded, if America does not take California, the French or English will. Diplomatic records later showed that neither country wanted to stir up trouble. But during the first half of the 19th century, no one in Mexico City, Monterey or Washington, D.C., knew that. Washington wanted prompt action, but there was no excuse for armed intervention.

U.S. presidents from Andrew Jackson on tried to buy California, or at least the northern half that included San Francisco Bay. The territory could enter the Union as a free state to balance the admission of Texas as a slave state. One emissary after another bungled the assignment. Jackson's agent openly tried to bribe officials in Mexico City and was ordered home. The Tyler administration was frustrated by an overeager commodore of the U.S. Pacific squadron.

Thomas Catesby Jones, sure that the English were about to annex California, sailed from Lima, Peru, and captured Monterey on October 19, 1842. Thomas Larkin, about to be appointed U.S. consul, convinced Jones that there was no war. Jones apologized profusely, but furious Mexican officials broke off negotiations. President Polk tried to revive the talks in 1845, but tensions over the annexation of Texas were so strong that Mexico refused to receive his messenger.

Polk thought that annexation might work in California, too. U.S. Consul Larkin was instructed to "arouse in their (Californios') bosoms that love of liberty and independence so natural to the American continent ... If the people should desire to unite their destiny with ours, they would be received as brethren."

Polk was too late. The new inland settlers had their own ideas, and they did not include caution. The plan, as it was explained around Sutter's Fort, was to encourage the flow of immigrants and then seize the colony by force. If Mexico did not resist, California would become American. If Mexico did resist, Washington would have to send the army to aid the endangered citizens, and California would become American.

Mexico responded to the annexation of Texas by ordering all aliens without valid passports out of California. The order included almost all of the new settlers. It was not immediately enforced, probably because winter was approaching and there was nowhere to go. But the threat of deportation did nothing to calm the settlers' anger and anxiety.

Nor did the arrival of Captain John Charles Fremont of the U.S. Corps of Topographical Engineers. It was Fremont's second trip to California. His first visit was in 1844, part of a trailscouting expedition to Oregon. After visiting Sutter's Fort and talking at length with Sutter and others, Fremont returned to Washing-

ton, D.C. His wife helped him turn the official story of his adventures into one of the decade's bestselling books.

Fremont returned with 68 heavily armed soldiers, a force strong enough to deal with any emergency – or to start one. Fremont told Mexican officials that he planned to winter in the San Joaquin Valley. Instead, he marched toward San José. The governor sent 200 troops to halt the advance. Fremont retreated north to Oregon but after receiving a message turned back to California. His sudden appearance stampeded the touchy settlers into open revolt. They began by stealing a herd of horses, then descended on the town of Sonoma where they captured General Vallejo. Vallejo favored joining California to the United States, but he had the misfortune to be the only Mexican official within easy reach.

The rebels jailed him at Sutter's Fort and declared California an independent republic. The flag raised over Sonoma carried a star and a crudely drawn bear (some observers thought it was meant to be a pig), giving the new nation the name "The Bear Flag Republic". Refined and romanticized, the two emblems remain on the California state flag today.

Fremont, never slow to seize the moment, threw his troops on the side of the rebels. In the end, it probably did not matter. The United States declared war on Mexico on May 13, 1846. By July, naval units had occupied every port in California. The Bear Flag Republic lasted one month. The war was over by January 1847, though another year passed before the two countries came to terms in the Treaty of Guadalupe Hidalgo.

War news did little to slow immigration. California attracted more settlers than Oregon for the first time in 1846. The foreign population took another leap with the arrival of 238 Mormons led by a fiery young man named Samuel Brannan. Brannan quickly settled into the limelight of San Francisco. He produced the city's

Right: "Wish you were here", panning for gold in the 19th century.

first newspaper, the *California Star*, performed the city's first American wedding, and was the defendant in the city's first lawsuit, a charge of misappropriating church funds. He also found time to open a store at Sutter's Fort.

The American takeover went reasonably smoothly. Mexican legal and civic institutions survived the transition, sometimes under American administrators, sometimes under Californios. California seemed to be sleeping into the Union easily and quietly, with Californios holding places of respect and influence.

The Gold Rush

Gold forever equated California with opportunity. It lured men into the mountains in such numbers that San Francisco was transformed from a windswept, flea-bitten village of 812 into a frenetic hive of 25,000 in two years. It lifted the population of California from less than 10,000 to 100,000 in the same time. Gold gave California the economic clout to avoid financial exploitation by the robber barons of the East; instead, California grew its own crop of exploiters. Gold changed California from a sleepy, pastoral backwater into a bustling leader of the world community. And gold gave California the political muscle to enter the Union on its own terms: The state was a functioning political unit, complete with constitution and elected officers, nearly a year before it was finally admitted to the Union.

California gave the United States its first major source of gold for coinage and monetary support. California was the first major supplier of the precious metal since the Spanish looted the Aztec and Inca empires in the 16th century.

The first recorded discovery of California gold was made in 1842 by a Mexican rancher near Los Angeles. In nine months, Mexican prospectors, most from Sonora, recovered gold worth $10,000 at the official Philadelphia Mint price of $18 an ounce. In 1843, they recovered $43,000 worth before the deposits played out. Like so much of California, Mexi-

cans got there first, but only Americans created the myth.

In California, there was faith in luck and mobility, a certainty that life will get better somewhere else. The attitude is reflected in the way Californians face failure. In California, more so than most other parts of the country, failure is accepted, not cursed. A person whose business fails is seen as more experienced, more likely to succeed in the future. Early miners lived on this optimism, but they were not above trying to shift the odds.

John Sutter's need for a sawmill set off *the* Gold Rush. Sutter's partner in the mill, James W. Marshall, had built a mill on the American River at a spot Indians called Culloma (now Columa), "beautiful vale". Marshall and other workers discovered bits of metal in the tailrace, the channel that carries water away from the revolving millwheel, between January 19

Above: Sonora, a gold boom town on Highway 49. Right: J. A. Sutter, near whose fort the first gold was found.

and January 24, 1848. Sutter tried desperately to keep the discovery secret, but word soon leaked out. California yawned at the news, at least until Sam Brannan strolled down San Francisco's Montgomery Street, a vial of gold dust in his hand, shouting, "Gold! Gold! Gold on the American River!" ... after he had bought up every pick, shovel, and bucket available.

Gold fever seized San Francisco, Monterey, even Oregon and Hawaii. San Francisco newspapers suspended publication for lack of readers, reporters, and printers. Half the male population of Oregon rushed south. Hawaiian adventurers sailed east, Mexicans and South Americans flocked north

Fields of Placer Gold

Luck played straight into the hands of the stampeders. Gold is usually difficult to mine, trapped in quartz veins deep below the surface. In California, nature did much of the hard work. Streams washed away soil and eroded bits of gold from the exposed veins. The metal, heavier than the surrounding sand and gravel, collected in quiet eddies behind boulders or in river bends. Deposits of metal, sand, and gravel are called *placer* gold, a Spanish term. In 1848, California was one of the richest and largst sources of placer gold in the world. The gold-fields covered nearly 35,000 square miles (90,000 sq km). Most deposits were with-in a few feet of the surface, in or near mountain streams that flowed year round. Temperatures during the rainless sum-mers made living outside not just tolera-ble, but pleasant. The work, though hard, was not complex. Once the Argonauts, as they were called, discovered that gold was heavier than sand and gravel, it be-came a simple matter of washing away lighter material with running water.

Dreams of Midas' golden touch came true, at least for the first few months. M.T. McClellan, an emigrant from Mis-souri who went straight to the goldfields in the fall of 1848, wrote to a friend that "my little girls can make from 5 to 25 dollars per day washing gold in pans ... My average income this winter will be about 150 dollars per day." Back east, a trained clerk earned $30 a month. Eastern clerks heard the news. So did President Polk, by way of William Tecumseh Sher-man, who sent reports and samples to Washington by courier. On December 5, 1848, Polk told Congress, "The accounts of the abundance of gold in that territory are of such an extraordinary character as would scarcely command belief were they not corroborated by the authentic re-ports of officers of the public service." It was the kind of pronouncement the pub-lic was waiting for – a match applied to a short fuse. Industrialization was disrupt-ing what had been an agrarian society. The war with Mexico had added a touch of restlessness. And for the first time, California was a feasible adventure.

In 1838, the journey over uncharted

mountains or distant seas was daunting. A decade later, whaling and trading fleets from Boston had made the sea lanes seem familiar. Government mail service via the Isthmus of Panama was about to begin. Years of Protestant missionary propa-ganda, the Mormon migration to Utah, and the march of hundreds of soldiers across the continent to fight Mexico had erased the terrors of an overland journey. California seemed an easy jaunt with as-sured riches at the other end.

Between 600 and 1,000 ships – no one bothered to count – dropped anchor in San Francisco in 1849 after rounding Cape Horn. Most were abandoned where they lay as passengers, officers, and crew rushed to the goldfields. Other thousands arrived via Panama and overland routes. In one year, the year of the '49ers, 80,000 arrivals is a conservative estimate. Al-most all of them were men. Women and children stayed home, waiting for the re-turn of newly rich husbands, fathers, and lovers. Federal census takers in 1850 found that males in their twenties made up more than half of California's population. In some mining camps, less than one per cent of the population was female. The census also found a well-educated population. The illiteracy rate for the country as a whole was 10.35 per cent; in California, it was 2.86 per cent. Only the better-educated and better-off could afford the cross-country trip.

Cradles, Long Toms, and Sluices

The easy gold was largely taken by the middle of 1849. The new arrivals needed something more efficient than panning, washing dirt and gravel away from flecks of gold in a broad, flat pan. Few Americans had any goldmining experience, but knowledgeable Mexicans provided early answers. They introduced the cradle, a large box on rockers that could be shaken back and forth as running water removed the lighter debris.

The next improvement was the Long Tom, a long box with wooden cleats nailed to the bottom. Water and paydirt went into the top. Heavy bits of gold were trapped behind the cleats. The miners developed sluice boxes, hundreds of feet long. Smaller bits of gold still washed away, but luck stepped in again.

Mercury, quicksilver to most of the miners, absorbs gold that can be separated again by boiling. And by happy coincidence, one of the largest mercury mines in the world, the New Almaden, opened near San José in 1845. Later, the miners formed working partnerships, financed largely by camp merchants. They built crude log dams to divert rivers, put flumes on stilts to carry water to remote hillsides, and dug long, unstable tunnels. By 1852, they were building mills to grind quartz gold ore. Next came hydraulic systems with cannonsized nozzles called monitors that washed away entire hillsides; then dredges that dug their own lakes as they crawled across the countryside.

Mining was an ecological disaster. Forests were stripped for lumber or burned off to expose the ground. Erosion, some natural, much the result of hydraulic mining, blocked streams and rivers. Silt clogged the Sacramento River, bringing annual floods. Salmon streams filled with debris. Oyster beds in San Francisco Bay were buried in the mud. A century later, fish from the Bay still carried traces of mercury from the quicksilver that escaped from sluice boxes in the Sierra foothills.

Mining was also a financial success, at least for a few. About 6,000 miners produced $10 million worth of gold in 1848. The take was $20 to $30 million the next year, but there were 40,000 miners. Total output was about $80 million during the peak year of 1852, with 100,000 miners in the goldfields.

Some of the miners who failed to find golden fortunes returned home. Others turned to the trades they already knew, working as farmers, clerks, and mechanics in the industries that were appearing. The world was learning of the difficulties of mining by 1850. Immigration dipped in 1851, then rebounded in 1852. The Gold Rush was over, but families were moving west. They were moving to the new State of California.

Statehood on Its Own Terms

California had been calm for a year when the official peace treaty was signed with Mexico. Another year, and the state still had no real government. The military was the only recognized authority, and Brigadier General Bennet Riley did not want the job.

Miners could not have cared less. They set up their own laws, based on conditions and leaders in each of more than 500 mining camps. The largely white

Right: The old Empire gold mine in Grass Valley, where dreams were mostly broken.

communities generally ruled that Mexicans, Chinese, Indians, and other "foreigners" could not own mining claims. The miners did not worry about land ownership, because no one wanted land, just gold. The federal government could keep title as long as the miners could keep on working. There was no government to provide roads, bridges, navigational aids, schools, streets, fire departments, or other services. Worst of all, nothing had been done about the huge Mexican land grants that tied up so many square miles of agricultural property that Americans felt was theirs by right of conquest, if not legal ownership.

General Riley decided to let Californians set up whatever kind of government they wanted. He may have had unofficial approval from Washington, and he knew he did not have enough troops to maintain order. In June 1849, he called elections to choose 48 delegates who would meet in Monterey to draw up a constitution. The delegates met and promptly split along regional lines. The 11 Southern California delegates opposed statehood. They feared, correctly, that the new state would support itself with taxes on land, not mines. They wanted to become a territory, administered and supported by Washington. Northern California wanted statehood, and they wanted it then. Six weeks later, they got it.

The constitution was signed on October 13 to the sound of the battery of Monterey firing a 31-gun salute. (It was premature, since it would be almost a year before Washington accepted the decision.) A month later, voters split 12,061 to 811 for statehood. If the United States did not want California, California would go it alone.

Golden riches also brought golden opportunities. Far more money was made supplying mines and miners than was ever grubbed from the earth. Miners who had more than one shirt sent them to Honolulu to be cleaned. One woman earned $18,000 a year baking pies for miners. George Briggs planted watermelons on 25 acres (10 hectares) of

41

Sacramento Valley land and sold the crop for $17,000. Six years later, an orchard he bought with the profits was earning $35,000 a year.

Rancheros who had been selling cattle for hides and tallow could sell them for ten times more at mining camp butcher shops. They rode home with bags bursting with gold slugs, privately minted coins. Many promptly went on wild spending sprees. It did not seem to matter if they overspent on silks and satins for their wives and silver saddles for themselves. Land and cattle seemed limitless, and merchants were happy to extend credit at five per cent per month, secured by land. Gold slugs were the result of an early shortage of money. Gold dust was not much of a substitute for hard cash. Purity varied, and there were few scales to weigh it. Prices were quoted in "pinches" of dust, leading to the phrase,

Above: Leland Stanford, responsible for railroads and a university. Right: Riverboats were part of the business cartel.

"How much can you raise in a pinch?"

Merchants and bankers used whatever was handy – American dollars, English pounds, Mexican pesos, Prussian florins, Indian rupees. Private mints began producing $20 and $50 gold slugs. Profits came from a "slight" difference between the face value and the assayed gold content.

It was called fiscal democracy, survival of the fittest, and anything went. Monopolies developed in haulage (Wells, Fargo & Co.), stagecoaches (California Stage Company), and riverboats (California Steam Navigation Company). San Francisco, the only port with access to the Central Valley, had a municipal monopoly on trade with interior California. The control of wholesale markets and transshipping to riverboats and coastal steamers turned into a stranglehold on California economic and political life that endured for decades.

The Great Land Grab

There were constant shortages of everything from flour to tobacco. The worst shortage was land. The Americans who moved to California expected an open frontier where they could obtain free or lowcost public land and build their own fortunes. In the 1850s, settlers could go into unsurveyed lands, create farms, and eventually buy 160 acres (65 hectares) for $200. When they got to California, they found more than 12 million acres (about 5 million hectares) already owned by, stories claimed, 813 Mexican grantees. As far as the wouldbe settlers were concerned, there was something distinctly un-American about so much land in so few hands. The Californios did not understand. They valued cattle, not land. Precise boundaries seldom mattered, for no one much cared just whose land a cow grazed as long as it was clear who owned the cow.

The Treaty of Guadalupe Hidalgo obli-

gated the U.S. to respect all legitimate land titles. But what was "legitimate"? Land grants by the last two Mexican governors were even sloppier than usual. The final governor had even made grants after the Americans landed at Monterey on July 7, 1846, then backdated the deeds. Thousands of American settlers simply squatted, assuming that physical possession would become legal title.

In 1851, Congress sent a land commission to San Francisco to fix the mess. Commissioners assumed that all titles were invalid until proven otherwise. Californios had to travel to San Francisco with witnesses and documents for legal proceedings the largest part of them did not understand. Not surprisingly, most of California ended up in American hands, either through commission decision or sales forced by legal expenses and debts.

The law became a tool for profit. John Fremont lost a commission ruling and appealed to the U.S. Supreme Court. The court, influenced by Fremont's political connections, reversed the decision. Fre-

mont promptly redrew the grant boundaries to include land where gold had been discovered. Several miners were killed and wounded in subsequent riots.

The state constitution forbade dueling, yet California had more duels and dueling deaths than any other state in the union between 1850 and 1860s. Crime, corruption, and poor administration drove the normally cynical citizens of San Francisco to form Committees of Vigilance in 1849, 1851, and 1856. The Vigilantes were colorful, but seldom efficient. As often as not, their targets were foreigners or Roman Catholics whose chief crimes were to be non-white, non-American, and non-Protestant.

Culture and Railroads

California grew up faster than any other frontier in the West. In five years, San Francisco went from a shanty town to the economic rival of New York and the cultural rival of Boston. All who could afford the good things in life

wanted them, and they wanted them *right away*. California's first regular newspaper, the weekly *Californian*, appeared in Monterey in 1846. A decade later, there were 132 periodicals in San Francisco alone. Their per capita circulation outstripped London or New York. By 1860, San Francisco had 50,000 residents, a population it had taken New York 190 years to reach. The goldfields were played out, but recession was swept away by a wave of silver riches from the Sierra. Placer gold had been found in the streams of western Nevada, but the flakes were embedded in a "wretched blue stuff" that clogged sluice boxes. In 1859, the blue stuff was identified as some of the richest silver ore ever assayed. It was the Comstock Lode, a vein that would produce $400 million before deposits played out in the 1880s. Silver mining was a rich man's game, for the ore was buried deep

Left: S. Brannan, Frisco's first newspaper editor. Right: C. Crocker, whose railroad connected California to N.Y. in four days.

beneath the Nevada mountains. San Francisco bankers provided the capital that poured into nearly 2,000 companies listed on the mining exchange. At the height of the market, there was more money in Comstock mining stocks than existed on the entire Pacific coast.

There was even more money to be made in railroads. The first serious proposals for a transcontinental line came in the 1840s when Eastern merchants in the China trade saw potential profits to be made carrying goods overland from Europe and Asia. The project got off the ground 20 years later. Theodore Judah found a practical route across the central Sierra and began raising capital for the Central Pacific Railroad. He was confident that the merchants of San Francisco would provide the rest.

His confidence was misplaced, for San Franciscans saw no quick profits. When Judah approached the Sacramento merchants, he changed his approach. The railroad, he pointed out, would capture the Comstock Lode traffic, ensuring immediate freight and passenger income. Presented with a concrete proposal and solid local backing, Congress would give cash construction subsidies.

The Big Four – Mark Hopkins, Collis Huntington, Leland Stanford, and Charles Crocker – agreed. The Central Pacific produced personal fortunes worth $200 million a few years later. It would build east from Sacramento, the Union Pacific west from Omaha. Both got generous loans and a checkerboard of thousands of square miles of government land along rights-of-way. Construction began in 1863, a year after Stanford had become governor of California. In true local style, he used his office in every possible way to advance the railroad. He appointed Charles Crocker's brother, Edwin, to the state supreme court, allowing him to continue as the Central Pacific's chief legal counsel.

It was not the last shady deal the four worked. Construction subsidies were considerably higher for work in the mountains than across the flat Sacramento Valley, so railroaders told Congress that the Sierra Nevada begins seven miles west of Sacramento. Supported by slanted testimony from a state geologist, the federal government accepted the new claim, and the four became known as the men who could move mountains.

The two railroads met at Promontory, Utah, on May 10, 1869. A century after the founding of the first Spanish settlement in California, the state was finally bound to the rest of the Union.

The Dream Fades

Charles Crocker celebrated the completion of the railroad in a way that every American could understand. He had originally traveled to California by land from the Missouri River in just over four months. His triumphant train return to New York took just over four days. In place of the rice, flour, jerky, and dried beans he carried west, Crocker escorted crates of strawberries, cherries, oranges, and roses, kept fresh by glacial ice from Alaska. Easterners were awed. It was the California dream come to life, fresh produce weeks out of season. And only Californians would have the audacity to tap a natural refrigerator on the Arctic Circle.

The state boomed. U.S. population rose 26 per cent from 1860 to 1870. California's population rose 47 per cent in the same decade. The national rate of growth remained constant in the 1870s, but California's grew to 54.3 per cent. San Francisco ruled an empire that stretched from Arizona and Nevada to Alaska and Asia. Manufacturing flourished. Shortages during the Civil War had forced the development of local industry. Agriculture blossomed, from truck farming to feed cities to vineyards that kept them drunk. Wheat grew like a weed in the wet, mild winters, then ripened to stony hardness in the dry, blistering heat of summer. It did not matter that the chief market was Liverpool, for European traders willingly paid a premium for "white gold".

Experimenters in Southern California started with three navel orange trees from Brazil and ended up with an annual crop of winter gold. Another amateur produced a balancing crop of summer gold by planting Valencia oranges in what is now Orange County. Hot on their heels came Luther Burbank, who spent 50 years improving and creating dozens of fruit and vegetable crops.

Expanding industries and productive mines, sophisticated networks of finance and commerce, California in the 1870s seemed to have it all – including a rising rate of bankruptcies, class struggles, racial conflict, and regional rivalries. California had dreamed more than it could deliver. Farmers, manufacturers, and wholesalers thought the new railroad would open vast new markets for their products and bring waves of job seekers

45

to drive down rising wages. Real estate promoters and construction workers envisioned a bonanza of new homes. Land prices doubled and tripled. New towns were created for the expected influx.

Business leaders formed the Immigrant Union, devoted to spreading the rosy tale of California. They found a receptive audience. The national economy was already sliding toward depression. Workers looking westward saw higher wages. Farmers imagined cheap land. More outsiders moved in between 1873 and 1875 than at any time since the Gold Rush.

The railroad had its own dreams. The old hope of controlling overland traffic between Europe and Asia revived. Determined that the traffic would ride their rails, the Central Pacific bought or crushed every local competitor. The Octopus, as the Central Pacific came to be known, extended lines north and south to block potential rivals from outside the

state. The most important was the Southern Pacific, linking San Francisco and Los Angeles via the San Joaquin Valley.

The dreams started falling apart when the Suez Canal opened in 1869, ending hopes of linking Europe and Asia by rail. The Big Four tried to unload their railroad at bargain prices, but there were no buyers. Manufacturers found that aggressive Easterners were flooding California, not buying California products. Farmers found that speculators had already bought nearly all of the arable land while urban developers were going out of business for lack of buyers at inflated prices.

The fevered economy crashed following a drought in 1876-77. Agriculture and hydraulic mining languished for lack of water. When a Comstock mine announced it would skip a dividend payment, depression hit full force. Farmers and workers swarmed into San Francisco to vent their wrath. With monopolies in land, water, transportation, corruption in government, and immigrant labor, they had plenty to choose from.

Above: The locomotive that powered freight, passengers and wild-west mythology.

The Central Pacific was the easiest target. It controlled all longdistance transportation in the state as well as transcontinental service. Free passes and outright bribes kept legislative reforms at bay. Towns that wanted rail service had to provide free land for depots and yards. Crooked tax assessors then undervalued the property.

The railroad had received more than 11 million acres (about 4.5 million hectares) in land grants in California alone. In order to turn a quick profit, the land was sold in large blocks to speculators.

Speculators also controlled huge tracts of "swampland" that had been intended for sale to individual farmers for drainage and cultivation. Local surveyors certified millions of prime Central Valley acres as swampland. Land agents then sold the supposed swamps for as little as $1 an acre. 280 landlords, most of them living in San Francisco, owned 11.45 million acres (4.63 million hectares), most of California's best farmland. It was the birth of agribusiness, factory farming, that still controls California agriculture.

Southern California Rises

Southern California tried to break away from the autocratic north three times in the 1850s. By 1914, business interests in San Francisco were trying to succeed.

That future was far from obvious in 1851. A shallow, poorly sheltered harbor was 20 miles (32 km) away in San Pedro. There were no navigable rivers. Paiute Indians raided outlying settlements. Outlaws retreated south when the law got too close in Northern California. There were 44 murders in a town of 2,300. It got worse. Earthquakes rocked the area in 1855 and 1857. Floods in 1861 and 1862 drowned cattle by the hundreds and thousands and wrecked adobe buildings. When the earth finally dried, it stayed dry for two years.

Anglo-Mexican tensions intensified as the ranchos crumbled in the drought. Social rules which allowed successful merchants to marry into landholding Californio families did not include common *vaqueros* and more recent hardcore Protestant immigrants. Californios rich and poor saw the land commission award their family lands to selfrighteous immigrants from the United States. Some reacted by forming outlaw gangs, which sparked vigilante action more savage than anything San Francisco ever experienced. But as the ranchos died, agriculture, watered by irrigation systems copied from the missions, prospered. Mormons bought El Rancho del San Bernardino, 35,500 acres (14,366 hectares), for $77,500. They built a thriving farming community, then sold it for almost nothing before returning to Utah in 1858.

Fifty German families invested $750 each in a new town they named Anaheim, and planted 400,000 grape vines. A few years later, they were exporting 120,000 gallons of wine and brandy to San Francisco every year. Then came the drought of 1862-64. Cattle ranches great and small died as mortgage holders foreclosed. The new owners, unwilling to restock, turned to other uses. Some raised sheep. Others planted wheat. And some subdivided for immigrants. Suddenly, immigrants were on the way. Most were from the shattered Confederacy, hoping to rebuild far from their defeat. Moving across Texas, New Mexico, and Arizona, California was as far as they could go. New towns like Downey, Pasadena, and Riverside sprouted across the Southland, watered by hundreds of wells drilled into immense underground aquifers. Since no longer affected by drought, agriculture thrived.

Dry weather also attracted sun lovers. As the national economy picked up in the 1880s, so did westward migration. The Southern Pacific eclipsed its parent Central Pacific by driving a line to New Orleans in 1883. When the Atchison, Topeka, and Santa Fé Railroad laid its own route to Los Angeles, coast-to-coast fares to Southern California fell to $1.

Frantic Growth

People poured in. San Diego went from 5,000 in 1884 to 32,000 three years later. Los Angeles boasted that it housed 100,000 the same year. Property sales in Los Angeles County topped the $200 million mark. The property bubble burst, but the City of Los Angeles still had more than 50,000 people in 1890, an increase of 351 per cent in 10 years. And the city knew how to keep growing, thanks to a frantic study of the forces promoting migration.

It extolled the virtues of sunny Southern California during cold Eastern winters. Nature provided the weather, but Californians applied the ingenuity, exuberance, aggressiveness, and slick talk to exploit their good luck. The alluring "California girl" was invented to popularize Southern California. Several Sunkist Orange campaigns promised to bring California sunshine to every American breakfast table.

And there was luck. Oil discoveries in residential Los Angeles sparked an economic boom in 1892. Henry Huntington sold his railroad interests in 1901 and invested in the embryonic streetcar system. Within a decade, the Los Angeles basin had the basic elements of a public transportation system that made it possible for workers to live 20, even 30 miles (32 to 48 km) from their jobs.

The business community supported forest reserves, now national forests, authorized by Congress in 1891. President Benjamin Harrison located California's first reserve in the San Gabriel Mountains north of Los Angeles. Angeli-

Right: The land of milk and honey, and of course oil as well.

nos were not trying to preserve timber but protect a vital watershed. Continued population growth spurred city engineers to propose an aqueduct. Their route lay under mountains and across deserts to the Owens Valley, to tap streams on the eastern Sierra. Some called the water project rape, others salvation, but Los Angeles got its water in 1913.

In the meantime, the Chamber of Commerce had been watching the changing demographics. They had begun by targeting farmers in search of better land. As the new century dawned, they realized that farming was losing its hold on the American psyche, especially on people who had grown up under its crushing physical burdens.

Rural youth were fleeing to the cities. Small Midwestern farm owners and businessmen were cashing in on rising land values and following their children. But they did not want to move to big cities like San Francisco.

Southern California created a halfway urban-rural mix of small towns with plenty of bungalows and lots which were large enough to raise oranges, lemons, walnuts, grapes, or almonds for supplemental income, without too much labor.

The Pacific Electric tram system was always nearby to whisk residents to the beach, to the mountains, or to downtown Los Angeles.

It was a good dream, but it degenerated into sprawling suburbs of single-family homes surrounded by front and back yards. Housing tracts in Los Angeles, Riverside, Pasadena, Anaheim, and other towns blended and congealed. Health, racial purity, temperance, religion, and a vague distrust of the Outside became daily reoccupations. Los Angeles had more churches than any other city of comparable size in the country. Southern California had changed, but residents felt they had lost control. They had not seen anything yet.

Quakes and Scandals

San Franciscans liked to think of their city as pleasure-loving, even romantically wicked. Between periodic economic crashes, it was. The Big Four moved to Nob Hill and began an orgy of mansion building. When mine engineer Andrew Hallidie invented the cable car in 1873, Nob Hill swells built a private line to haul endless streams of grand pianos, classical statuary, teak furniture, and rich friends up the steep slopes.

The growing middle class staged their own immoderate boom. Rows of Victorian homes marched from the original city center. Sober was unthinkable, flamboyance was a bare minimum. Wooden baubles, brackets, spindles, decorative shingles, towers topped with witch's cap roofs, bay windows, iron fences, and stained glass dripped from tens of thousands of façades. They were simple massproduced houses, but catalogs of equally massproduced ornaments turned each exterior into a unique creation.

Money attracted literary talent as well. Rudyard Kipling called San Francisco "a mad city, inhabited for the most part by perfectly insane people whose women are of a remarkable beauty." Mark Twain, Bret Harte, and Ambrose Bierce cut their literary and journalistic teeth in San Francisco. So did William Randolph Hearst, whose *Examiner* perfected the art of yellow journalism.

None of them lacked for subjects. San Francisco was a private dukedom for a procession of businessmen and politicians. Wrote the *San Francisco Call* in 1887: "To hold one of the principal city offices for two years is equivalent to obtaining a large fortune." Vice and corruption were a fine art. One of the city's largest brothels was nicknamed "The Municipal Crib" for the number of city politicians it supported. The same streets gave birth to the words "shanghai," "hoodlum", "hatchman", and "gangster".

It all came to an abrupt end at 5:12 a.m. on April 18, 1906. The San Andreas earthquake fault slipped, sending shock

waves rippling through the landfill that lies beneath much of the city. Streetcar rails became twisted steel snakes. Buildings collapsed. Enrico Caruso was scared voiceless, and the new city hall crumbled, more a victim of poor materials and embezzlement than of the earthquake. Damage could have been worse, and soon was.

With water mains shattered, fire fighters watched a growing conflagration march westward. The proud Palace Hotel, all but untouched by the tremors, was engulfed in flame. So were the elegant Fairmont and the mansions of Nob Hill. San Francisco was a field of flame for three days. Finally, Presidio commander General Frederick Funston ordered houses along the west side of Van Ness Avenue dynamited to create a fire break. Wine soaked burlap saved buildings on Telegraph Hill, but three quarters

Above: A Californian nightmare, the earthquake of April 18, 1906. Right: A repeat performance in 1989.

of the city's homes and businesses were gone. The solid granite U.S. Mint was almost the only building left standing south of Market Street. More than 200,000 people camped out in the city parks.

But the spirit that rebuilt after half a dozen goldrush fires prevailed. Relief workers and army troops fed thousands. To no one's surprise, one of the first businesses to reopen was a bordello. Reconstruction began while the ruins were still smoking. San Francisco remained one of the busiest ports in the world. Profits still flowed through Montgomery Street, the Wall Street of the West. When ground was broken for the Panama-Pacific Exposition in 1911, President William Howard Taft dubbed San Francisco, "The City That Knows How."

It also knew how to have fun, if somewhat more sedately. A wave of reform swept corrupt bosses from power, building on a reform movement that had given Los Angeles voters the referendum, initiative, and recall in 1903. In 1910, voters statewide elected the reform Governor

Hiram Johnson. Women got the right to vote the next year. A Red Light Abatement Act was passed in 1913, closing the more ostentatious brothels.

Movies and Cars

Another influence was creeping into California: the movies. The first film crew set up shop in 1908 to shoot *The Count of Monte Cristo*. A few years later, several independent production companies discovered the Los Angeles suburb of Hollywood. The nearby Mexican border was a decided advantage, for early filmmakers were hounded by agents of Thomas Alva Edison and others who held patents on the new entertainment medium. Cameras and film could be loaded into cars and rushed across the border to safety at a moment's notice, and often were.

But there were more permanent advantages, as D.W. Griffith found when he came west in 1910. Even indoor scenes had to be shot in sunlight, and Southern

California had more sunny days than the East. Any location a script writer could imagine could be found nearby, from alpine forests to the Sahara Desert. Hollywood created Southern California's romantic appeal as the place where all things are possible.

The automobile made it possible to get there. There was only a handful of horseless carriages in 1900, but many of them were in California. Under pressure from the new Automobile Club of Southern California and the California State Automobile Association, the state floated a bond issue in 1910 to begin a statewide system of paved highways.

Luck played a role, too. The rich pools of oil discovered in Los Angeles in the 1920s turned out to be rich in gasoline. Earlier, gasoline had been a bothersome byproduct, important only because it was hard to get rid of. As the number of cars rose, so did gas consumption. In Los Angeles County, for example, the population more than doubled from 1920 to 1930. The number of registered cars

51

quintupled. In 1925, Los Angeles had one car for every three residents, the most car-conscious city in the world. Los Angeles was also the first metropolis to develop during the automobile era. The car intensified the move toward decentralization begun by the Pacific Electric, freeing citizens from densely populated urban centers. Los Angeles soon had the lowest population density of any major city in the United States. The modern supermarket, designed to serve customers with their own transportation, was born in Los Angeles. So were service stations, motels, shopping centers, freeways, and the brown haze called smog.

Depression, War, and Internment

Even the Great Depression could not squelch the car. It was no longer love; it was dependency. Driving continued to increase through the 1930s, especially in California. City workers and migrant agricultural workers needed their vehicles to get to whatever work might be available. The agonies of the Depression lit the fires of social and labor unrest. In San Francisco, police and National Guard troops were used to break a dockworkers' strike amidst charges of Communism. The move sparked a general strike that paralyzed the entire Bay Area and left labor a potent political force.

World War II changed California forever. Federal spending more than tripled personal income between 1939 and 1945, even allowing for 30 per cent inflation and 30 per cent population growth. The military became a permanent fixture in everyday life. Aircraft and shipbuilding industries, chronically short of workers, offered extraordinary opportunities for women, racial minorities, and other groups previously excluded from the economy. But when the

Right: Most Californians take a loving look at themselves in their T-shirt culture.

boys came home in 1945, they got their old jobs back. The quickly displaced minorities were left with little more than bitter memories.

Pearl Harbor also brought rabid anti-Japanese feelings to the surface. About 112,000 Japanese, 93,000 of them in California, were "relocated" to inland camps surrounded by barbed wire, watchtowers, and armed guards. Most of the internees were U.S. citizens by birth; the rest had been residents since at least 1924, when Congress banned immigration from Japan. Japanese property was not confiscated, but they were ordered to sell or abandon nearly all of their possessions.

The internees received an apology of sorts from the War Relocation Authority in 1946. Earl Warren, who supported the internment as California attorney general, apologized for his actions after he was appointed Chief Justice of the U.S. Supreme Court. In 1988, Congress finally approved reparation payments to the surviving internees.

Revolt

The entire nation seemed to doze off during the 1950s, California included. Immigration mushroomed as thousands of exservicemen returned to the warm climate and relaxed lifestyle they had seen during World War II. But the slumber did not last. The first murmurings of protest came from San Francisco. Gossip columnist Herb Caen called them "beatniks", hanging out in cheap North Beach coffee houses, listening to jazz music, reading poetry, discovering marijuana, and trying to decipher the meaning of life.

It was a murmur that changed the world. "The beatnik begat the hippy", wrote novelist Herbert Gold, "and the hippy begat a life style that touches us in ways that extend from fashion and drugs and sexuality to politics and race and a sense of what America might be".

The change has moved in two diver-

gent directions. The New Left protests of the 1960s began when the House un-American Activities Committee, meeting in San Francisco City Hall, was met by hundreds of noisy protesters. Police moved in with clubs and water cannon. The event set a pattern of confrontation that spread to college campuses across the state and around the country, changing forever the way Americans see government and themselves. The hippy revolution took a less active course, preaching a vague amalgam of peace, love, and drugs. The Haight-Ashbury district of San Francisco became the center of "flower power", with Golden Gate Park next door for blissful wanderings. Sunset Boulevard in Hollywood saw a similar blossoming. Beat figures such as Allen Ginsburg, Neal Cassady, and Ken Kesey flowed easily into the hippy world. New Journalists like Tom Wolfe and Hunter Thompson dove deeply into the experience, translating the feelings of a growing subculture through subjective eyes.

The Haight, Sunset Boulevard, Telegraph Avenue in Berkeley, and other hippy havens became tourist attractions as hip turned fashionable. The hippies, like the beats before, succumbed to their own success and excess. Some scrambled bodies and brains on drugs. Others fell into the clutches of religious cults and charismatic maniacs. But most eventually cut their hair out of economic necessity and joined the "me generation" of the 1980s. Both influences remain. The New Left helped make political activism acceptable, while the hippies forever altered attitudes toward religion, sex, drugs, and personal relationships.

In the 1820s, Horace Greeley advised, "Go West, young man". When Greeley finally took his own advice, he went to California and found an extravagant place that held the seeds of the future. Extravagance has not retreated in the last 150 years, and as the focus of economic might shifts from the Atlantic to the Pacific Ocean, California is still leading the way.

MAKING THE UNEXPECTED EXPECTED

SAN FRANCISCO
THE BAY AREA
WINE COUNTRY
MONTEREY - BIG SUR

SAN FRANCISCO

Poised at the mouth of a giant bay on the edge of the North American continent, San Francisco occupies a hilly, scenic peninsula often eclipsed by Pacific Ocean fog. For all its fame, it is a relatively small and extremely compact city of only 46 square miles (119 sq km) and fewer than 800,000 people. Discovered by the Spanish and established by Mexicans, it was settled by English, French, Germans and Chinese, and fought over by Russians and Americans. Its citizens boast a reputation for liberalism, sophistication, and a high level of acceptance of different beliefs, cultures, and religions.

From its beginning, San Francisco was known as the untamed metropolis of the Wild West. Today, despite its stature as a center for international business and finance, it retains some of its freewheeling pioneer spirit. The city – and many of its citizens – often seem larger than life.

Preceding pages: The "ribbon of highway" by Lone Pine. Dwarfed by the prehistoric dimension of the grand redwoods in Kings Canyon National Park. Traffic jam on the Golden Gate Bridge, hallmark of San Francisco. Left: A friendly meeting at the entrance of Macy's.

The City by the Bay

The discovery of **San Francisco Bay** in 1769 was, in fact, an accident. A Spanish entourage led by José de Ortega, pathfinder for Gaspar de Portola's expedition, sailed from San Blas to north of Monterey, where the waters flowing through the Golden Gate halted their progress. Ortega became the first white man to see the entrance to the bay. He called it *La Boca del Puerto de San Francisco.* It was renamed the Golden Gate by General John Fremont in 1848.

Another Spaniard, Juan Manuel de Ayala, sailed into the hidden bay in 1775, opening the way for the full incorporation of the area into Spain's American empire. Two islands named by Ayala retain those names today. "Island of Our Lady of Angels" is popularly referred to as **Angel Island**, now a recreational park managed by the State of California. Ayala named another island in the bay "Island of the Pelicans"; in 1851 it was taken over by the U.S. government and its Spanish name (La Isla de los Alcatraces) changed to **Alcatraz**. Rising precipitously out of the waters of the bay, the rock was first considered the ideal location for a lighthouse; it came into operation in 1854, warning shipping of the dangers of the foggy region. At the same

SAN FRANCISCO

0   1 km

0   1 mile

time the government built a fortress, one which was never threatened by an aggressor. As of 1861 the exposed location was used as a military prison and even then enjoyed an infamous reputation. Once the island became a federal prison in 1934 its notoriety increased, striking fear to the hearts of even the most hardened criminals. The inhospitable place played host for many years to Al Capone, George "Machine Gun" Kelly, Mickey Cohen and other such reluctant guests. The guards ruled with a rod of iron, any attempt to escape was considered hopeless. For the happy-go-lucky inhabitants of San Francisco, however, the prison represented a blemish on their horizon. In 1963 it was therefore closed. Between 1969 and 1971 Indians used the island as the site of a long demonstration. Today it is an impressive if somewhat spine-chilling destination for day-trippers: More than half a million visitors cross every year from Pier 41 – and are only too happy to be able to leave again for the mainland only two hours later.

The establishment of Father Junipero Serra's **Mission Dolores** in a sheltered valley in 1776 (now 16th and Dolores Streets) was one of three major points of early settlement. The others included the Presidio (west of the Marina district, near the Golden Gate Bridge), a rough military installation at the southern mouth of the bay, and a trading post secured in 1835 in Yerba Buena Cove, a sandy-bottomed inlet named after a local wild mint. It was located where Chinatown is situated today.

A year after Mexico declared its independence from Spain in 1821, the town of **Yerba Buena** was founded by Captain William A. Richardson, an English-born captain determined to establish a port town at the cove. His tent, the first habitation recorded to have been erected on the peninsula, was replaced in 1835 by a house in the 800 block of Grant Avenue (then Dupont Street).

Richardson was described as "the solitary settler" by Richard Henry Dana in *Two Years Before the Mast*. He was soon followed by other settlers, mostly Anglo-Saxon and American, and then by American soldiers aboard the *U.S.S. Portsmouth* in 1846. A plaque placed by the Native Sons of the Golden West in 1916 at the corner of Clay and Montgomery streets commemorates Captain John B. Montgomery's arrival to seek possession of the town and the frontier to the north.

The nearby Mexican plaza at **Portsmouth Square** was quickly transformed into an international commercial hub, replete with gambling halls and saloons. Dana wrote: "The docks into which we drew, and the streets about it, were densely crowded with express wagons and handcarts to take luggage, coaches, and cabs for passengers. ... Through this crowd I made my way, along the well-built and well-lighted streets, as alive as by day."

From the very beginning, San Francisco had an international flavor. Its expansion to metropolitan status, however, was given several major boosts by outside events that changed its shape and its image in the eyes of the world.

Assault of the Argonauts

Described by one writer as "the city that was never a town", San Francisco began its boom in 1847 as Manifest Destiny was drawing the emerging United States from the Atlantic coast toward the Pacific. The decade kicked off by the Gold Rush of 1849 transformed the West as no other single event had.

In the months following the discovery in the Sierra foothills, countless thousands of Argonauts descended upon the Gold Country and San Francisco, its natural port. From all over the United States,

Right: Close encounters between the old and new skylines.

from Latin America and eventually from Europe, gold diggers heard the news and devoted themselves to striking it rich.

What they found in San Francisco was a city just struggling to its feet. In 1847, the town government had hired a civil engineer named Jacob O'Farrell to lay out the land surrounding the original Mexican grid, in order to parcel it off. O'Farrell, setting his sights on Twin Peaks to the southwest, laid out a wide boulevard named **Market Street**. It remains a confusing and artificial dividing line between San Francisco districts.

North of Market, the scale of the blocks is European, designed for pedestrian use. South of Market, the blocks are wider, designed for the wheeled traffic soon to become American tradition. Thus the northern neighborhoods became known as the preferable addresses for commerce and banking; the southern area was home to blue-collar workers and light industry. These distinctions remain in evidence today. Even the South of Market construction of William (Bank of California) Ralston's famed Palace Hotel – now the **Sheraton-Palace**, recently renovated – was not enough to buck the trend.

As gold strikes burgeoned, the young town mushroomed. Wooden shacks and temporary tents sprang up overnight. The city's population soon exploded to some 20,000 as it began changing from a makeshift city to a real one of bricks and timber. Eventually, it developed into a turn-of-the-century hub which was strongly influenced by Victorian architecture. That eclipsed the more sober Greek Revival styles evident in the **Jackson Square Historic District**, now a prime area for antique shopping.

Landfill expanded the city on its northern waterfront as well as the east. In 1848, a New York lumberman named Henry Meiggs brought a shipload of timber to the West Coast. He stayed on to become a prominent citizen. Five years

later, he built Meiggs Wharf in the area that ultimately became San Francisco's best-known tourist attraction: **Fisherman's Wharf**.

Today, the wharf is famous for its open markets and food stalls selling fresh crab cocktails and sourdough bread. Numerous bay cruises leave from the wharf; fine restaurants abound; attractions like the **Wax Museum** and **Ripley's "Believe It or Not" Museum** beckon; street entertainers mime, juggle, and otherwise fascinate passers-by on the sidewalks. Nearby extend **The Cannery** and **Ghirardelli Square**, worthseeing shopping and entertainment centers in restored 19th century chocolate factories.

Bawdy and Boisterous

The region near **The Embarcadero** evolved into a rough-and-ready district known as the Barbary Coast. Close to the passenger ship docks, it filled up with transients from all over the world. At its center was Pacific Street, packed with dance halls, boarding houses, saloons, and bordellos. The area got its name from the infamous pirate-infested North African coast. Today, it is quite different: the $375 million **Embarcadero Center** shopping, restaurant and entertainment complex dominates the district.

One street over, **Broadway** became the modern-day equivalent of the Barbary Coast a little more than a century later, as all-night clubs and topless dancing revues lined the street in the late 1960s and early 1970s. Their numbers have declined, but many of the **North Beach** clubs remain today.

Not that dancing girls constituted the city's entire cultural scene. As early as 1851, operas were being presented on local stages. The few women who had migrated to the boomtown were especially appreciated on the stage. Even the least talented among them could count on regular work and frequent bonuses, sometimes in the form of a veritable shower of gold nuggets strewn on the planks at the end of a performance.

65

The bay, hitherto lapping the shores at the end of Clay Street, was invaded with wharves and eventually settled with landfill. As the city grew, its epicenter migrated from Portsmouth Square onto fill land east of Montgomery Street. The banks established in this quadrant were the foundation for what became known as "Wall Street West", the **Financial District**. Restaurants such as the **Tadich Grill,** on California Street, opened to serve the community; the Tadich remains popular 150 years later.

In close proximity, banks and other centers of commerce were established. Wells Fargo, California's oldest bank and perhaps its most famous, began as a banking and express business in 1852 on Montgomery Street, only a few feet from where the **Wells Fargo Bank History Room** is located today. It displays artifacts from the days of the Gold Rush, in-

Above: His ancestors worked long and hard for the state's glory. Right: Cable cars – facilitating travel since the 1870's.

cluding a red-and-yellow stagecoach. Showcases are filled with gold nuggets, strongboxes, and other mementoes of the city's mid-19th century history.

Union Square, surrounded by Powell, Stockton, Geary, and Post Streets, was always regarded as the city's geographical center. In 1850, it was deeded for public use. Today, the square is at the hub of San Francisco's shopping and theater district. All of the city's major department stores – Macy's, Saks, Nordstrom, I. Magnin, Neiman-Marcus, and The Emporium – are here, along with fine smaller shops, outstanding European-style hotels, and great restaurants. Facing Union Square on the west is the **Westin St. Francis Hotel**, built in 1904 by Charles Crocker; eight U.S. presidents and half a dozen foreign heads of state have stayed at this imposing architectural delight.

Railroads and Chinese

The "Big Four" of the Central Pacific Railroad also invested large sums in great city mansions and fantastic country ranches. Stanford, Huntington, Hopkins, and James G. Fair bought large properties around **Nob Hill**. It later became known as Nabob Hill, as elegant hotels with their names attached were constructed on top.

There was a dark side to the railroad construction that linked San Francisco with the east and south. Thousands of Chinese immigrants were pressed into virtual slave labor. Once in California, many ended up working for longer hours and lower wages than would their Occidental brethren. By 1872, it is estimated, Chinese men held 50 per cent of the factory jobs in San Francisco, swelling the population of the ghetto known as **Chinatown** to approximately 47,000 by 1875.

The area now bordered by Grant Avenue, Broadway and Powell Street remains one of the most intriguing neighborhoods in San Francisco. Grant Avenue throngs with Chinese arts and crafts shops, restaurants, and markets. Saturday mornings, especially, are a riot of color, people, sounds and smells as the community spills out onto the narrow streets to shop for the week's meals. With the influx of Hong Kong Chinese in recent decades, Chinatown has spilled over into North Beach, once dominated by Italians.

The Gold Rush, and then the discovery of silver in the hills of Nevada, dramatically changed San Francisco's profile far beyond the confines of the financial community. The hundreds of ships that began arriving in port in 1849 carried missionary preachers as well as gold seekers. By the summer following the discovery of gold, spiritual life had established a strong foothold in San Francisco, with these missionaries and their myriad successors playing major roles in education and government as well. Presbyterians, Methodists, Episcopalians and Catholics all had their places of worship.

St. Francis Church, located at the intersection of Vallejo Street and Columbus Avenue, is second only to Mission Dolores as the oldest Roman Catholic parish in town, having been founded the year of the discovery of gold. San Francisco's first Catholic cathedral, **Old St. Mary's Church**, was dedicated in 1854 at the corner of Grant Avenue and California Street. Built with bricks brought around Cape Horn and with stone imported from China, it was replaced in 1891 by another cathedral to the southwest, which was destroyed by fire in 1962. Old St. Mary's nearly succumbed to the fire of 1906; only its walls remained until it was rebuilt and rededicated in 1909.

The site of the first Jewish religious services in San Francisco, on the west side of Montgomery Street near Columbus Avenue, is marked by a plaque noting the date in September 1849 when 40 pioneers came together to celebrate Yom Kippur.

Climbing the Hills

Naturally, the city evolved from its birthplace on the waterfront. Communities of Australians, then Latin and other immigrants, sprouted wherever they could. The Anglo-Saxon Protestant population, originally centered west of Portsmouth Square, slowly migrated towards Nob and Russian Hills. But the hills themselves, currently some of the most desirable real estate in San Francisco, posed a natural barrier to early construction: They were too steep.

The renowned **cable cars** now synonymous with tourism in San Francisco were invented in the 1870s. Both Europeans and Americans were working on improving passenger transit systems for expanding cities on either side of the Atlantic. Andrew Smith Hallidie, a London-born mechanic, is generally credited with inventing the cable car line in 1873. He may better be described as the premier developer of the system. "One of the principal developments of mechanical genius in San Francisco is the extensive and perfect system of cable street railways, of which the Clay Street line was the pioneer", wrote C. P. Heininger in his 1889 guide to San Francisco. "The system is unique, and a triumph of inventive genius and engineering skill, of which San Francisco has just cause to be proud." Proud it was, and proud it is. Three major lines remain, running on cable looped beneath 69 blocks of city streets along California, Powell, Hyde, and Mason Streets, every day from six in the morning till midnight. Massive renovations closed the popular system in the early 1980s, but the cable cars and their clanging bells are once again an integral part of the San Francisco experience. Visitors fascinated with these modes of transportation can visit the free **Cable Car Museum** at Washington and Mason Streets to see the world's first cable car, the system's winding machinery, and a film.

The city edged west, transforming more than 1,000 acres (405 hectares) of sand dunes into beautifully landscaped **Golden Gate Park** in 1868. The finer addresses were the palatial Victorian buildings in what is now **Pacific Heights**, in the north central part of the city. Hundreds of large residential sites were established west of Van Ness Avenue and between California and Pacific Streets.

The social pecking order had barely been established when upheaval came in the form of the great earthquake and fire of 1906. The vast majority of the city's homes were destroyed, either by the April 18 quake itself, or by the fires that erupted in its wake. A giant trench was dug as a firestop along Van Ness Avenue; as a result, it is one of the widest boulevards in the city today.

San Francisco's civic symbol is a phoenix rising from the ashes. Naturally,

Right: Haight-Ashbury, the famous and infamous center of the hippy movement.

it began to rebuild immediately. A Beaux Arts-style **City Hall** and other civic buildings became part of the massive reconstruction effort.

An Architectural Boom

By 1915, the city was hosting the Panama-Pacific International Exposition, whose legacy includes the Hellenic-style **Palace of Fine Arts** in the Marina district. Today it contains the **Exploratorium**, an acclaimed hands-on science-and-technology museum.

Other buildings have been inspired by the Palace of Fine Arts – notably the **M.H. de Young Memorial Museum** in Golden Gate Park. It houses a great number of European treasures, including paintings by El Greco and Rembrandt, and Flemish tapestries. There is a gallery of American art as well as exhibits from Oceania and Africa. A separate wing, the **Asian Art Museum**, is devoted to collections of Oriental porcelain, sculptures, and other artwork, spanning 6,000 years of history from China and Japan to the Middle East.

Besides the museums, **Golden Gate Park** contains numerous gardens (with about 6,000 species of plants). On sunny weekends, it is packed with all manner of San Franciscans at play, and is a great place for people-watching.

By 1932, San Francisco opera aficionados had their temple, the **War Memorial Opera House** on Van Ness Avenue at Grove Street. It is now part of an enormous Civic Center complex that includes the **Davies Symphony Hall**, the **San Francisco Museum of Modern Art**, and **Herbst Theater**, where the U.N. Charter was signed in 1945.

Coit Tower, a white cylindrical landmark atop arty **Telegraph Hill** on the northeast side of the city, was built in 1933 as a monument to San Francisco's firemen. An elevator carries visitors up 210 feet (64 m) to a superb viewpoint.

In 1936, the world's longest steel bridge, the **San Francisco-Oakland Bay Bridge**, was built across the 8.2-mile (13.2-km) wide bay, linking the peninsula to the mainland opposite. The following year, the landmark **Golden Gate Bridge** traversed the mile-wide entrance to the bay, extending from Fort Point north to the southern boundary of Marin County.

True to tradition, San Francisco always harbored and fostered dissenting points of view. After all, the **Bohemian Club** was founded here in 1872 by a group of newspapermen, writers, and artists. In its golden age in the early 1900s, the club counted among its members Ambrose Bierce, Sinclair Lewis, Jack London, and Frank Norris. Today the clubhouse is situated in the vicinity of Post and Taylor Streets, though it has become essentially a club for businessmen and politicians. The 1950s version of the bohemians of the previous century was the Beat Generation, including men like Jack Kerouac and Allen Ginsberg, who found,

in the cafés of North Beach, camaraderie and expression for their idiosyncratic literature and jazz. In the 1960s, the hippy invasion culminated in the Summer of Love in 1968. The movement was centered in the **Haight-Ashbury** district, a neighborhood that retains the live-and-let-live characteristics of a generation ago: long hair, avant-garde music, and an extremely casual lifestyle. Within a few years, San Francisco's liberal attitudes had made it a mecca for gay men and women. Throughout the 1980s, the city always had at least one avowed gay on its 11-member Board of Supervisors, helping to ensure a voice for one of the city's most vocal and creative subcultures.

The **Castro District** today is known as the city's foremost gay neighborhood, just as Chinatown is associated with Chinese; North Beach with Italians and artists; Pacific Heights with the Social Register; Richmond with the growing influx of Asian immigrants; South of Market with light industry and small arts-and-crafts concerns.

SAN FRANCISCO
Accommodation

All addresses in city; zip (postal) code is noted. Unless stated, hotels are near Union Square. Telephone numbers have 415 area codes; toll-free numbers indicated by 800 prefix. Rates (1990) for two.

LUXURY: **Campton Place**, 340 Stockton St. 94108 (Tel. 781-5555, 800-647-4007). **Fairmont**, 4 Nob Hill 94106 (Tel. 772-5000, 800-527-4727). **Four Seasons Clift**, 495 Geary St. 94102 (Tel. 775-4700, 800-332-3442); **Hilton**, 1 Hilton Square 94102 (Tel. 771-1400, 800-445-8667); **Hyatt Regency**, 5 Embarcadero Center 94111 (Tel. 788-1234, 800-228-9000); **Le Meridien**, 50 Third St. 94103 (Tel. 974-6400, 800-543-4300); **Mandarin Oriental**, 222 Sansome St. 94104 (Tel. 885-0999, 800-622-0404) Financial District; **Mark Hopkins**, 1 Nob Hill 94108 (Tel. 392-3434, 800-327-0200); **Marriott**, 1250 Columbus Ave. 94133 (Tel. 775-7555, 800-228-9290), Fisherman's Wharf; **Sheraton**, 2500 Mason St. 94133 (Tel. 362-5500, 800-325-3535), Fisherman's Wharf; **Stanford Court** 905 California St. 94108 (Tel. 989-3500, 800-227-4736); **Westin St. Francis**, 335 Powell St. 94102 (Tel. 397-7000, 800-228-3000).

MODERATE: **Bedford**, 761 Post St. 94109 (Tel. 673-6040, 800-227-5642); **Holiday Inn Financial District/Chinatown**, 750 Kearny St. 94108 (Tel. 433-6600, 800-465-4329); **Holiday Inn Fisherman's Wharf**, 1300 Columbus Ave. 94133 (Tel. 771-9000, 800-465-4329); **Howard Johnson's**, 580 Beach St. 94133 (Tel. 775-3800, 800-654-2000), Fisherman's Wharf; **Kensington Park**, 450 Post St. 94102 (Tel. 788-6400, 800-553-1900); **Miyako**, 1625 Post St. 94115 (Tel. 922-3200, 800-533-4567), Japanese-style, Japan Center; **Monticello Inn**, 80 Cyril Magnin St. 94102 (Tel. 392-8800, 800-669-7777); **Villa Florence**, 225 Powell St. 94102 (Tel. 397-7700, 800-553-4411). **Vintage Court**, 650 Bush St. 94108 (Tel. 392-4666, 800-654-1100).

BUDGET: **Atherton**, 685 Ellis St. 94109 (Tel. 474-5720, 800-227-3608). Civic Center. **Essex**, 684 Ellis St. 94109 (Tel. 474-4664). Civic Center. **Geary**, 610 Geary St. 94102 (Tel. 673-9221, 800-227-3352). **Grant Plaza**, 465 Grant Ave. 94108 (Tel. 434-3883, 800-472-6805). Chinatown. **Mark Twain**, 345 Taylor St. 94102 (Tel. 673-2332, 800-227-4074). **Mosser Victorian Hotel of Arts and Music**, 54 Fourth St. 94103 (Tel. 986-4400, 800-227-3804). **Virginia**, 312 Mason St. 94102 (Tel. 397-9255).

Bookstores and Libraries
City Lights (poetry, new editions), 261 Columbus Ave. (Tel. 368-8193); **European Book Co.** (foreign-language), 500 Sutter St. (Tel. 981-1666); **Harold's** (international), 484 Geary St. (Tel. 474-2937); **Land of Counterpane** (children), 139 Kearny St. (Tel. 986-7745); **Sierra Club Bookstore** (outdoor), 730 Polk St. (Tel. 923-5600). *LIBRARY:* **Main Public Library,** Civic Center (Tel. 558-3191).

Hospitals
Children's, 3700 California St. (Tel. 386-0830); **Mount Zion**, 1600 Divisadero St. (Tel. 567-6600); **Pacific Medical Center**, 2320 Sacramento St. (Tel. 563-4321); **Saint Francis**, 900 Hyde St. (Tel. 775-4321); **San Francisco General**, 1001 Potrero Ave. (Tel. 431-2800); **University of California**, 500 Parnassus Ave. (Tel. 666-9000).

Museums and Art Galleries
American Carousel Museum, 633 Beach St. (Tel. 928-0550), 10am-6pm daily; **Asian Art Museum**, Golden Gate Park (Tel. 668-8921), 10am-5pm Wed-Sun; **Cable Car Museum,** Washington and Mason streets (Tel. 474-1887), 10am-5pm daily; **California Academy of Sciences**, Golden Gate Park (Tel. 221-5100), 10am-5pm daily; **California Palace of the Legion of Honor**, Lincoln Park (Tel. 750-3600), 10am-5pm Wed-Sun; **Chinese Historical Society of America Museum**, 650 Commercial St. (Tel. 391-1188), 12-4pm Wed-Sun; **M.H. de Young Memorial Museum**, Golden Gate Park (Tel.750-3600), 10am-5pm Wed-Sun; **Exploratorium/Palace of Fine Arts**, 3601 Lyon St. (Tel. 561-0360), 10am-5pm Wed-Sun; **Friends of Photography Museum**, Ansel Adams Center, 250 Fourth St. (Tel. 495-7000), 11am-6pm Tue-Sun; **Museum of Modern Art**, 401 Van Ness Ave. (Tel. 863-8800), 10am-5pm Tue-Wed and Fri, 10am-9pm Thu, 11am-5pm Sat-Sun; Old Mint, Fifth and Mission streets (Tel. 974-0788), 10am-4pm Mon-Fri; **Ripley's "Believe It or Not!" Museum**, 175 Jefferson St. (Tel. 771-6188), 10am-10pm daily winter, 9am-12am daily summer; **Wax Museum at Fisherman's Wharf**,145 Jefferson St. (Tel. 885-4975), 10am-10pm daily winter, 9am-11pm daily summer; **Wells Fargo Bank History Museum**, 420 Montgomery St. (Tel. 396-2619), 9am-5pm Mon-Fri; **Whittier Mansion**, 2090 Jackson St. (Tel. 567-1848), 1-4:30pm Tues-Sun.

Other Attractions
Coit Tower, Telegraph Hill (Tel. 362-8037), 10am-5:30pm daily June-Sept, 9am-4:30pm daily Oct-May; **Golden Gate Na tional Recreation Area**, Park Headquarters, Building 201, Fort Mason (Tel. 556-0560), includes Alcatraz Island

and sites in three counties; **Golden Gate Park**, McLaren Lodge, Fell and Stanyan streets (Tel. 558-4268); **Performing Arts Center,** 401 Van Ness Ave. (Tel. 621-6600), tours 10am-2:30pm Mon; **Presidio**, Building 37, Presidio (Tel. 5561-2211), 10am-5pm daily; **S.S. Jeremiah O'Brien**, Fort Mason, Pier 3 East (Tel. 441- 3101), 9am-3pm daily; **S.F. Maritime National Historical Park**, Hyde Street Pier (Tel. 556-3002), 10am-5pm daily winter, 10am-6pm daily summer; **San Francisco Zoo**, Sloat Blvd. and 45th Ave. (Tel. 661-2023), 10am- 5pm daily.

Postal Services

Main Post Office, Seventh and Mission streets (Tel. 550-0100). There are about 50 other postal stations in the city.

Restaurants

AMERICAN: **Hamburger Mary's**, 1582 Folsom St. (Tel. 626-5767); **Hard Rock Cafe**, 1699 Van Ness Ave. (Tel. 885- 1699); **Lehr's Greenhouse**, 740 Sutter St. (Tel. 474-6478); **MacArthur Park**, 607 Front St. (Tel. 398-5700); **Palm Restaurant**, 586 Bush St. (Tel. 981-1222); **Top of the Mark**, Mark Hopkins Hotel, California /Mason Streets (Tel. 392-3434). *CALIFORNIA:* **Billboard Cafe**, 299 Ninth St. (Tel. 558-9500); **Cafe Majestic**, 1500 Sutter St. (Tel. 776-6400); **Clement Street Bar & Grill**, 708 Clement St. (Tel. 386-2200); **Edible Delights Cafe**, 1916 Hyde St. (Tel. 673-6632). *CHINESE:* **The Celadon**, 881 Clay St. (Tel. 982-1168); **Dynasty Fantasy**, 6139 Geary Blvd. (Tel. 386-3311); **Empress of China**, 838 Grant Ave., 6th floor (Tel. 434-1345); **Imperial Palace**, 919 Grant Ave. (Tel. 982-4440); **Ocean City**, 640 Broadway (Tel. 982-2328); **The Pot Sticker,** 150 Waverly Place (Tel. 397-9985). *CONTINENTAL:* **Amelio's**, 1630 Powell St. (Tel. 397-4339); **Doros**, 714 Montgomery St. (Tel. 397-6822); **Magic Pan**, 341 Sutter St. (Tel. 788-7397) and Ghirardelli Square (Tel. 474-6733); **Maxwell's of San Francisco**,Ghirardelli Square (Tel. 441-4140); **Sears Fine Foods**, 439 Powell St. (Tel. 986-1160). *FRENCH:* **Brasserie Chambord**, 150 Kearny St. (Tel. 434- 3688); **Christophe**, 320 Mason St. (Tel. 433-7560); **Ernie's**, 847 Montgomery St. (Tel. 397-5969); **L'Olivier**, 465 Davis Court, Jackson Square (Tel. 981-7824); *GERMAN:* **Beethoven**, 1701 Powell St. (Tel. 391-4488); **Schroeder's**, 420 Front St. (Tel. 421-4778). *INDIAN:* **India House**, 350 Jackson St. (Tel. 392-0744); **Peacock,** 2800 Van Ness Ave. (Tel. 982-7001). *ITALIAN:* **Bardelli's**, 243 O'Farrell St. (Tel. 982-0243); **Columbus Italian Food**, 611 Broadway (Tel. 781-2939); **Kuleto's**, 221 Powell St. (Tel. 397-7720); **Tutto Bene**,

2080 Van Ness Ave. (Tel. 673-3500). *JAPANESE:* **Benkay**, Nikko Hotel, Mason/ O'Farrell streets (Tel. 394-1111); **Sushi Boat**, 389 Geary St. (Tel. 781-5111); **Yamato**, 717 California St. (Tel. 397-3456). *MEXICAN:* **Border Cantina**, 1192 Folsom St. (Tel. 626-6043); **Corona Bar & Grill**, 88 Cyril Magnin St. (Tel. 392-5500); **Las Guitarras**, 3200 24th St. (Tel. 285-2684); **Las Mananitas**, 850 Montgomery St. (Tel.434-2088). *SEAFOOD:* **Cliff House**, 1090 Point Lobos Road (Tel. 386- 3330); **Maye's Steak & Oyster House**, 1233 Polk St. (Tel. 474-7674); **Pacific Green**, 2424 Van Ness Ave. (Tel. 771-3388); **Tarantino's**, 206 Jefferson St. (Tel. 775-5600). *THAI:* **Franthai**, 939 Kearny St. (Tel. 397-3543); **Thai Inspiration**, 1217 Sutter St. (Tel. 441-5003). *VIETNAMESE:* **Mekong**, 730 Larkin St. (Tel. 928-8989); **Pearl Garden**, 1715 Union St. (Tel. 673-5765).

Shopping

Union Square is surrounded by upscale department stores like **Macy's, Saks, Nieman-Marcus** and **I. Magnin**.
Near Fisherman's Wharf are four shopping-dining-entertainment complexes: **The Cannery**, 2801 Leavenworth St., a former peach cannery; **Ghirardelli Square**, 900 North Point St., a restored chocolate factory; **Pier 39** and **The Anchorage**. **Embarcadero Center**, Battery and Sacramento streets, is a new complex of offices, shops and restaurants.

Tourist Information

San Francisco Visitor Information Center, Hallidie Plaza, Market and Powell streets (Tel. 391-2000); **San Francisco Convention and Visitors Bureau**, 201 Third St., Suite 900 (Tel. 974-6900); activities are recorded daily in English (Tel. 391- 2001), French (Tel. 391-2003), German (Tel. 391-2004), Japanese (Tel. 391-2101), and Spanish (Tel. 391-2122).

Transportation

The **San Francisco Municipal Railway (Muni)** comprises three cable-car routes ($2 fare); electric buses and motor coaches (85 cent); and underground light-rail (85 cent).
The **Bay Area Rapid Transit (BART)** links eight city stations with 25 in East Bay in a 71-mile (114-km) network. Trains operate 6am-midnight Mon-Sat, 9am-midnight Sun; fare is $2.60. Buses to San Francisco International Airport are run by the **San Mateo County Transit District (SamTrans)** from its TransBay Terminal at First and Mission streets (Tel. 761-7000). Boat trips from Fisherman's Wharf by **Blue & Gold Fleet**, Pier 39 (Tel. 781-8790), or **Red & White Fleet**, Pier 41 (Tel. 546-2655).

SAN FRANCISCO BAY AREA

0 ___ 5km
0 ___ 5 ___ 10miles

THE BAY AREA

For a relatively small city-county, San Francisco exerts a tremendous influence over its suburban neighbors. All of the other eight counties that touch San Francisco Bay are larger, but when Californians refer to "the City", they are talking about San Francisco. Each of the nine Bay Area counties – San Mateo, Santa Clara, Alameda, Contra Costa, Solano, Napa, Sonoma, and Marin – has its own personality.

San Mateo County, directly south of San Francisco, is a dormitory community for workers commuting to the city or south to Silicon Valley. It is home to San Francisco International Airport, National Aeronautics and Space Administration research facilities, and the Moffett Field Naval Air Station.

The 1906 earthquake prompted many prominent families to relocate to San Mateo County from the City. Much of the county was originally settled as farmland. One such area, owned by Senator Leland Stanford, in 1891 became today's prestigious **Stanford University,** considered the home of America's high-technology industry. With their many columns and arches, the Romanesque sandstone buildings of the university precinct convey the impression almost of a Spanish mission, their tranquility contrasting sharply with the activity of researchers within. The **Memorial Church** stands in a central courtyard. The walls of the domed church are richly decorated with biblical scenes; stained-glass windows scatter the light in the interior.

Visitors can get an environmental overview of the Bay Area at San Mateo's **Coyote Point Museum**, a bayfront park slightly south of the airport. In microcosm and in imaginative exhibits, it

Right: The rambling house of Sarah Winchester, who was told she would never die if she kept building on to her house.

shows the natural history and contours of the various bay environments. Small coastline towns such as **Half Moon Bay** still evoke the slow pace of times long past. In neighboring **Princeton-by-the-Sea**, it is possible to charter cruises during the winter months to observe the migrations of the Pacific gray whale.

Most of the large inland estates have been divided and remain private, but an exception is **Filoli,** open for scheduled tours. Built in 1916 for an influential water baron, the 16-acre (6.5-hectare) grounds and 43-room mansion are remembered by millions of television viewers as the fictional home of the Carrington family of *Dynasty* fame.

A Mission and High Technology

Santa Clara County demonstrates how far the Bay Area has evolved in two centuries. Founded in 1777 by the Franciscan padres, the **Mission Santa Clara de Asis** was the eighth and most successful of the 21-mission California chain. It

is now located on the campus of **Santa Clara University**. Some of the original adobe structures, as well as a replica of a mission church, can be seen on the campus. The **De Saisset Museum** contains artifacts and photographs relating to the mission and its restoration.

Santa Clara is the home of the **Great America** theme park, with five sections recalling different periods of U.S. history. There are rides, stage shows, restaurants, and shops, spread across 100 acres (40 hectares).

Modern-day Santa Clara is a vast metropolis of low-rise buildings and traffic congestion that is largely caused by the legions of workers toiling in **Silicon Valley**, the greatest concentration of advanced technology in the United States. Visitors can ponder on new and emerging technologies at the **Technology Center** of Silicon Valley in San José.

Above: The San Francisco Oakland Bay Bridge. Right: Moorish architecture lends spice to the harbor of Sausalito.

Busy, booming **San José** may have more unusual attractions to turn tourists' heads than any Bay Area city besides San Francisco. Chief among them are the **Winchester Mystery House,** a strange 160-room mansion whose paranoiac owner feared she would be harmed by evil spirits if she did not keep carpenters working steadily for 38 years; and the **Rosicrucian Egyptian Museum**, a huge private collection belonging to the mystical religious sect of the same name.

The **San Francisco-Oakland Bay Bridge** connects the City with **Alameda County** and its hub cities of Oakland, which always had the image of second best, and Berkeley.

The Merits of East Bay

Oakland boasts an enormous urban saltwater lake, the 155-acre (62-hectare) **Lake Merritt.** Protected in 1870 as the country's oldest waterfowl refuge, its attractions include walking, jogging, sailing, canoeing, and a children's amuse-

ment park. Nearby, the **Camron-Stanford House** hosts cultural and horticultural events in a restored 1876 Italianate Victorian mansion.

The **Paramount Theatre,** a restored 1931 Art Deco masterpiece, presents ballet productions, touring shows, and various recitals and rock concerts. Other notable older structures in Oakland are the **Dunsmuir House**, built in the 1890s, and the **Claremont Hotel,** a landmark resort that is visible from miles away.

Pioneering educator Dr. Cyrus Mills gave his name to **Mills College,** the premiere women's liberal arts college in the Bay Area. Much of northern California's history can be traced in the **Oakland Museum**, which includes exhibits on natural history as well as art. Author Jack London, who spent many years in Oakland, is honored by **Jack London Square**, a popular waterfront complex housing various restaurants and a bevy of boutiques and other retail establishments.

The **University of California** was established in **Berkeley** in 1873. Today, it is the head campus, and the most prestigious, of a nine-campus statewide complex. Originally designed by the noted landscape architect Frederick Law Olmstead, it defines life in Berkeley today. Tens of thousands of students give Telegraph Avenue a permanent aura of impermanence. This was, after all, the birthplace of the Free Speech Movement in the 1960s. The faculty is no less a factor in Berkeley's complexion. They comprise an influential core of the community, considered one of the most left-leaning in California.

The **Campanile** is Berkeley's landmark, a 307-foot (93 m) clock tower where visitors can get 360-degree views. The **University Art Museum**, the largest university museum in the country, exhibits its works by Cezanne, Picasso, Renoir, Rubens, Miro, and many modern American artists. It also has the world's largest collection of paintings by German-born abstract expressionist Hans Hoffman, who donated paintings and money that helped create the museum.

Shattuck Avenue has become known as a "gourmet ghetto", thanks to a restaurant called **Chez Panisse**, credited with introducing the concept of "California cuisine". An eye-catching sight is the fairy-tale-like **Claremont Resort Hotel**, built in 1915 – a good place to spend a refreshing afternoon.

Contra Costa and Marin

North and east of Alameda County, Contra Costa County's far-flung suburbs are booming. More and more businesses have moved from San Francisco and established satellite offices closer to the homes of commuters, eager to avoid the high real-estate prices, congestion and fog of San Francisco.

Marin County, the southernmost of the North Bay counties, has long been a popular summer retreat for well-to-do San Francisco families. But the 1937

Above: The Pacific Ocean's incessant wash at Point Reyes National Seashore.

spanning of the mile-wide Golden Gate heralded a new era in suburban development. Known for innovative lifestyles and high incomes, Marin is the least populated of the Bay Area counties. That blessing was enhanced by the establishment in 1972 of the **Golden Gate National Recreation Area**. Congress set aside some 34,000 acres (13,750 hectares) stretching from the San Francisco waterfront through much of Marin, including mountains and portions of the bay and ocean.

The **Point Reyes National Seashore** is a vast peninsula featuring trails for hiking and horseback riding. It was in this vicinity that Sir Francis Drake landed in the 16th century. Today, Marin is also known for picturesque towns such as **Sausalito** and **Mill Valley**, as well as for **Mount Tamalpais,** a scenic state park with peaks nearing 2,500 feet (760 m). On the slopes of this mountain, which is extremely popular with hikers and mountain bikers, is a vast preserve of native redwoods, **Muir Woods National Monument**.

BAY AREA
BURLINGAME / AIRPORT
Accommodation
LUXURY: **Sofitel**, 223 Twin Dolphin Drive, Red wood City 94065 (Tel. 415-598-9000, 800-221-4542); *MODERATE:* **Embassy Suites**, 150 Anza Blvd., Burlingame 94010 (Tel. 415-342-4600, 800-362-2779). *BUDGET:* **La Quinta**, 20 Airport Blvd., South San Francisco 94080 (Tel. 415-583-2223, 800- 531-5900).

Attractions
Coyote Point Museum, Coyote Point, S. Mateo (Tel. 415-342-7755), 10am-5pm Wed-Fri, 1-5pm Sat-Sun. **Filoli House**, Canada Rd, Woodside (Tel. 415-364-2880), 10am-4pm, Tue-Sat, Feb-Nov.

Tourist Information
San Mateo County Convention and Visitors Bureau, 11 Anza Blvd., Suite 410, Burlingame, CA 94010 (Tel. 415-348-7600, 800-288-4748).

EAST BAY
Accommodation
LUXURY: **Berkeley Marina Marriott**, 200 Marina Blvd., Berkeley 94710 (Tel. 415-548-7920, 800-228-9290); **Claremont Resort**, Ashby and Domingo avenues, Oakland 94623 (Tel. 415-843-3000). *MODERATE:* **Boatel Waterfront Inn**, 88 Jack London Sq., Oakland 94607 (Tel. 415-836-3800); **Durant**, 2600 Durant Ave., Berkeley 94704 (Tel. 415-845-8981). *BUDGET:* **Best Western Berkeley House**, 920 University Ave., Berkeley 94710 (Tel. 415-849-1121, 800-528-1234); **Jack London Inn**, 444 Embarcadero West, Oakland 94607 (Tel. 415-444-2032).

Restaurants
AMERICAN: **Oakland Grill**, 3rd and Franklin streets, Oakland (Tel. 415-835-1176); **Chez Panisse**,1517 Shattuck Ave., Berkeley (Tel. 415-548-6004); **Santa Fe Bar and Grill**, 1310 University Ave., Berkeley (Tel. 415-841-4740). *CONTINENTAL:* **Fourth Street Grill**, 1820 Fourth St., Berkeley (Tel. 415-849-0526). *ITALIAN:* **Bay Wolf**, 3853 Piedmont Ave., Oakland (Tel. 415-655-6004). *SEAFOOD:* **Scott's**, 73 Jack London Sq., Oakland (Tel. 415-444-3456).

Attractions
Eugene O'Neill and John Muir National Historic Sites, 4202 Alhambra Ave., Martinez (Tel. 415-228-8860), 10am-4:30pm daily. **Oakland Museum**, 1000 Oak St., Oakland (Tel. 415-273-3401), 10am-5pm Wed-Sat, 12-7pm Sun.

Tourist Information
Oakland Convention and Visitors Bureau, 1000 Broadway, Suite 200, Oakland, CA 94607 (Tel. 415-839-9000, 800-444-7270).

MARIN COUNTY
Accommodation
LUXURY: **Tiburon Lodge**,1651 Tiburon Blvd., Tiburon 94920 (Tel. 415-435-3133, 800-842-8766). *MODERATE:* **Howard Johnson's**, 160 Shoreline Drive, Mill Valley 94941 (Tel. 415-332-5700). *BUDGET:* **Alvarado Inn**,6045 Redwood Hwy., No vato 94947 (Tel. 415-883-5952).

Restaurants
AMERICAN: **Lark Creek Inn**, 234 Magnolia Ave., Larkspur. **Casa Madrona**, 801 Bridgeway, Sausalito (Tel. 415-331-5888); **Butler's**, 625 Redwood Hwy., Mill Valley *SEAFOOD:* **North Sea Village**,300 Turney St., Sausalito .

Attractions
Muir Woods National Monument, via Hwy. 101, Mill Valley, 8am-sunset daily. **Point Reyes National Seashore**, Point Reyes. **Richardson Bay Audubon Center**, 376 Greenwood Beach Road, Tiburon, 9am-5pm Wed-Sat.

Tourist Information
Marin County Chamber of Commerce and Visitors Bureau, 30 N. San Pedro Road, Suite 150, San Rafael, CA 94903 (Tel. 415-472-7470).

SAN JOSÉ / SILICON VALLEY
Accommodation
LUXURY: **Fairmont Inn,** 170 Market St., San Jose 95113 (Tel. 408-998-1900). *MODERATE:* **Hyatt Rickeys,** 4219 El Camino Real, Palo Alto 94306 (Tel. 415-493-8000). *BUDGET:* **Comfort Inn,** 1215 S. First St., San Jose, 95110 (Tel. 408-280- 5300).

Restaurants
CONTINENTAL: **La Foret**, 21747 Bertram Rd. San Jose. *FRENCH:* **Liaison**, 4101 El Camino Real, Palo Alto. *MEXICAN:* **El Charro**, 2169 S. Winchester Blvd., Campbell.

Attractions
De Saisset Museum, Santa Clara University, Santa Clara (Tel. 408-554-4528), 11am-4pm Tue-Sun. **Great America**, Santa Clara (Tel. 408-988-1800), daily summer. **Mission Santa Clara de Asis**, 920 Alviso St., Santa Clara (Tel. 408-554-4023), 7am-7pm daily. **Rosicrucian Museum**, Park/Naglee Avenues, San Jose (Tel. 408-287-2807), 9am-5pm Tue-Sun. **Technology Center of Silicon Valley**, 95 S. Market St., San Jose (Tel. 408-279-7150); **Winchester Mystery House**, 525 S. Winchester Blvd., San Jose (Tel. 408-247-2101), daily.

Tourist Information
San Jose Convention and Visitors Bureau, 333 W. San Carlos St., Suite 1000, San Jose, CA 95110 (Tel. 408-295-9600, 800-726-5673).

THE WINE COUNTRY

Wine grapes are grown in many areas throughout California. But the premium varieties grown in the region north of San Francisco Bay have earned Sonoma and Napa Counties the joint title "California Wine Country".

Chardonnay, sauvignon blanc, and cabernet sauvignon, in particular, have helped to create a multimillion-dollar industry. Since the 1960s, some California wines have been compared favorably with their French counterparts, laying to rest the myth that New World wines are inherently inferior.

With thousands of acres devoted to vineyards, the Wine Country is one of the state's most beautiful tourist destinations. The Napa Valley, a 21-mile (33-km) swath running north from the bay to the town of Calistoga, is the best-known wine-growing region in California. But neighboring Sonoma County, west across the Mayacamas Mountains, boasts several distinct regions within its boundaries, which extend west to the Pacific Ocean and north to Geyserville.

Startling Sonoma

With nearly 1,600 square miles (about 4,000 sq km), **Sonoma** is not only the larger but the more historic of the two counties. The entire breadth and sweep of the California winemaking saga can be traced here. A huge, colorful cast of characters, international intrigue, armed rebellion, and numerous innovations in agriculture and viticulture make this first century of Sonoma's development as complex as a full-length novel.

Two centuries separate the discovery of the Sonoma coast, in 1602 by the expedition of Sebastian Vizcaino, and its first habitation by hunters. In 1775, Fran-

Left: Napa Valley grapes have earned world-wide recognition.

cisco de Bodega charted what is now Bodega Bay and nearby Tomales Bay.

But it was Russians who settled here first, establishing a community called Romazov. They used it as a base for hunting the sea otter and for growing food to supply their colony in Alaska. In 1812, they established Fort Ross, naming it after their motherland "Rossiya", and began hunting seals off the Farallon Islands, which lay on the horizon. The old block buildings and a Russian church are still visible at **Fort Ross State Park**.

After Spain relaxed its hold on the colonies, the Mexican government, concerned about encroachment from the Russians, advised Father Jose Altimira to consolidate two southern-lying missions into a single mission farther north.

Sonoma was chosen as an ideal site: close to the Russian encampments yet also convenient for the Indian neophytes of the mission. Today, the only vestige of the original Indian inhabitants is the town's name, which recalls a chieftain named Zanoma.

The Mission San Francisco Solano in Sonoma was the last and northernmost of the California missions, and the only one built under the Mexican government. For more than a decade, the small, whitewashed adobe **Sonoma Mission** served as a distant outpost. Now the restored stucco-clad structure houses an outstanding collection of clerical vestments, historical relics, and paintings.

Under orders from Mexico, General Mariano Vallejo secularized the mission in 1833 in an attempt to banish the Russians once and for all. A native Californio, Vallejo, went on to establish a *presidio* and map out the town plaza, which remains the center of Sonoma today.

Among the adobe buildings facing the square, the two-storey, balconied **Sonoma Barracks** is a state historic monument. The nearby mansion where Vallejo lived, Casa Grande, burned down, but a long, low adobe in back, used as a

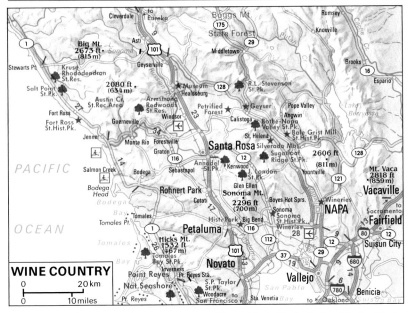

kitchen and for servants' quarters, remains in the hands of the state.

Numerous other 19th century structures also remain. The **Swiss Hotel**, built by Vallejo's brother Salvador in 1840, was remodeled and converted into a commercial establishment in the 1880s. On a nearby corner, the **Sonoma Hotel** began life as a two-storey building occupied by shops, grocery stores, and saloons, with a meeting hall on the upper floor. Samuele Sebastiani, a noted winemaker, eventually added a third floor and balcony. The popular hotel boasts one room decorated with furnishings that were once Vallejo's sister's.

Vallejo built a Gothic Revival-style home a few blocks to the west of Casa Grande. Old magnolia trees still shade Lachryma Montis ("Tears of the Mountain"), where Vallejo lived until his death in 1890. The house, part of **Vallejo**

Right: Robert Mondavi represents one of the latest generations of Napa Valley vintners.

Home State Park, is furnished with the general's possessions.

The First Grape Vines

In 1824, Father Altimira planted more than 1,000 grapevines to produce sacramental wine for the new mission. After the mission closed, General Vallejo replanted vines around the plaza to ensure enough wine for his own use. Despite a disappointing first vintage, Vallejo persevered with such success that he is now remembered almost as much for his wine-growing ability as for founding the town. It remained for a Hungarian count named Agoston Haraszthy to solidly establish the California wine industry. In 1856, he moved his grape-growing operations north from San Mateo County to acreage now known as the **Buena Vista Winery** on the east edge of town. Using Chinese labor, he had several tunnels dug into the hillside for storing wine. They are part of the winery tour now, more than a century later.

Haraszthy was the first vintner to use California redwood for aging casks and the first to discover that vines planted in coastal regions did not need irrigation to thrive. These innovations made Sonoma the early headquarters for viticultural experimentation and development. But he is best known for introducing European grape varieties into California, following trips to several countries to gather vine cuttings.

Haraszthy's introduction of European grape varieties was very nearly the downfall of the wine industry when Sonoma was hit with phylloxera, a root louse that attacked the imported vines. Even the great horticulturist, Luther Burbank, who later became known as the "plant wizard of Santa Rosa" for his pioneering work in developing some 800 new plants, could not halt the advance of the louse. Eventually, native rootstock – which is resistant to the louse – saved the wine industry. By the end of the 19th century, more than 100 wineries flourished in the region.

The new vintners came from all over the world. **Italian Swiss Colony**, for instance, began in 1881 as a cooperative agricultural association for jobless Swiss and Italian immigrants. After Prohibition, the colony near Asti, north of Geyserville, became one of the top three wineries in America.

Nearby **Alexander Valley** has evolved into a distinct wine-growing region of its own, as has the **Russian River** area, home to such wineries as **Korbel** and **Iron Horse**. The most recent region to emerge is **Carneros**, along the southern boundaries of both Sonoma and Napa counties. Vallejo's in-laws, the Carrillos, settled presentday **Santa Rosa**, which succeeded Sonoma as the county seat and is now by far the biggest city in the county. Following on from wine, two other vital components of fine French cuisine have also settled in Sonoma. The **Sonoma Cheese Factory**, the **Vela**

Cheese Company, not far from the Plaza, and the **French Bakery** provide the other essentials for a picnic.

Napa Newcomers

In 1835, George Yount settled in the Napa Valley on land granted by Vallejo. **Yountville** today is a small town known for wineries such as **Domaine Chandon** and for a large shopping and dining complex called **Vintage 1879**.

Up the valley, English surgeon Edward Turner Bale built a grist mill, a picturesque landmark located near the highway northwest of St. Helena. Built in 1846, the **Bale Grist Mill State Park** is a popular picnic spot for tourists. Although Yount planted vineyards, it was not until the 1860s that vintners began building imposing structures of stone and brick reminiscent of those in France and Germany. Fascinating examples include **Charles Krug**, **Beringer**, **Inglenook** and **Greystone Cellars**, all of which offer interesting tours and wine tastings today.

In 1859, San Franciscan Sam Brannan created a grand resort and spa at the northern end of the valley near Mount St. Helena. Local legend says he intended to name it "Saratoga", but a slip of the tongue caused him to say, "This will be the **Calistoga** of Sarifornia." The name stuck. The hot mineral waters here continue to make it a premium Napa Valley destination.

Esteemed author Robert Louis Stevenson honeymooned near here. His sojourn on the mountain and near the neighboring Silverado Trail found expression in *Treasure Island* and *Silverado Squatters*. In **St. Helena**, the heart of the Napa Valley wine region, the **Silverado Museum** contains memorabilia of the author.

It has been said that Napa is more similar to France, Sonoma to Italy. Likewise, if Napa is Stevenson land, Sonoma belongs to Jack London. The prolific author of such classics as *The Sea Wolf*

Above: Californian wine ripens in the labyrinthan cellars at Stag's Leap Vineyard.

and *The Call of the Wild* made his home in the Sonoma Valley. In Glen Ellen, he built his dream house, an estate called Wolf House. Sadly, it burned down in 1913 before he could move into it. Today, much London memorabilia and the remains of Wolf House can be seen at **Jack London State Park**.

Both Sonoma and Napa Counties were devastated by phylloxera, only to recover and face the economic effects of Prohibition. It was not until the middle of the 20th century that the wine industry fully recuperated. Now, fascinating examples of architecture – such as **Clos Pegase** and **Sterling Vineyards** in Napa, and **Gloria Ferrer Champagne Caves** and **Viansa Winery** in Sonoma – can be visited on tours that include more venerable winemaking concerns.

Sonoma County and the Napa Valley are among the state's most popular tourist destinations today, with a plethora of inns, hotels, restaurants, shops, and recreational opportunities, including horseback riding and hotair ballooning.

(All local phone numbers have 707 area code.)

NAPA COUNTY
Accommodation
LUXURY: **Meadowood Resort**, 900 Meadowood Lane, St. Helena 94574 (Tel. 963-3646, 800-458-8080); **Napa Valley Lodge**, Highway 29 at Madison St, Yountville 94599 (Tel.944-2468, 800-528-1234); **Silverado Country Club**, 1600 Atlas Peak Road, Napa 94558 (Tel. 257-0200, 800-532-0500); **Vintage Inn**, 6541 Washington St., Yountville 94599 (Tel. 944-1112, 800-982-5539).
MODERATE: **The Chateau**,4195 Solano Ave, Napa 94558 (Tel. 253-9300, 800-253-6272); **Clarion Inn**, 3425 Solano Ave., Napa 94558 (Tel. 253-7433); **John Muir Inn**, 1998 Trower Ave, Napa 94558 (Tel. 257-7220, 800-5222-8999).
BUDGET: **Comfort Inn**, 1865 Lincoln Ave., Calistoga 94515 (Tel. 942-9400, 800-228-5150); **Magnolia Hotel**, 6529 Yount St., Yountville 94599 (Tel. 944-2056).

Restaurants
AMERICAN: **Calistoga Inn**, 1250 Lincoln Ave., Calistoga (Tel. 942-4101); **The Diner**, 6476 Washington St., Yountville (Tel. 944-2626).
CALIFORNIA: **California Cafe**, Cement Works, 3111 N. St. Helena Hwy. (Tel. 963-5300); **Miramonte**, 1327 Railroad Ave., St. Helena (Tel. 963-3970).
FRENCH: **La Belle Helene**, 1345 Railroad Ave., St. Helena (Tel. 963-1234); **Le Rhone**, 1234 Main St., St. Helena (Tel. 963-0240).

Attractions
Bale Grist Mill State Historic Park, 3 miles north of St. Helena on Highway 29 at Highway 128 (Tel. 963-2236); **Napa Valley Wine Train**, 1275 McKinstry St., Napa (Tel. 253-2111), open year-round, fares from $25.
Old Faithful Geyser of California, 1299 Tubbs Lane, Calistoga (Tel. 942-6463), open 9am-5pm daily, $2.50.
Petrified Forest, 4100 Petrified Forest Road, Calistoga (Tel. 942-6667), open 9am-5pm daily, $3. **Robert Louis Stevenson State Park**, 7 miles north of Calistoga on Highway 29 (Tel. 942-4575); **Silverado Museum**, 1490 Library Lane, St. Helena (Tel. 963-3757). Open 12-4pm Tue-Sun, free.

Tourist Information
Napa Valley Chamber of Commerce, 1556 First St. (P.O. Box 636), Napa, CA 94559 (Tel. 226-7455).
St. Helena Chamber of Commerce, 1080 Main St. (P.O. Box 124), St. Helena, CA 94574 (Tel. 963-4456).

SONOMA COUNTY
Accommodation
LUXURY: **Sonoma Mission Inn and Spa**, 18140 Sonoma Hwy. 12, Sonoma 95476 (Tel. 938-9000, 800-358-9022); **Timber Cove Inn**, 21780 North Coast Hwy. 1, Jenner 95450 (Tel. 847-3231). *MODERATE:* **Fountaingrove Inn**, 101 Fountaingrove Pkwy., Santa Rosa 95403 (Tel. 578-6101, 800-222-6101); **Los Robles Lodge**, 925 Edwards Ave., Santa Rosa 95401 (Tel. 545-6330, 800-552-1001); **Sheraton Round Barn Inn**, 3555 Round Barn Blvd., Santa Rosa 95401 (Tel. 523-7555); **Sonoma Valley Inn**, 550 Second St. W., Sonoma 95476 (Tel. 938-9200, 800-334-5784). *BUDGET:* **Dry Creek Inn**, 198 Dry Creek Rd, Healdsburg 95448 (Tel. 433-0300); **Heritage Inn**, 870 Hopper Ave., Santa Rosa 95403 (Tel. 545-9000, 800-553-1255); **Petaluma Inn**, 200 S. McDowell Blvd., Petaluma 94952 (Tel. 763-0994, 800-528-1234).

Restaurants
AMERICAN: **Sandy Creek Gardens**, 415 First St. W., Sonoma. **John Ash & Co.**, 2324 Montgomery Drive, Santa Rosa.
CONTINENTAL: **Salt Point Lodge**, 23255 North Coast Hwy. 1, Jenner. *FRENCH:* **Provencal**, 18140 Sonoma Hwy., Sonoma.
SEAFOOD: **Inn at the Tides**, 800 North Coast Hwy. 1, Bodega Bay.

Attractions
Armstrong Redwoods State Reserve, 17000 Armstrong Woods Road, Guerneville (Tel. 869-2015), open 8am-sunset daily. **Fort Ross State Historic Park**, 12 miles north of Jenner on Highway 1 (Tel. 847-3286), open daily. **Healdsburg Museum**, 221 Matheson St., Healdsburg (Tel. 431-3325), 12-5pm Tue-Sat. **Jack London State Historic Park**, 2400 London Ranch Road, Glen Ellen (Tel. 938-5216), open 8am-sunset daily. **Luther Burbank Memorial Garden and Home**, 415 Steele Lane, Santa Rosa (Tel. 576-5115), 10am-4pm Wed-Sun. **Petaluma Adobe State Historic Park**, 3325 Adobe Rd, Petaluma (Tel. 762-4871), open 10am-5pm daily. **Sonoma Cheese Factory**, 2 Spain St., Sonoma (Tel. 996-1000), 9:30am-5:30pm daily. **Sonoma County Museum**, 425 Seventh St., Santa Rosa (Tel. 579-1500), 11am-4pm Wed-Sun. **Sonoma State Hist. Park and Mission San Francisco Solano**, Spain St., Third St. W., Sonoma (Tel. 938-1519), daily.

Tourist Information
Sonoma County Convention and Visitors Bureau, 10 Fourth St., Suite 100, Santa Rosa, CA 95401 (Tel. 575-1191); **Sonoma Valley Visitors Bureau**, 453 First St., East Sonoma, CA 95476 (Tel. 996-1090).

MONTEREY BAY AND BIG SUR

Located almost at the exact center of the California coast, **Monterey Bay** offers a little of everything that band of coastline is known for. In the north are redwood forests and wide sandy beaches blessed by sun and gentle surf. In the south are deep green forests of Monterey cypress and fog-swept rocky promontories falling into an untamed sea.

The bay's northern tip begins at **Santa Cruz**. The two-hour drive south from San Francisco is most pleasantly made by following bucolic coastal Highway 1. Although much of Santa Cruz's charming Victorian-era downtown was ravaged by the October 1989 earthquake, there is still much for the visitor to enjoy in the mountains and beaches surrounding the city.

One of Santa Cruz's oldest and best-known attractions, the **Santa Cruz Boardwalk,** survived the earthquake and

Above: Recalling John Steinbeck: Fisherman's Wharf. Right: The Lone Cypress.

was open for business within days of the disaster. Unharmed was the Giant Dipper roller coaster, which has thrilled millions of riders since 1924, and the lovely merry-go-round, with its carousel animals carved by Charles Loof in 1911. Elsewhere on the old-fashioned boardwalk are two dozen other rides and turn-of-the-century amusements. Fronting the boardwalk is a mile-wide swath of sandy beach bordered by **Municipal Wharf,** the longest pier on the Pacific Coast. It supports a lively jumble of seafood restaurants and markets.

A less commercial coastal attraction in Santa Cruz is **Natural Bridges State Park.** A sandstone arch overlooking the beach gives the park its name. The loop trail is especially delightful in fall and winter when clusters of monarch butterflies hang in long fluttering veils from the eucalyptus trees.

Above the city, the **University of California at Santa Cruz** sits on 2,000 acres (4,940 hectares) of redwood forest and rolling grasslands. The campus, founded in 1965, is worth a visit both for its spectacular setting, with sweeping views of Monterey Bay, and for its eight colleges with their distinct architectural styles and academic focuses.

Heading south from Santa Cruz, Highway 1 leads past several pleasant beach parks open both for day use and overnight camping. Among them are **New Brighton State Beach** and **Seacliff State Beach.** Also worth a stop is the **Elhorn Slough,** a federal bird sanctuary near Moss Landing. A 2-mile (3-km) walk along the meandering canals and wetlands can reveal swans, pelicans, loons, herons, egrets, and even pink flamingoes.

The 17-Mile Drive

A good way to begin exploration of the Monterey area is to take the **17-Mile Drive.** The main entrances are off Lighthouse Avenue in Pacific Grove and North San Antonio Avenue in Carmel. Although some sightseers balk at the $5-per-car entrance fee, it is well worth the price to explore these 8,400 acres (3,400 hectares) of forest and coastal splendor.

Among the natural treasures are many prime examples of the rare Monterey cypress, trees so gnarled and twisted that Robert Louis Stevenson once described them as "ghosts fleeing before the wind". Most photographed is the **Lone Cypress,** a weather-sculpted tree growing out of a rocky outcropping pounded by the surf below. Two other natural landmarks are **Seal Rock** and **Bird Rock,** two islands teeming with harbor seals, sea lions, cormorants, and pelicans.

The drive is also known for the palatial homes and resorts situated along its meandering curves. Most impressive of the stately mansions is the **Crocker Marble Palace,** a waterfront estate designed after a Byzantine castle.

In **Monterey,** one can explore the historic roots of the entire state of California. Under Spanish rule in the late

18th century, Monterey was both the military and ecclesiastical capital of Alta California, an important center.

Although Monterey's political importance waned soon after Commodore John Sloat had raised the American flag over the Custom House on July 7, 1846, the remnants of its past glory can be observed at **Monterey State Historic Park,** a collection of handsomely preserved adobe buildings and other landmarks. Far from being an isolated period museum, some of the park's buildings are an integral part of the town, still in use as government offices, restaurants, and private residences. Others are museums open to the public, vivid illustrations of life in the raw young seaport.

The best way to enjoy the park is on a 2-mile (3-km) self-guided walking tour outlined in a brochure called "The Path of History", available at the chamber of commerce or at many of the buildings in the park. Among the highlights are the **Custom House,** built by the Mexican government in 1814 and considered the

oldest government building west of the Rockies, and the **Larkin House,** a lovely blend of Mexican and New England architecture with rooms furnished in period antiques brought from New Hampshire by the Larkin family. Also in the park is **Colton Hall,** furnished as it was when a convention of delegates met in 1848 to draft the first state constitution.

Inevitably, visitors are drawn toward the waterfront in Monterey, if only because the mournful barking of sea lions heard throughout the town is a constant reminder of its presence. The whiskered marine mammals are best enjoyed while walking along **Fisherman's Wharf,** an aging pier crowded with souvenir shops, fish markets, and seafood restaurants.

From the wharf, a footpath along the shore leads to **Cannery Row,** a street characterized by old tinroof sardine canneries that thrived until the sardines mys-

teriously disappeared from the bay in the 1940s. Today, the canneries have been converted into restaurants, art galleries, and shops, and the fame they gained in John Steinbeck's novel is kept up by the name of one fish restaurant, "Steinbeck Lobster Grotto".

By far the most popular attraction on the Row is the **Monterey Bay Aquarium,** a spectacular window on the sea waters just outside its back doors. Devoted to the plant and marine life found in Monterey Bay, the museum's most impressive exhibit is the three-storey, glass-enclosed **Kelp Forest**, the only one of its kind in the world. Other highlights include a bat-ray petting pool, where the flat, velvety creatures can be touched as they swim past; a 55,000-gallon (208-cubic meter) sea otter tank; and an enormous outdoor artificial tidepool filled with starfish, anemones, and other invertebrate creatures.

More coastal delights lie to the immediate south in **Pacific Grove.** An inviting walking path follows a 3-mile (5-km)

Above: A relic from the Spanish years, the Carmel mission. Right: The wilderness of the Big Sur coastline.

stretch of flower-skirted coastline along Ocean View Boulevard. **Lovers Point Park,** located midway along the waterfront, is a pleasant grassy area for picnics. Another beautiful coastal area is **Asilomar State Beach** on Sunset Drive, a 100-acre (40-hectare) region of sand dunes, tidepools, and pocket-sized beaches.

Pacific Grove is also known as "Butterfly Town USA", because of the thousands of orange-and-black monarch butterflies that migrate there each year between October and March. The best place to see them is **Washington Park** at the corner of Lighthouse Avenue and Alder Street. When the butterflies are not in residence, the **Pacific Grove Museum of Natural History** on Forest Avenue gives a good approximation of the annual miracle. In addition to a finely crafted butterfly tree exhibit, the museum features a collection of 400 mounted birds native to the region.

In much the same way as Pacific Grove attracts butterflies, **Carmel,** a few miles south, is a magnet for shoppers and browsers. Classic sportswear, gourmet cookware, and original art are among the best buys along, Ocean Avenue, and its cross streets. Just as notable is the architecture of many of the shops, a charming mishmash of ersatz English Tudor, Mediterranean, and other styles.

Before it became an art colony in the early 20th century, and long before it became a tourist mecca, Carmel was an important religious center in the days of Spanish California. That heritage is preserved in the **Carmel Mission** on Rio Road. Founded in 1770 and serving as headquarters for the California mission system under Father Junipero Serra, the Carmel Mission exists today with its stone church and tower dome beautifully restored. Adjoining the church is a tranquil garden planted with California poppies, and a series of museum rooms that depict an early kitchen, Father Serra's sleeping quarters, and the oldest college library in California.

Some late 20th century movie fans still consider a visit to Carmel to be a re-

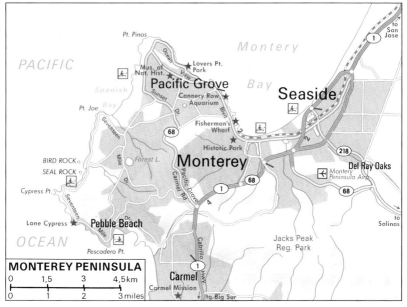

MONTEREY PENINSULA

| 0 | 1,5 | 3 | 4,5 km |
| 0 | 1 | 2 | 3 miles |

ligious pilgrimage. The townspeople elected resident he-man actor Clint Eastwood as their mayor in 1988.

Carmel's greatest landmarks are those left behind by nature. Located at the foot of Ocean Avenue is **Carmel River State Park,** which stretches 106 acres (43 hectares) along Carmel Bay with a sugar-white beach and, on sunny days, water nearly as turquoise as the Caribbean Sea.

A few miles south is **Point Lobos State Reserve,** a 1,250-acre (505-hectare) headland with an impressive network of hiking trails. Especially good choices are the Cypress Grove Trail, which leads through a forest of rare Monterey cypresses clinging to the rocks above an emerald-green cove, and Sea Lion Point Trail, from which sea lions, harbor seals, otters, and (in winter) migrating whales can be observed.

South from Point Lobos, Highway 1 leads to **Big Sur,** a 65-mile (105-km) stretch of coastline that one-time resident Henry Miller described as "the face of the earth as the creator intended it to look".

With the Santa Lucia Mountains on one side and the Pacific Ocean on the other, the drive through Big Sur affords thrilling vistas around each of the tortuous hairpin turns. Building a highway through this formidable territory was a grand achievement, particularly the stunning **Bixby Bridge,** the longest single-span concrete bridge in the world. South of the bridge is **Nepenthe,** a legendary restaurant and bookstore with an outdoor patio – designed by a student of Frank Lloyd Wright – that offers spectacular views of mountains unfolding into the sea.

Big Sur is a hiker's delight. It encompasses several state parks with trails and guided nature walks. Among these is **Julia Pfeiffer Burns State Park** which rewards even novice hikers with views of Waterfall Cove and Saddle Rock after just an easy five-minute walk. More challenging trails in the 3,543-acre (1,434-hectare) park afford exploration of redwood groves and high chaparral country, still a sanctuary for coyotes and black-tailed deer.

SANTA CRUZ

(All local phone numbers have 408 area code.)

Accommodation

LUXURY: **Pajaro Dunes**, 2661 Beach Rd, Watsonville 95076 (Tel. 722-9201, 800-772-5276). *MODERATE:* **Inn at Pasatiempo**, 555 Highway 17 95060 (Tel. 423-5000). *BUDGET:* **Travel Lodge**, 525 Ocean St. 95060 (Tel. 426-2300).

Attractions

Big Basin Redwoods State Park, 20 miles north of Santa Cruz via hwy 9 and 236 (Tel. 338-6132); **Long Marine Laboratory**, 100 Shaffer Rd (Tel. 429-4308), open 1-4pm Tue-Sun, tours; **Roaring Camp & Big Trees Narrow-Gauge Railroad**, Felton (Tel. 335-4484), trains depart noon Mon-Fri, also 1:30 and 2:45pm Sat-Sun; **Santa Cruz Beach Boardwalk**, 400 Beach St. (Tel. 423-5590), from 11am daily summer, weekends spring and fall.

Tourist Information

Santa Cruz County Conference and Visitors Council, 105 Cooper St., Suite 243 (P.O. Box 8525), Santa Cruz, CA 95061 (Tel. 423-1111).

SALINAS

Accommodation

MODERATE: **Ramada Inn**, 808 N. Main St. 93906 (Tel. 424-8661). *BUDGET:* **Laurel Inn**, 801 W. Laurel Drive 93906 (Tel. 449-2474).

Attractions

Mission Nuestra Senora de la Soledad, Fort Romie Rd, Soledad, 10am-4pm Wed-Mon; **Mission S. Juan Bautista**, 408 S. Second St., S. Juan Bautista, (Tel. 623-2127), 9:30am-4:30pm daily; **Monterey County Hist. Museums**, 333 Boronda Rd, Salinas (Tel. 757-8085), 9am-noon Mon-Fri, 1-4pm Sun; **Pinnacles Nat. Monument**, via Soledad, open daily; **San Juan Bautista State Hist. Park**, S. J. Bautista, 10am-4:30pm daily.

Tourist Information

Salinas Area Chamber of Commerce, 119 E. Alisal St. (P.O. Box 1170), Salinas, CA 93901 (Tel. 424-7611).

MONTEREY

Accommodation

LUXURY: **Monterey Plaza**, 400 Cannery Row, 93940 (Tel. 649-4234, 800-325-3535); **Pacific**, 300 Pacific St., 93940 (Tel. 373-5700, 800-225-2903). *MODERATE:* **Mariposa Inn**, 1386 Munras Ave. 93940 (Tel. 800-824-2295); **Victorian Inn**, 487 Foam St. 93940 (Tel. 373-8000, 232-4141). *BUDGET:* **Arbor Inn**, 1058 Munras Ave. 93940 (Tel. 372-3381, 800-351-8811); **Travel Lodge**, 2030 Fremont St. 93940 (Tel. 373-3381, 800-255- 3050).

Restaurant

SEAFOOD: **The Whaling Station Inn**, 763 Wave St., Monterey (Tel. 373-3778).

Attractions

Cannery Row, 765 Wave St. (Tel. 649-6690); **Colton Hall Museum**, Civic Center, Pacific St. (Tel. 375-9944), 10am-5pm daily; **Fisherman's Wharf**, 885 Abrego St. (Tel. 373- 3720); **Monterey Bay Aquarium**, 886 Cannery Row (Tel. 648-4926), 10am-6pm daily; **Monterey State Historic Park**, 525 Polk St. (Tel. 649-7118), hours and days vary; **Museum of Art**, 559 Pacific St. (Tel. 372-7591), 10am-4pm Tue-Sat, 1-4pm Sun.

Tourist Information

Monterey Peninsula Visitors and Convention Bureau, 380 Alvarado St. (P.O. Box 1770), Monterey, CA 93942 (Tel. 649-1770).

CARMEL

Accommodation

LUXURY: **Highlands Inn**, Hwy. 1 (P.O. Box 1700), 93921 (Tel. 624-3801, 800-538-9525); **The Inn at Spanish Bay**, 17-Mile Drive, Pebble Beach 93953 (Tel. 647-7500, 800-654- 9300); **The Lodge at Pebble Beach**, 17-Mile Drive, Pebble Beach 93953 (Tel. 624-3811). *MODERATE:* **Carmel Mission Inn**, 3665 Rio Road, 93922 (Tel. 624-1841, 800-242-8627).

Attractions

Mission San Carlos Borromeo de Carmel, Rio Road. **Point Lobos State Reserve**, Route 1 (Tel. 624-4909), open daily; **17-Mile Drive**, Pacific Grove to Pebble Beach. **Tor House**, Carmel Point (Tel. 824-1813), tours 10am-3pm Fri-Sat, reservations required.

Tourist Information

Carmel Valley Chamber of Commerce, 9 Del Fino Place, Suite 5 (P.O. Box 288), Carmel Valley, CA 93924 (Tel. 659-4000).

BIG SUR

Accommodation

LUXURY: **Ventana**, Highway 1, 93920 (Tel. 667- 2331). *MODERATE:* **Big Sur Lodge**, Hwy 1 (P.O. Box 190), 93920 (Tel. 667-2171).

Attractions

Garapata State Park, Highway 1, 18 miles north (Tel. 667-2315). **Pfeiffer Big Sur State Park**, Highway 1, one mile south (Tel. 667-2315).

Tourist Information

Big Sur Chamber of Commerce, P.O. Box 87, Big Sur, CA 93920 (Tel. 667-2100).

CITIES
IN THE SUN

LOS ANGELES
ORANGE COUNTY
SAN DIEGO
CENTRAL COAST

LOS ANGELES

To many who do not know the city, Los Angeles conjures visions of two things: freeways and smog. The macadam ribbons that tie up rush-hour traffic for hours twice daily are legendary. For people not used to driving them regularly, the legends may be more scary than enticing. But freeways are the means of getting to the disparate delights of this meandering megalopolis, and they are well-marked and easy to navigate.

As for smog, well, it is true that in summer, mainly June and July, when the heat builds up and there are no strong winds to help automobile and industrial emissions out to sea, or rains to wash the skies clean, the area can seem an all-over yellowish gray. But much of the year, L. A. resides under a canopy of blue sky.

That said, it is not hard to understand how the city's convention and visitors, bureau could boast "L. A.'s the Place" in its brochures. Los Angeles has a lot going for it.

There is its size, for one thing. The city of Los Angeles has a population of 3.4 million and covers 464 square miles (1,202 sq km). Los Angeles County

Previous pages: No one walks anymore in Los Angeles.

stretches over a whopping 4,083 square miles (10,575 sq km).

Covering all that ground are a multitude of manmade and natural delights. There are mountains, ocean and desert; there are museums and theaters and amusement parks; and there are so many neighborhoods and communities (nearly one hundred) – each with its own sights and sites – that it would take years to explore them all.

In maneuvering the freeways, remember that they are referred to both by number and name. The freeway's name can change, depending upon where you encounter it. So, get a good road map: the *Thomas Bros. map book*, available at local stores, is outstanding. Auto club maps work well, too, as do the quick-reference maps often given out free by car-rental companies.

Downtown L. A.

Many people equate Los Angeles with urban sprawl at its extreme. It often escapes notice that the city has a "downtown" of its own. That is somewhat surprising, as L. A.'s City Hall, business towers, Music Center and other enclaves of culture and history that make up the heart of L. A. are easy to spot from the Hollywood Freeway.

One of the best overviews of the city can be obtained from the observation deck that circles the top of **City Hall,** downtown's best-known landmark. (It has made several television appearances, among them as the *Daily Planet* newspaper offices in the *Superman* series and as the police station in *Dragnet*.)

City Hall is bordered by Spring, Main, First and Temple streets. It takes two elevators, an express to the 22nd floor and another to the tower, to reach the breezy balcony that on a clear day offers not only a bird's eye look at L. A.'s city center, but a commanding view of the entire Los Angeles basin.

At ground level, the building's marble lobby houses a giant holographic photo of Los Angeles Mayor Tom Bradley as well as modern paintings and a Shinto shrine – a gift from Nagoya, Japan, one of Los Angeles' sister cities.

Across from City Hall, at Temple and Main Streets, extends **Fletcher Bowron Square,** where the city's **Children's Museum** is located. Among the exhibits in this hands-on, learn-by-doing place are "The Sticky Room", where every object coheres to the walls or ceilings, and "The Strobe Light Room", where animated images of children are "frozen" on the walls.

A few blocks north of City Hall on Spring Street is **Pueblo de Los Angeles State Historic Park,** preserving the plaza where Los Angeles began in 1781. It was at this site that Spanish Governor Felipe de Neve founded El Pueblo de Nuestra Senora la Reina de Los Angeles. Today, visitors can see a lacy, wrought-iron bandstand in the plaza, where the local Hispanic community celebrates its holidays to the trumpet blare of *mariachi* music; a graceful old church; L. A.'s first firehouse; and **Olvera Street,** the last concentration of traditional Spanish architecture left in downtown. Olvera Street has become a souvenir-shopping and restaurant district.

Practically next door to this paean to early Hispanic Los Angeles is **Chinatown** (at Hill and Spring Streets and Sunset Boulevard). Shopping centers like Mandarin Plaza, Chinatown Plaza, and Bamboo Plaza wear Oriental façades and offer such items as silk suits and dresses, exotic herbs and potions. The Asian-style **Phoenix Bakery,** an institution in Chinatown for more than 50 years, is worth a visit, too; just follow the aroma to 969 N. Broadway. For lunch or tea, try one of the numerous restaurants serving Cantonese and other Chinese dishes.

Los Angeles is not so much a melting pot as an international stew, with each cultural ingredient keeping its own character but adding to the flavor of the whole. Another such place of interest downtown is **Little Tokyo** (between First, Third, Los Angeles and Alameda streets). This three-block area of shops and restaurants is also home to the **Japanese American Cultural Center** with its James Irvine Garden, a refreshing bit of greenery in a concrete jungle.

Downtown areas of large cities are typically noted for their shopping possibilities, and L. A. is no exception. Of special interest are the **Jewelry District** (along Broadway near Seventh Street), where there are bargains galore on baubles; and the **Grand Central Market** (Broadway between Third and Fourth Streets), where everything from ethnic foods to cowboy boots is available. The **Garment District**, with dozens of retail shops selling fine clothes at a discount, is located between Seventh and Eighth, Main and Los Angeles Streets. More than 2,000 additional clothing manufacturers and representatives can be found in the 3 million square feet (278,000 sq m) of space that make up the **California Mart** (Eighth and Ninth, Main and Los Angeles Streets).

There are shops, too, in many of the buildings that are changing L. A.'s skyline as well as its shopping and browsing

habits. The clutch of skyscrapers in the area bordered by Third and Eighth Streets, Grand Avenue and the Harbor Freeway are business towers, not galleries or oases, yet many have softened their ultra-modern aspects. They have sculptures and other artworks, greenery and fountains, and have filled their lobbies and subterranean levels with shops.

Some of the more interesting downtown buildings to see for any or all of the above reasons are the **Wells Fargo Center** (333 S. Grand Ave.), **ARCO Plaza** (between Figueroa and Flower, Fifth and Sixth Streets), **Citicorp Plaza** (Figueroa and Seventh Streets), **Security Pacific Plaza** (Third and Fourth, Hope and Flower Streets), and the **Home Savings Tower** (Seventh and Flower Streets). The futuristic **Westin Bonaventure Hotel** was created by the architect John Port-

Above: Peace and quiet in the stocks of the University of Southern California. Right: Downtown L.A. from the USC campus. Far right: Streetlife in Los Angeles.

man. Its message seems to be that nature can only be protected within giant buildings. So he included 35 acres (14 hectares) of waterfalls and ponds in the lobby area. At the same time you can use the exterior glass elevators to watch the skyscrapers grow. These downtown highrises signal Los Angeles' status as a major international business and financial center. In fact, if L. A. were its own country, its gross national product would rank sixth in the world. But L. A. is a cultural center, too. Few people give modern Los Angeles credit for that aspect of its lifestyle. At the city's cultural epicenter is the **Music Center**, 135 N. Grand Ave. It contains the Dorothy Chandler Pavilion, a 3,000-seat facility best-known to TV viewers as the home of the annual Academy Awards ceremonies; the pavilion is also home to the Los Angeles Philharmonic Orchestra, the Los Angeles Master Chorale, the Los Angeles Civic Light Opera, and the Joffrey Ballet. Also at the Music Center is the 2,000-seat Ahmanson Theater, which presents inter-

national premieres as well as classic dramas and comedies; and the intimate, 700-seat Mark Taper Forum, home of the Center Theater Group known for its contemporary dramas and new works.

The greater Los Angeles area boasts any number of other theater and music options. The L. A. Philharmonic gives music-under-the-stars concerts each summer in the **Hollywood Bowl**; also in Hollywood is the **Pantages Theater.** The **Shubert Theater** is in Century City.

The **Huntington Hartford Theater** and **Wilshire Theater** present original productions as well as touring Broadway plays. And there are small (300 to 500-seat) houses, among them the **Gallery, L.A. Stage Company, Solari, Mayfair, Westwood Playhouse** and **Coronet.**

Some of the city's museums provide rich cultural experiences, too. Indeed, greater Los Angeles has some of the world's richest museums. The **J. Paul Getty Museum,** for instance, has an endowment believed to be in excess of $750 million. This and other city art museums are covered in a separate article later in this book.

Another museum worth seeing is the **Gene Autry Western Heritage Museum** in Griffith Park. It chronicles the cultural and historical legacy of the American West from the sixteenth century to the present. A heroic-sized bronze sculpture of movie cowboy Autry and his "wonder horse", *Champion,* stands at the entrance. Autry was the driving force behind the museum and some of the 16,000 artifacts come from his own collection. The displays include the art of Charles Russell and Frederic Remington, historic firearms (including a rifle Teddy Roosevelt used on his ranch and a 174-piece Colt Industries collection with weapons), and clothing, toys and furnishings used by early settlers.

For the technically inclined, there is the **California Museum of Science and Industry** in Exposition Park. It includes an Aerospace Complex with planes, rockets and satellites; a McDonald's Computer Chef exhibit giving a behind-

**METROPOLITAN
LOS ANGELES**

```
0        7,5      15 km
0        5        10 miles
```

the-scenes look at the fast-food business; a display showing the inner workings of the body; and a hatchery for baby chicks. Kids love it; so do adults.

At the **Natural History Museum of Los Angeles County,** also in Exposition Park, dioramas and displays present natural history in the form of gems and minerals, North American and African mammals, crafts and artifacts giving insight to the lives of various cultures. The structures that house it are every bit as interesting as the exhibits, especially the Spanish Renaissance main building, which contains inlaid marble floors, travertine columns and walls, and domes.

Walking is an easy and pleasurable way to get around L. A.'s fairly compact downtown. Buses run frequently. Coming in 1993 will be Metro Rail, an underground public transportation system connecting downtown to the "suburbs".

A work of art without art-historical credentials can be seen at 1765 E. 107th Street. **Watts Towers** were built by Simon Rodia, an Italian immigrant. For decades Rodia collected anything and everything he could get for free and then, with this as his building material, erected 30m-high towers in his garden. In 1954, having completed his work, Rodia disappeared, leaving art historians guessing. What remains is an almost inexplicable collection of junk in a dilapitaded part of town: truly art for art's sake.

Hollywood and Beverly Hills

Perhaps no other town fascinates the world as does **Hollywood,** the spiritual home (if no longer the actual home) of moviemaking. It is easy to find Hollywood. Just look for the "Hollywood" sign on the hillside overlooking the community, visible for miles. The original sign read "Hollywoodland" and was put there by a land-development company in 1923 to tout a real-estate promotion; it lost its last four letters in the 1940s. Now,

from a position on Mount Lee, the 50-foot (15-m) letters benevolently gaze across its namesake town long after the company became just a vague memory.

The hub of Hollywood in the days when the name spelled glamour – back when the town was filled with major movie studios, starlets and leading men – was the corner of Hollywood and Vine Streets. Though today it is a seedy street corner in a seedy town (Hollywood is in the process of redevelopment), it remains a good spot to orient yourself for a tour of local sights, such as the **Capitol Records** building just to the north at 1756 N. Vine Street. Shaped like a stack of records – a suggestion of singer Nat King Cole and songwriter Johnny Mercer, both under contract to Capitol in the middle 1950s when the building was constructed – the building also has a chimney meant to resemble a stylus.

Above: Many great actors have left their marks at Mann's Chinese Theater. Right: The other side of paradise.

Also on any Hollywood tour should be **Mann's** (formerly Grauman's) **Chinese Theater**, 6925 Hollywood Blvd., for a look at the forecourt filled with signatures (and sometimes hand and foot prints) of many of Hollywood's elite. Before Sid Grauman built the Chinese Theater, he built another elaborate movie palace, the **Egyptian Theater** at 6712 Hollywood Blvd. Its courtyard was lined with palms and Middle Eastern flavored shops in its heyday, and its stage was flanked by columns and sphinxes. The Egyptian Theatre still shows first-run films, now under the auspices of United Artists. Although it has lost some of its flamboyance, enough remains to make it seem an exotic bit of Hollywoodiana.

Buildings are not all Hollywood has to offer. Its **Walk of Fame,** that part of Hollywood Boulevard between Sycamore and Gower, and Vine Street between Sunset and Yucca, is another favorite with visitors. More than 1,500 bronze stars carrying the names of celebrities are imbedded in the sidewalks there.

You would prefer to see the celebrities, not just their names? You could try **Beverly Hills** – perhaps at the **Beverly Hills Hotel,** 9641 Sunset Blvd. Also called the Pink Palace, it has been a favorite home-away-from-home for visiting movie-industry people for years. Especially popular with the film moguls – and the people who want to see them – is the hotel's Polo Lounge, said to be Hollywood's deal-making headquarters.

Another celebrity hangout – perhaps promenade is a better word – is **Rodeo Drive** in Beverly Hills. One of the most fashionable shopping streets in the United States, it is a relatively short, three-block stretch filled with elegant and expensive designer boutiques, jewelry shops and art galleries. If you do not want to shop, visit Rodeo Drive anyway to watch other people shop.

Not quite so elegant, but also a worthwhile Beverly Hills shopping experience, is **Farmer's Market**, Third and Fairfax Streets. Once an open field where farmers came to sell their crops, Farmer's

Market is now a large fruit and vegetable sales area with more than 160 shops and food stalls. You can browse through the produce or find various delectables for a late breakfast or lunch. Beverly Hills was built to be a strictly upper-class residential community, as can be seen by the sprawling mansions with their well-manicured lawns. So were the nearby communities of **Bel-Air, Trousdale Estates** and **Brentwood.** Many movie people call these communities on L.A.'s west side home. The Hollywood landmark tours of tour companies include drives through this area in their itineraries. Also on L. A.'s west side is **Westwood,** home of the University of California-Los Angeles (UCLA). Its sculpture garden, library and student cafés are worth a visit. Westwood village has lots of interesting shops, not just for books.

Beaches and Beach Cities

Santa Monica, stretching as it does along the Pacific, was once known as the

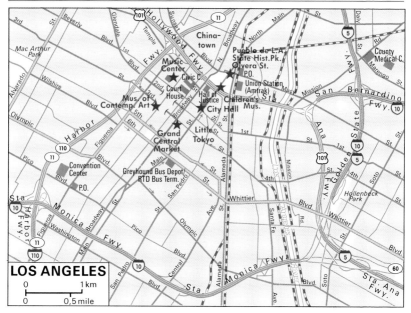

LOS ANGELES

0   1 km

0   0,5 mile

"Gold Coast". Many of Hollywood's biggest names have made their homes here. In the 1930s, for instance, Mary Pickford and Douglas Fairbanks Sr. lived at 705 Palisades Beach Road.

The most-visited landmark along this strip is the **Santa Monica Pier,** built in 1909. It is best known for its fully restored, turn-of-the-century carousel, featured in the movie *The Sting.* The pier has been a location for other movies and TV shows as well. It is a popular fishing spot for locals, and a favorite among people just out for a pleasant stroll, or maybe looking for a meal with a water view. There are any number of dining and drinking spots, bumper cars, video and pinball games, and a psychic ... besides the carousel.

Santa Monica State Beach forms the town's western boundary. It has playground equipment, picnic and volleyball facilities and excellent swimming. Other

Right: The most important pastime in California is keeping fit on the beach.

popular beaches nearby include **Will Rogers State Beach,** at the foot of Sunset Boulevard on Pacific Coast Highway, for swimming and windsurfing; and **Las Tunas State Beach,** about 6 miles (10 km) northwest of Santa Monica along Pacific Coast Highway, for skindiving and spear fishing.

Probably because of the "Gidget" movies and television shows – and because it is where the movie people play these days – **Malibu** *means* L. A. beach life. Although a fence cordons off the elite **Malibu Colony** homes of the stars, stargazing is still as popular here as swimming and surfing.

South of Santa Monica is **Venice.** In 1909, Abbot Kinney purchased 160 acres (64 hectares) of marshy tidal flats here with the intention of replicating Venice, Italy. Kinney imported gondolas, singing gondoliers and arched Venetian bridges; still his idea did not really take. With the popularity of the car, which could move faster than gondolas, the canals were given over to streets.

Then in 1950, the beat generation discovered the area. The sixties brought hippies. Today Venice is trendy and chic, with dozens of boutiques and restaurants. It is also the place to find an ecclectic assortment of people. Stroll along the boardwalk and view them building their bodies in a compound on the beach, or wheeling by on roller skates. As likely as not, you will be joined by strolling musicians and magicians.

South from Venice, you will find **Marina del Rey,** the largest small-craft harbor in the world. This is a good place to take a harbor cruise, or souvenir shop and dine in full view of a water-borne forest of masts at **Fisherman's Village.**

Manhattan Beach, Redondo Beach, and **Hermosa Beach** are farther south still, and have fine reputations with the surf, sand, and fun crowd. **San Pedro,** the port of Los Angeles, is where the cruise ships call. You can see them – and wave – from **Ports O'Call Village,** a nautically themed shopping center whose weathered-wood boutiques and eateries give a New England look to the Pacific Coast.

Long Beach

Long Beach, the farthest south of L. A.'s beach cities, was called the "Coney Island of the West" in the 1920s – not just because it had a popular beachside amusement park, but also because the long, sheltered beaches sang siren songs to hordes of Angelenos. Meanwhile the amusement park is gone, although **Shoreline Village,** a waterfront shopping and dining complex, does have a carousel, but the city has numerous other attractions, a couple of which are usually described in superlatives.

Long Beach is home to Howard Hughes' flying boat, the all-wood **Spruce Goose.** The world's largest plane, it has a wingspan longer than a football field. Permanently docked next door is the **Queen Mary,** one of the largest ocean liners ever built. During the early twentieth-century heyday of this art deco treasure, everybody who was anybody sailed on it at least once. Photos on board show some of the famous passengers, including Winston Churchill and Spencer Tracy. Both the *Queen Mary* and the *Spruce Goose* are open daily for tours. Adjacent is **London Towne,** rows of shops and pubs meant to give visitors a flavor of "merrie old England." Aboard the *Queen Mary* is a mini version of the much famed London department store, Harrods.

Santa Catalina Island

The view of the crescent-shaped harbor at **Avalon,** Santa Catalina's main city, alone is worth the 90-minute sea journey. This 74-square-mile (192 sq km) island, 26 miles (42 km) off the coast, can be reached from Long Beach and San Pedro by ferry (Catalina Express or Catalina Cruises) and helicopter (Helitrans or Island Express).

101

Santa Catalina once was owned by chewing-gum magnate William Wrigley, Jr. He bought it in 1919 and through much of his residence it was off-limits to the public. But by 1929, when the island's landmark Casino opened its doors, people were finding their way there: especially people interested in dancing. The Casino became nationally known for radio broadcasts featuring performers like Benny Goodman and Kay Kyser. The Casino still serves as the island's entertainment center. Daily tours show off its history and architecture. Each spring, summer and fall, dancers crowd in for big band events.

There is a small beach in Avalon, shops and restaurants. At the green pleasure pier not far from where the ferries dock, you can buy a ride on a glass-bottomed boat for a look at the underwater

Above: The Queen Mary cheek-by-jowl with the dome housing Hughes' wooden flying machine, the Spruce Goose. Right: Cooling it at Venice Beach.

life in this picturesque harbor. Other tours take you through the island's interior, with its wild boars, goats, mule deer and bison. The countryside is rugged enough that you might expect to see cowboys riding over the hills: In fact, it is often used for location shooting of Western movies.

San Fernando and San Gabriel

Today's "Hollywood" has moved north and inland from downtown Los Angeles, to the San Fernando Valley. The film industry put this part of Los Angeles County on the map. Movie pioneer D.W. Griffith "discovered" the valley in the early 1900s, and filmed his famous movie, *Custer's Last Stand,* on the grounds of the San Fernando Mission. Today, many of the major movie and television studios are located here across the Santa Monica Mountains from Los Angeles. NBC, Universal and Burbank studios offer tours (see Film Industry feature, later in this book); Columbia and Warner Bros. are also in the valley.

It was Padre Fermin, though, who really discovered the San Fernando Valley. He built the **San Fernando Mission** in what is now the city of San Fernando in 1797.

The graceful building is noted for its 21 classic arches and adobe walls 4 feet (1.22 m) thick. Visitors can see a replica of the original mission chapel. Among the mission museum's displays worth seeing is an intricately handcarved and gold-leaf-decorated altar dating to the seventeenth century.

Six Flags Magic Mountain, a family-fun theme park, is located in the valley town of **Valencia.** Among its more than 100 rides, shows and attractions are "Tidal Wave," a plunge over a 50-foot (15-m) waterfall, and "Free Fall", which drops you some 98 feet (30 m) at speeds of up to 55 mph. Both are truly breathtaking. There are two roller coasters: "Revolution", which makes a 360-degree loop, and "Ninja", the West's only suspended coaster.

Griffith Park, at the southeastern end of the San Fernando Valley, is a 4,000-acre (1,600-hectare) mountainside recreational area that offers bridle and wilderness trails, a planetarium, picnic areas, a miniature train ride, full-size rail cars to tour, and the 80-acre (32-hectare) **Los Angeles County Zoo.**

East of the San Fernando Valley is the **San Gabriel Valley**. Its best-known city is **Pasadena**, nestling at the base of the San Gabriel Mountains about 11 miles (18 km) out of downtown Los Angeles.

Pasadena is the home of the **Rose Bowl,** a 104,000-seat football stadium where, each New Year's Day, the best university team on the West Coast (Pacific-10 Conference) tests the champion of the Great Lakes region (Big-10 Conference). This rivalry, which often sees L. A.'s University of Southern California or University of California-Los Angeles in the host team's role, has been going on since 1915. Kicking off the festivities is the Tournament of *Roses Parade,* perhaps America's best-known procession.

LOS ANGELES
DOWNTOWN AND HOLLYWOOD
(All telephone area codes are 213).
Accommodation
LUXURY: **Century Plaza**, 2025 Ave. of the Stars, 90067 (Tel. 277-2000, 800-228-3000); **L' Ermitage**, 9291 Burton Way, Beverly Hills 90210 (Tel. 278-3344, 800-424-4443); **Westin Bonaventure**, 404 S. Figueroa St., 90071 (Tel. 624-1000, 800-228-3000). *MODERATE:* **Beverly Crest**, 125 Spalding Dr., Beverly Hills 90212 (Tel. 274-6801); **Plaza Suites**, 7230 Franklin Ave. (Tel. 278-9310), and 7940 Hollywood Blvd., 90046 (Tel. 656- 4555, 800-421-0745). *BUDGET:* **Courtesy Inn**, 2011 N. Highl. Ave., Hollywood 90068 (Tel. 851-1800); **Park Plaza**, 607 S. Park View St., 90057 (Tel. 384-5281).
Hospitals
Cedar-Sinai, 8700 Beverly Blvd. (Tel. 855-5000); **City of Hope**, 1500 E. Duarte Blvd. (Tel. 359-8111); **Hollywood Presbyteriand,** 1300 N. Vermont Ave. (Tel. 660-3530).
Museums and Art Galleries
California Museum of Science and Industry, Exposition Park (Tel. 744-7400), 10am-5pm daily. **Gene Autry Western Heritage Museum,** Griffith Park (Tel. 666-9005), 10am-5pm Tue-Sun. **George C. Page Museum of La Brea Discoveries**, 5801 Wilshire Blvd. (Tel. 936-2230), 10am-5pm Tue-Sun; **Museum of Art**, 5905 Wilshire Blvd. (Tel. 857-6222), 10am-5pm Tue-Fri, 10am-6pm Sat-Sun; **Museum of Contemporary Art**, 250 S. Grand Ave. (Tel. 626-6222), 11am-6pm Tue-Sun. **Natural Hist. Museum**, Exposition Park (Tel. 744-3466), 10am-5pm Tue-Sun; **Southwest Museum**, 234 Museum Dr. (Tel. 221-2163), 11am-5pm Tue- Sun.
Other Attractions
Chinatown, 900 block N. Broadway; **El Pueblo de Los Angeles Historic Monument**, 845 N. Alameda St. (Tel. 628-1274), 10am- 7:30pm daily; **Exposition Park**, 700 State Dr. at Harbor Fwy. (Tel. 744-7400); **Farmers Market**, 6333 W. Third St. (Tel. 933- 9211), 9am-6:30pm daily; **Griffith Park**, Los Feliz Blvd. and Riverside Dr. (Tel. 665-5188), includes Griffith Observatory and L.A. Zoo. **Hollywood Walk of Fame**, Hollywood Blvd. and Vine St.; **Mann's Chinese Theatre** 6925 Hollywood Blvd., Hollywood (Tel. 461- 3311), daily.
Postal Services
Main Post Office, 900 N. Alameda Ave. (Tel. 688- 2290).
Restaurants
AMERICAN: **Intermezzo**, 6919 Melrose Ave., Hollywood; **Philippe the Original**, 1001 N. Alameda St.; **Tribeca**, 242 N. Beverly Dr., Beverly Hills. *CALIFORNIAN:* **Indigo**, 8222 W. 3rd St.; **Menagerie**, 3347 Motor Ave.; **Muse**, 7360 Beverly Blvd. *CHINESE:* **Mon Kee**, 679 N. Spring St. *CONTINENTAL:* **Chasen's**, 9039 Beverly Blvd.. **L.A. Rose Cafe**, 4749 Fountain Ave. *FRENCH:* **Cassis French Grill**, 8450 W. 3rd St.; **L'Orangerie**, 903 N. La Cienega Blvd. *GERMAN:* **Veronika**, 8164 W. 3rd St. *ITALIAN:* **Palato**, 6840 Hollywood Blvd., Hollywood. *JAPANESE:* **Asakuma**, 11701 Wilshire Blvd. *MEXICAN:* **Tamayo**, 5300 E. Olympic Blvd., E. Los Angeles. *SEAFOOD:* **Del monico's**, 9320 W. Pico Blvd., W. Los Angeles; **Fisherman's Outlet**, 529 S. Central Ave.
Shopping
Many visitors find it hard to bypass exclusive **Rodeo Drive** in Beverly Hills, at least for window shopping. Close to downtown are two ethnic shopping areas: **Olvera Street** at W. 17th St. (Mexican) and **Little Tokyo**, 1st and San Pedro (Japanese).
Tourist Information
Los Angeles Convention and Visitors Bureau, 515 S. Figueroa St., 11th floor, 90071 (Tel. 624-7300); **Visitor Information Center** (downtown), 695 S. Figueroa St. (Tel. 689- 8822); **Visitor Information Center** (Hollywood), 6541 Hollywood Blvd. (Tel. 461-4213); **Beverly Hills Visitors Bureau**, 239 S. Beverly Drive, Beverly Hills, 90212 (Tel. 271-8174, 800-345- 2210).
Transportation
The **Southern California Rapid Transit District (RTD)** (Tel. 626-4455), offers tourists bus passes for unlimited travel on its extensive routes at just $2 a day (minimum three days). Public bus travel is normally 50 cents a ride.

BEACH COMMUNITIES
(All telephone area codes are 213.)
Accommodation
LUXURY: **Portofino Inn**, 260 Portofino Way, Redondo Beach 90277 (Tel. 379-8481, 800-338-2993).
MODERATE: **Pacific Shore**, 1819 Ocean Ave., Santa Monica 90401 (Tel. 451- 8711, 800-241-3848).
BUDGET: **Hacienda**, 525 N. Sepulveda Blvd., El Segundo 90245 (Tel. 615-0015).
Restaurants
AMERICAN: **DC 3**, 2800 Donald Douglas Loop N., Santa Monica (Tel. 399-2323).
CONTINENTAL: **St. Estephe**, 2640 Sepulveda Blvd., Manhattan Beach (Tel. 545-1334).
SEAFOOD: **Tony's on the Pier**, 210 Fisherman's Wharf, Redondo Beach (Tel. 374-9246).

Attractions

J. Paul Getty Museum, 17985 Pacific Coast Hwy., Malibu (Tel. 458-2003), 10am-5pm Tue-Sun. **Marina del Rey Harbor**, 4701 Admiralty Way (Tel. 305-9545), 9am-5pm daily; **Wayfarers Chapel**, 5755 Palos Verdes Dr., Rancho Palos Verdes (Tel. 377-1650), 9am-5pm daily; **Will Rogers State Historic Park**, 14253 Sunset Blvd., Pacific Palisades, 8am-6pm daily.

Tourist Information

Santa Monica Conv. and Visitors Bureau, P.O. Box 5278, S. Monica, 90405 (Tel. 393-7593). **Redondo Beach Marketing Council**, P.O. Box 270, Redondo Beach, 90277 (Tel. 318- 0630).

LONG BEACH AREA

(All telephone area codes are 213).

Accommodation

LUXURY: **Hyatt Regency**, 200 S. Pine Ave. 90802 (Tel. 491-1234, 800-228-9000). *MODERATE:* **Queen Mary**, Pier J, 90801 (Tel. 435-3511, 800-421-3732). *BUDGET:* **Vegabond Inn**, 185 Atlantic Ave., 90802 (Tel. 435-3791, 800-522-1555).

Restaurants

CALIFORNIAN: **Collage**, 762 Pacific Ave. *CONTINENTAL:* **Nizetich's**, Ports o'Call Village, San Pedro. *SEAFOOD:* **Rusty Pelican**, 6550 Marina Dr.

Attractions

Cabrillo Marine Museum, 3720 Stephen White Dr., San Pedro (Tel. 548-7562), 12-5pm Tue-Fri, 10am-5pm Sat-Sun; **Queen Mary and Spruce Goose**, Pier J (Tel. 435-3511), 10am-6pm daily.

Tourist Information

Long Beach Convention and Visitors Council, 1 World Trade Center, Suite 300, Long Beach, 90831 (Tel. 436-3645, 800- 234-3645).

Transportation

Catalina Channel Express, Berth 95, San Pedro (Tel. 513-7957, 800-257-2227), 90-min. cruises to Avalon, $27.70 round trip, also from Long Beach and Redondo Beach.; **Catalina Cruises**, 320 Golden Shore, San Pedro (Tel. 514-3838), 2-hour cruises to Avalon, $24.30 round trip.

SAN FERNANDO VALLEY

(All telephone area codes are 818).

Accommodation

LUXURY: **Sheraton Universal**, 333 Universal Terrace Pkwy., Universal City 91608 (Tel. 980-1212, 800-325- 3535). *MODERATE:* **Burbank Airport Hilton**, 2500 Hollywood Way, Burbank 91505 (Tel. 843-6000). *BUDGET:* **Comfort Inn**, 2300 W. Colorado Blvd., Eagle Rock 90041 (Tel. 256-1199, 800-228- 5150).

Restaurants

AMERICAN: **Moonlight Tango Cafe**, 13730 Ventura Blvd., Sherman Oaks. *CONTINENTAL:* **Cafe Polo**, 480 Riverside Dr., Burbank. *SEAFOOD:* **Piero's**, 2825 W. Olive Ave., Burbank (Tel. 842-5150).

Attractions

Burbank Studios VIP Tour, 4000 Warner Blvd., Burbank (Tel. 954-1744), tours 10am and 2pm Mon-Fri; **Mission San Fernando Rey de Espana**, 15151 S. Fernando Mission Blvd., Mission Hills (Tel. 361-0186), 9am-4pm daily; **NBC Studios Tour**, 3000 W. Alameda Ave., Burbank (Tel. 840-3537), 8:30am-4pm Mon-Fri, 10am-4pm Sat, 10am-2pm Sun; **Six Flags Magic Mountain**, 26101 Magic Mountain Pkwy., Valencia (Tel. 805-255-4111), from 10am summer, weekends and holidays rest of year; **Univ. Studios Hollywood**, 3900 Lankershim Blvd., Universal City (Tel. 508-9600), 10am-3:30pm Mon-Fri, 9:30am-4pm Sat Sun, 7-hour tour.

Tourist Information

Glendale Chamber of Commerce, 200 S. Louise St. (P.O. Box 112), Glendale, 91209. **S. Fernando Chamber of Commerce**, 519 S. Brand Blvd., S. Fernando, 91340.

SAN GABRIEL VALLEY

(All telephone area codes are 818).

Accommodation

LUXURY: **Industry Hills & Sheraton Resort**, 1 Industry Hills Pkwy., City of Industry 91744 (Tel. 965-0861, 800-325-3535). *MODERATE:* **Embassy Suites**, 211 E. Huntington Dr., Arcadia 91006 (Tel. 445-8525, 800-362-2779). *BUDGET:* **Pasadena Inn Royale**, 3600 E. Colorado Blvd., Pasadena 91107 (Tel. 793-0950, 800-528-1234).

Restaurants

AMERICAN: **Crocodile Cafe**, 140 S. Lake St., Pasadena. *CONTINENTAL:* **Brown Derby**, 911 E. Colorado Blvd.. *SEAFOOD:* **Cameron's**, 1978 E. Colorado Blvd. , Pasadena.

Attractions

Huntington Library, Museum and Gardens, 1151 Oxford Rd., San Marino (Tel. 405-2100), 1-4:30pm Tue-Sun; **Mission San Gabriel**, 537 W. Mission Dr., San Gabriel (Tel. 282-5191), 9:30am-4:30pm daily. **Norton Simon Museum of Art**, 411 W. Colorado Blvd., Pasadena (Tel. 449-3730), 12-6pm Thu-Sun; **Pacific Asia Museum**, 46 N. Los Robles Ave., Pasadena (Tel. 449-2742), 12-5pm Wed-Sun.

Tourist Information

Pasadena Conv. and Visitors Bureau, 171 S. Los Robles Ave., Pasadena, CA 91101.

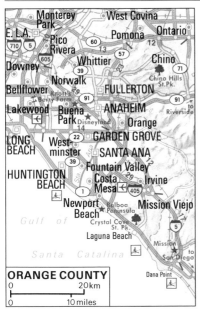

ORANGE COUNTY

0   20km

0   10 miles

ORANGE COUNTY

Not many places live up to their picture-postcard images. Orange County does. This area, which sprawls between the Pacific Ocean and Los Angeles, San Diego and Riverside Counties, epitomizes what Southern California is known for today: seemingly perpetual blue skies and entertainment options galore.

Orange County offers in abundance the very things this part of the state sells via postcards that visitors write home. "Wish you were here?!" they declare to stay-behinds after a day at one of the county's popular theme parks. The card shows Mickey Mouse standing in front of Sleeping Beauty's Castle at Disneyland, or maybe a big-nosed white beagle waving from the Camp Snoopy kids' area at Knott's Berry Farm. Another card, this one showing a stretch of sand and water somewhere along the county's 42 miles

Right: The Gothic style in California can only be found at Disneyland in Anaheim.

(68 km) of beach, declares "Wow!" after the senders have tried riding the local waves.

Of course, in its 782 square miles (2,025 sq km), Orange County offers much more than exciting amusement parks and luring beaches. There are resort towns, too, and shopping and culture – anything and everything vacationers might be looking for.

Southern California is at its most diverse in Orange County. That gives visitors opportunities difficult to find elsewhere: opportunities to hike in the Santa Ana Mountains in the morning, for instance, then spend the afternoon sailing or swimming in the Pacific off Newport Beach.

For the evening, there is fine dining, sunset watching, gallery hopping, world-class music or drama at the Orange County Performing Arts Center. It is not surprising, then, that 35 million people a year visit the county.

Not that people come to Orange County only to play. It is true that the county maintains a certain casualness of attitude and attire not often found in other business centers: Men often sit down to power lunches jacketless and in open-necked shirts, for instance.

But Orange County has an economic base that makes its more than 2 million residents some of the wealthiest in the United States, with an average household income of more than $35,000 a year. High-rise business blocks and industrial parks spread in an ever-widening circle from the county core cities of Costa Mesa, Newport Beach, and Irvine. They have changed Orange County from a rural expanse to one whose aerospace, high-technology and other industries draw an international clientele. Those business high-rises and the county's booming tourist attractions would amaze the area's early farming residents. But today, Orange County is a prosperous region due to its main tourist destinations.

Anaheim and Buena Park

Anaheim, probably the county's best known city, was once California's wine capital. In the late 1800s, the orange industry took root. Now, although orange groves can still be found, tourism is Anaheim's primary industry.

No. 1, of course, is **Disneyland.** The 76-acre (30-hectare) theme park celebrated its 35th anniversary in 1990 with a year-long birthday party. There are seven themed areas here, each of them enchanting: Adventureland, Bear County, Fantasyland, Frontierland, Main Street, New Orleans Square and Tomorrowland. Most popular at the moment are a 3-D space-fantasy motion picture starring rock music star Michael Jackson, and "Star Tours," a space-adventure ride in Tomorrowland which is based on famous Hollywood director George Lucas' *Star Wars* movies.

Disneyland is filled with fun. On turn-of-the-twentieth century **Main Street**, you can watch as an animated Abraham Lincoln delivers his Gettysburg Address. Moving and sound-making robots like these, called audio-animatronics, are an invention of the late Walt Disney and form a characteristic attraction of the park. In 19th century **Frontierland**, children can travel like young Mark Twain to **Tom Sawyer Island**, where there are rafts to pole and caves to explore. In **Adventureland**, you can exit frolicking New Orleans Square aboard a ride that takes you through a den of devilish pirates, or ride a boat past gaping hippopotamus and crocodiles on a tropical river. In **Bear County** one can join a lively jamboree or explore America's wilderness in a canoe. Children, of course, will be fascinated by **Fantasyland**, where they will encounter many of the famous Disney cartoon figures and go on a variety of exciting rides. Voyages through outer and inner space as well as journeys under the sea are all available at **Tomorrowland**.

From the cartoonlike Fantasyland to twenty-first century Tomorrowland, no

matter where you wander, there are rides that take you through a haunted house or up Matterhorn Mountain; movies that surround you with the sights and sounds of the U.S. and China and more exotic places; parades filled with familiar Disney characters like Snow White, Donald Duck, and many more. Should hunger strike, there are a great number of snack bars and restaurants to choose from. The only thing one will not find anywhere in the park is alcohol. You need at least a day at Disneyland – a long day.

Walt Disney opened his park and put Anaheim on the tourism map in 1955. Long before he got to Orange County, **Knott's Berry Farm,** in adjacent Buena Park, was already well established.

Knott's comes by its name honestly: It started as an authentic berry farm in the 1920s. Walter and Cordelia Knott later opened a restaurant in the family living

Above: A live performance at Knott's Berry Farm. Right: The business of religion: the Crystal Cathedral in Anaheim.

room, serving fried-chicken dinners that became so popular people would wait three and four hours for them. To keep customers occupied during that period, Walter recreated an Old West ghost town on his land.

Walter Knott's old ghost town is just one of the themed areas of this 150-acre (60-hectare) park. Others include Fiesta Village, the Roaring Twenties Airfield, and Camp Snoopy. There is a Good Time Theater, where musical variety shows are staged; and the Pacific Pavilion, which features aquatic shows with performing dolphins. And there are rides, of course, everything from gentle merry-go- rounds to parachutes that drop you from the sky to the ground but keep your stomach dangling. In the chicken-dinner restaurant you will have to wait in line for a meal, just as the Knotts' early customers did.

Like Disneyland, all rides and attractions (but no meals) are included in Knott's admission price. It takes another full day to tour this park. But take a tip: Do not make it the day after your Disney-

and visit. Unless you are particularly hardy, it is wise to put some time between the two amusement park visits.

There is more to Anaheim and Buena Park than the two theme parks. Two professional sports teams, baseball's *California Angels* and football's Los Angeles Rams, play at **Anaheim Stadium,** just a mile or so from Disneyland. The nearby **Anaheim Convention Center** hosts such special events as rock concerts, circuses and ice-skating extravaganzas.

In Buena Park, the **Movieland Wax Museum** immortalizes in wax Hollywood stars like George Burns, Clint Eastwood, Katherine Hepburn and Paul Newman, showing them in scenes from their famous movies. Across the street is **Medieval Times**, an unusual dinner theater that regularly stages jousting tournaments on horseback.

Just south of Anaheim, in **Garden Grove,** one of America's best known televangelists orates from the pulpit of the **Crystal Cathedral,** near Interstate-5 at Chapman Avenue at Lewis Street. The Rev. Robert Schuller, who started preaching "possibility thinking" in 1955 with a drive-in church for the motorized generation, built, from the donations of his followers, a multimillion-dollar 12-storey glass-and-steel church and a 32-acre (13-hectare) arboretum complex.

The Business Center

The central Orange County area once was noted mainly for quiet beaches, farm fields, and the 102,000-acre (41,278-hectare) **Irvine Ranch**. Today, it is the third largest "downtown" in California in terms of office space, behind only Los Angeles and San Francisco.

Much of the county's business is conducted here, in the high-rises and industrial parks surrounding **John Wayne/Orange County Airport.** But there are other draws. Culture is one, in the form of the **Orange County Performing Arts Center**, 600 Town Center Drive, Costa Mesa. The $65 million facility brings first-rate drama and music to the area.

Shopping is another. In Costa Mesa, where Bristol Street meets the I-405 freeway, **South Coast Plaza** has eight major department stores, more than 200 specialty shops, and higher annual sales than any other shopping center in the nation. Its tourism figures rival Disneyland's. Shops like Polo/Ralph Lauren and Courreges draw tourists as well as local customers. **Fashion Island**, Pacific Coast Highway and MacArthur Boulevard in Newport Beach, is anchored by five leading department stores and boasts 120 speciality shops – among them Amen Wardy, where women can buy designer clothes, designer jewelry, and complete make overs of hair and makeup to set them off properly. Wardy dispatches limousines to pick up customers in Beverly Hills, driving right past that city's own exclusive shopping mecca, Rodeo Drive, to reach the portal.

Above: Newport Beach offers ideal conditions for surfing and sailing. Right: Art for sale and for free on the beach in L. A.

Newport Beach is Orange County's Beverly Hills, an attractive and upscale residential area. Unlike Beverly Hills, though, many of Newport's palatial homes have an ocean view.

The Pacific is the focus of Newport Beach life. The sandy stretches here have been well known since the early 1900s. At that time the Pacific Electric Railroad's big red cars began bringing land locked Angelenos to this waterfront wonderland for a day of swimming and sun-bathing.

Newport's beaches are broad, and extend along a finger of land called the **Balboa Peninsula**. Water action at various places along the peninsula causes waves beloved by surfers and marshes fancied by waterfowl. The latter can be found in **Upper Newport Bay**, a wildlife preserve. As for the surfing waves, they can be found just about anywhere along this coast, especially at **Corona State Beach** in the Newport neighborhood known as Corona del Mar. In the shadow of **Newport Pier**, you can find a fleet of dory

fishermen, probably the last such fleet on the California coast. Since 1890, the dory fishermen have been angling for flounder, red snapper, sea trout, and rock cod in the waters off Newport; they chug out before dawn, and by 10 a. m. or so are back, pulling their colorful wooden boats onto the sand and setting up an open-air fish market. Among their customers are chefs from the local restaurants, so seafood on Newport menus is guaranteed fresh. **Balboa Pier** is nearby; so is **Newport Harbor,** one of the busiest yacht harbors in the world and easily one of the most picturesque. Harbor cruise tours point out the homes of one-time Orange County residents like John Wayne and "King Gillette" (known for his safety razor).

Harbor tours are easily available on the **Pavilion Queen** or the **Showboat**, docked in Balboa's Fun Zone. The nearby Balboa Pavilion contains the Tale of the Whale restaurant and Davey's Locker, where you can buy a trip on a sportfishing boat. The **Fun Zone** also has a merry-go-round, Ferris wheel, souvenir shops, and video games.

Balboa is one of the islands in Newport Bay. It can be reached by road off the Pacific Coast Highway, or by three-car ferry (a five-minute trip, and you do not have to be in a car to ride it). Among its pleasures is a "boardwalk", actually a concrete walkway paralleling the beach. Locals often roller-skate their way along it; a stroll is pleasant, too.

The California Riviera

The beach towns south of Newport make up the California Riviera, so called because the flatland beaches give way here to cliffs. The clifftops are bedecked with homes, giving the area a look of the French Riviera.

The first town south of Newport is **Laguna Beach,** Orange County's artist colony. Dozens of art galleries line the Pacific Coast Highway here, or are tucked away in funky arcades across the street from the beach, or on the bluffs

above it. Laguna is also a good place to find crafts, antiques, swimsuits and resort wear. Among the places for browsing and buying are **The Pottery Shack, Laguna Mercado, The Collection, The Colonnade,** and **Laguna Village.**

Each summer, Laguna Beach stages a seven-week-long **Festival of the Arts and Pageant of the Masters.** During this period, hundreds of artists and craftspersons exhibit and sell their works. Pageant of the Masters is a display of "living artworks": Local residents recreate famous paintings through painted backdrops and live, seemingly breathless poses, accompanied by orchestral music and narration.

Laguna's recently remodeled **Museum of Art,** 307 Cliff Drive, displays revolving exhibits of the works of American artists. Laguna's beach, in the center of town, is excellent for swimming.

Above: Beach life on the San Francisco bay. Right: The mission at San Juan de Capistrano, Orange county's oldest town.

In **Dana Point,** south of Laguna, the swimming is fine, too, but the boating is even better. Dana Point has one of Southern California's most scenic boat basins. Sailor and author Richard Henry Dana, who wrote *Two Years Before the Mast* a century and a half ago, described it as the most romantic spot along the California coast. In the 1920s, when developers began opening this area to landowners, the name was changed from Bahia Capistrano in Dana's honor.

Recreation in Dana Point centers on its harbor. Sportfishing, whalewatching (in winter) and parasailing launches leave from **Dana Wharf.** The **Orange County Marine Institute**, Dana Point Harbor Drive and Del Obispo, gives glimpses of local sea life through tidepools, exhibits and lectures. **Mariners Village** offers shopping and dining with a nautical flavor, and the seafood is excellent.

For a panoramic seascape, head for the clifftop **Dana Point Resort** or to the viewpoint on **Street of the Blue Lantern.** Extending 200 feet below you (60

m) is the town and the Pacific coast. In the distance to the south, you can see **San Clemente,** Orange County's southern boundary and the location of former President Richard Nixon's "western White House". You cannot really see the building, which is well hidden by towering palms; but you can see where it is located from San Clemente's municipal pier.

A stroll along the pier is a perfect way to spend an afternoon here, for it opens the town to view as well. San Clemente is built in Spanish style, with white stucco and red-tile roofs, their lines softened by plants and shrubs. Ole Hanson, who founded the town in 1925, thought of it as his canvas. Indeed, it looks as if it were painted on the coast.

San Juan Capistrano

Inland from San Clemente is **San Juan Capistrano.** The county's oldest town, it is noted for a Spanish mission, at the corner of Ortega Highway and Camino Capistrano, that dates to 1776 and was founded by Father Junipero Serra.

A popular song of the 1940s, about birds that migrate to and from South America, *When the Swallows Come Back to Capistrano*, makes **Mission San Juan Capistrano** one of California's better-known missions to tourists. They come to see its eighteenth-century church – which replaced the original Great Stone Church destroyed in an 1812 earthquake – and an even more ancient compound that depicts the lifestyle of the priests, soldiers, and Indians who once resided here. Living quarters, kitchens, and workrooms are open to view.

San Juan Capistrano is every bit the modern Orange County town, enjoying the kind of building boom a stable economy brings. Still, there is some history on view here besides the mission. On Sundays, members of the local historical society lead visits to the circa-1790s **Montanez Adobe** and to a Victorian-era structure, the **O'Neill Museum,** which houses local memorabilia.

ANAHEIM

(All local phone numbers have 714 area code.)

Accommodation

LUXURY: **Disneyland Hotel**, 1150 W. Cerritos Ave., 92802 (Tel. 635-8600, 800-642-5391); **Marriott**, 700 W. Convention Way, 96802 (Tel. 750-8000, 800-228-9290); **Pan Pacific**, 1717 S. West St., 92802 (Tel. 999-0990, 800-821-8976); **Residence Inn**, 1700 S. Clementine Ave., 92802 (Tel. 533-3555, 800-331- 3131).

MODERATE: **Grand**, 1 Hotel Way, 96802 (Tel. 772-7777, 800-421-6662); **Ibis**, 100 W. Freedman Way, 92802 (Tel. 520-9696, 800-982-4247); **Inn at the Park**, 1855 S. Harbor Blvd., 96802 (Tel. 750-1811, 800-421-6662); **Sheraton**, 1015 W. Ball Rd., 96802 (Tel. 778-1700, 800-325-3535). *BUDGET:* **Desert Inn**, 1600 S. Harbor Blvd., 96802 (Tel. 772-5050, 800-433-5270); **Nendels Anaheim Ascot Inn**, 2145 S. Harbor Blvd., 92802 (Tel. 971-5556, 800-547-0106); **Penny Sleeper Inn**, 1441 S. Manchester Ave., 96802 (Tel. 991-8100, 800-854-6118); **Raffles Inn**, 1331 E. Katella Ave., 96802 (Tel. 750-6100, 800-233-6583).

Restaurants

AMERICAN: **The Original Cattleman's Wharf**, 1160 W. Ball Rd.; **Ramzi's House of Ribs**, 323 N. State College Rd., Fullerton; **Mr. Stox** 1105 E. Katella Ave.. **The Cellar**, 305 N. Harbor Blvd., Fullerton. *CONTINENTAL:* **Lafayette Cafe**, 12532 Garden Grove Blvd., Garden Grove; **Ruby Begonia's**, 1500 S. Raymond Ave., Fullerton. *FRENCH:* **Chez Cary**, 571 S. Main St., Orange; **La Brasserie**, 202 S. Main St., Orange. *JAPANESE:* **Akachan**, 9906 Katella Ave., Garden Grove (Tel. 534-0153); **Benihana**, 2100 E. Ball Rd.. *MEXICAN:* **Casa Gamino**, 5638 E. La Palma Ave.

Attractions

Crystal Cathedral, 12141 Lewis St., Garden Grove (Tel. 971-4073), tours 9am-3:30pm Mon-Sat, 12-3:30pm Sun. **Disneyland**, 1313 Harbor Blvd. (Tel. 999-4565), 10am-6pm Mon-Fri, 9am-midnight Sat-Sun; **Hobby City Doll** and **Toy Museum**, 1238 S. Beach Blvd. (Tel. 527-2323), 10am-6pm daily except holidays; **Richard Nixon Library and Birthplace**, Yorba Linda. **Seaports of the Pacific**, 1150 W. Cerritos Ave. (Tel. 778-6600).

Tourist Information

Anaheim Area Visitor and Conv. Bureau, 800 W. Katella Ave., Anaheim 92802 (Tel. 999-8999).

Transportation

Orange County Transit District, Garden Grove (Tel. 636-RIDE);

BEACH COMMUNITIES

Accommodation

LUXURY: **Newport Beach Marriott**, 900 Newport Center Dr., Newport Beach 92660 (Tel. 640-4000, 800-228-9290); **Ritz-Carlton**, 33533 Ritz-Carlton Dr., Laguna Niguel 92677 (Tel. 240-2000); **Waterfront Hilton,** 21100 Pacific Coast Hwy., Huntington Beach 92648 (Tel. 960-7873, 800-445-8667). *MODERATE:* **Hotel Laguna,** 425 S. Coast Blvd., Laguna Beach 92651 (Tel. 494- 1151); **Meridien**, 4500 MacArthur Blvd., Newport Beach 92660 (Tel. 476-2001, 800-543-4300); **San Clemente Inn**, 2600 Ave. del Presidente, San Clemente 92672 (Tel. 492-6103, 800- 874- 8770). *BUDGET:* **Capistrano Inn**, 27174 Ortega Hwy., San Juan Capistrano 92675 (Tel. 493-5661, 800-528-1234); **Huntington Shores Motel**, 21002 Pacific Coast Hwy., Huntington Beach 92648 (Tel. 536-8861).

Restaurants

AMERICAN: **MacArthur Park**, 16390 Pacific Coast Hwy., Huntington Beach (Tel. 846-5553); **Tivoli Terrace**, 650 Laguna Canyon Rd., Laguna Beach (Tel. 494-9650).

CALIFORNIA: **The Ritz,** 880 Newport Center Dr., Newport Beach (Tel. 720-1800).

CONTINENTAL: **El Adobe de Capistrano**, 31891 Camino Capistrano, San Juan Capistrano (Tel. 830- 8620); **Five Crowns**, 3801 E. Pacific Coast Hwy., Corona del Mar (Tel. 760-0331); **Magic Island**, 3050 Via Oporto, Newport Beach (Tel. 645-7600).

JAPANESE: **Koto**, 4300 Von Karman Ave., Newport Beach (Tel. 752-7151).

MEXICAN: **Las Brisas**, 361 Cliff Dr., Laguna Beach (Tel. 497-5434).

SEAFOOD: **Ben Brown's**, 31106 Pacific Coast Hwy., South Laguna (Tel. 499-2663); **Newport Landing**, 503 E. Edgewater Rd., Newport Beach (Tel. 675- 2373).

Attractions

Crystal Cove State Beach, Hwy 1 between Corona del Mar and Laguna Beach (Tel. 494-3539).

Laguna Art Museum, 307 Cliff Dr. Laguna Beach (Tel. 494-6531), 11am-5pm Tue-Sun.

Mission San Juan Capistrano, Ortega Hwy. and Camino Capistrano, San Juan Capistrano (Tel. 493-1424), 7:30am-5pm daily.

Newport Center Fashion Island, 1045 Newport Center Dr., Newport Beach (Tel. 721- 2022), 10am-9pm Mon-Fri, 10am-6pm Sat, 12-5pm Sun.

Festival of Arts and Pageant of the Masters, Laguna Canyon (Tel. 494-1145), early July-late August.

Sherman Library and Gardens, 2647 E. Coast Hwy., Corona del Mar (Tel. 673-2261), 10:30 am-4pm daily.
Upper Newport Bay Ecological Reserve, Newport Beach (Tel. 590-5158).

Tourist Information
Huntington Beach Conference and Visitors Bureau, 2213 Main Street, Suite 32, Huntington Beach 92648 (Tel. 536-8888).
Laguna Beach Chamber of Commerce, 357 Gleneyre St. (P.O. Box 396), Laguna Beach 92652 (Tel. 494-1018).
Newport Beach Conference and Visitors Bureau, 3700 Newport Blvd., Suite 107, Newport Beach 92663 (Tel. 675-7040).
San Juan Capistrano Chamber of Commerce, 31682 El Camino Real, San Juan Capistrano 92675 (Tel. 493-4700).

BUENA PARK
Accommodation
LUXURY: **Embassy Suites**, 7762 Beach Blvd., 90620 (Tel. 739-5600).
MODERATE: **Buena Park**, 7675 Crescent Ave., 90620 (Tel. 995-1111, 800-854-8792); **Days Inn**, 3 Centerpointe Dr., 90623 (Tel. 670-1400, 800-325-2525); **Holiday Inn**, 7000 Beach Blvd., 90620 (Tel. 522-7000, 800-465-4329).
BUDGET: **Farm de Ville Motel**, 7800 Crescent Ave., 90620 (Tel. 527-2201, 800-882-8846); **Hampton Inn**, 7828 Orangethorpe Ave., 90620 (Tel. 714-670-7200, 800-426-7866); **Travelers Inn**, 7121 Beach Blvd., 90620 (Tel. 670-9000, 800-538-0006).

Restaurants
AMERICAN: **Mrs. Knott's Chicken Dinner Res taurant**, Knott's Berry Farm, 8039 Beach Blvd. (Tel. 220-5080).
CONTINENTAL: **Medieval Times**, 7662 Beach Blvd. (Tel. 521- 4740).
SEAFOOD: **Seafood Show Restaurant and Sushi Bar**, 50 Centerpointe Dr., La Palma (Tel. 670-0137).

Attractions
Knott's Berry Farm, 8039 Beach Blvd. (Tel. 220-5200), 10am-6pm Mon-Fri, 10am-10pm Sat, 10am-7pm Sun, extended summer hours. **Movieland Wax Museum**, 7711 Beach Blvd. (Tel. 522-1154), daily and nightly; **Museum of World Wars and Military History**, 7884 E. La Palma Ave. (Tel. 952-1776), 10am-6pm Mon-Sat, 12-6pm Sun.

Tourist Information
Buena Park Convention and Visitors Office, 6280 Manchester Blvd., Suite 103, Buena Park 90621 (Tel. 994-1511).

COSTA MESA-SANTA ANA-IRVINE
Accommodation
LUXURY: **Irvine Hilton**, 17900 Jamboree Blvd., Irvine 92714 (Tel. 863-3111, 800-445-8667); **Registry**, 18800 MacArthur Blvd., Irvine 92715 (Tel. 752-8777, 800-247-9810); **Westin South Coast Plaza**, 666 Anton Blvd., Costa Mesa 92626 (Tel. 540-2500, 800-228-3000).
MODERATE: **Beverly Heritage**, 3350 Avenue of the Arts, Costa Mesa 92626 (Tel. 751-5100, 800-443-4455); **Country Side Inn**, 325 Bristol St., Costa Mesa 92626 (Tel. 594-0300, 800-332-9992); **Ramada**, 2726 S. Grand Ave., Santa Ana 92705 (Tel. 966-1955, 800- 854-2608).
BUDGET: **Costa Mesa Inn**, 3205 Harbor Blvd., Costa Mesa 92626 (Tel. 557-8360, 800-522-1555); **Executive Lodge Suites**, 2909 S. Bristol Ave., Santa Ana 92704 (Tel. 540-2300); **La Quinta Inn**, 14972 Sand Canyon Ave., Irvine 92718 (Tel. 551- 0909, 800-531-5900).

Restaurants
CALIFORNIA: **Gemmell's**, 3000 Bristol St., Costa Mesa (Tel. 751-1074); **Grand Teton Chelet**, 695 Town Center Dr., Costa Mesa (Tel. 432-7791). *CONTINENTAL:* **Nieuport 17**, 1615 E. 17th St., Santa Ana (Tel. 547-9511); **Restaurant at Cameron Court**, 2 Hutton Centre Dr., Santa Ana (Tel. 540-8615). *MEXICAN:* **The Hacienda**, 1725 College Ave., Santa Ana (Tel. 558-1304). *SEAFOOD:* **Monterey Bay Canners**, 15483 Culver Dr., Irvine (Tel. 552-3474).

Attractions
Bower's Museum, 2002 N. Main St., Santa Ana (Tel. 972-1900), open 10am-5pm Tue-Sat, 12-5pm Sun; **Orange County Performing Arts Center**, 600 Town Center Dr., Costa Mesa (Tel. 556-2787); **Santa Ana Zoo**, 1801 E. Chestnut St., Santa Ana (Tel. 835-7484), 10am-5pm daily; **South Coast Plaza**, San Diego Fwy. at Bristol St., Costa Mesa (Tel. 241-1700); **Wild Rivers Waterpark**, 8800 Irvine Center Dr., Laguna Hills (Tel. 768-9453), mid May- Sept.

Tourist Information
Costa Mesa Chamber of Commerce, 1901 Newport Blvd., Suite 135, Costa Mesa 92627 (Tel. 650-1490).
Irvine Chamber of Commerce, 2815 McGaw St., Irvine 92714 (Tel. 660-9112).
Santa Ana Chamber of Commerce, 600 W. Santa Ana Blvd., Suite 202 (P.O. Box 205), Santa Ana, 92701 (Tel. 541-5353).

Transportation
John Wayne/Orange County Airport (SNA), 18741 Airport Way N., Santa Ana 92707 (Tel. 834-6631), served by numerous national and commuter airlines.

THE INLAND EMPIRE

Just 45 minutes east of the glitz and plastic of Los Angeles lies the real West: the Inland Empire. Here, real life and middle America move at a slower pace. The Inland Empire offers a slice of history, of cowboys and Indians, as well as the natural beauty of what remains of the Old West. There are still open spaces to enjoy. Here, lakes, parks, and recreational areas abound.

This vast, diverse area includes 30-plus communities in Riverside and San Bernardino Counties. The latter is, geographically, the largest county in the United States, bigger than the states of Rhode Island, Connecticut, and Delaware combined. During the 1980s, this was the fastest growing area in the United States. Affordable houses lure families to settle, a favorable business climate provides

Above: The beautiful San Bernardino mountains, where locals find some rest and recuperation.

jobs, and a pleasant Mediterranean climate makes outdoor living easy.

In the early 1950s, James Guthry and George Savage conceived the Inland Empire. It was high time, they felt, to get out of the shadow of big-brother Los Angeles County. By joining forces with Riverside County under the name "Inland Empire" they believed they would have more clout to build both the population and the business community.

Today, within the boundaries of these two counties are several colleges and universities, the world-famous Loma Linda Medical Center, Ontario International Airport, several Air Force bases and other military reserves, and even ski resorts.

The Inland Empire encompasses scenic mountains and lakes, high and low deserts, farmland and vineyards. Its communities, as diverse in character as the landscape, have a common thread: Most of them were originally part of Spanish land grants sold off over the years.

Along the foothills of the **San Bernardino Mountains** are a string of towns, all

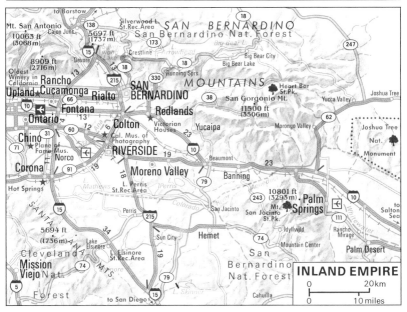

of them about 1,000 feet (305 m) above sea level. They enjoy warm days and cool nights, and get about 15 inches (38 cm) of rain, mainly between November and March. In summer, the temperature is often over 90 °F (32 °C) and dry. That is also the smoggy season, especially if the wind blows in from the west, from Los Angeles.

San Bernardino, incorporated in 1854, is 59 miles (95 km) east of Los Angeles. It is a transportation hub where four major railroad lines and several freeways converge. An arrowhead, appropriately, is the city's logo: Indians played an important role in its early history, and there are still several reservations nearby, as well as collections of Indian artifacts.

Riverside, first known as the Santa Ana River Valley, was originally inhabited by Chuilla and Serrano Indians. Visited in 1774 by Juan Bautista de Anza, it was included in the 32,000-acre (13,000-hectare) **Rancho Jurupa** land grant to Juan Bandini in 1838. Its core became a mile-square township called

Jurupa; in 1871, the name was later changed to Riverside.

In the heart of downtown stands the **Mission Inn Garden Hotel,** a state historical monument and registered U.S. landmark renowned for its Spanish Mission architecture and charm. It was closed in early 1990 for extensive remodeling, but was scheduled to reopen late in the year. The mission theme is carried further in the city's symbol, a replica of Father Junipero Serra's bell and cross.

With about 180,000 people, Riverside is the largest city between Los Angeles and Phoenix, Arizona. It is home to four colleges and universities, nine golf courses, more than 30 parks, two major shopping centers, and seven museums, including the **California Museum of Photography,** 3824 Main St.; the **Riverside Municipal Museum** of human and natural history, 3720 Orange St.; and the **March Field Museum** at nearby March Air Force Base, with vintage planes and flying memorabilia. An impressive air show is held at the base annually in

March. (There is another fine vintage aircraft collection in the **Plane of Fame** museum at **Chino,** on the western edge of San Bernardino County.)

Most importantly from a state historical standpoint, Riverside was the birthplace of California's multimillion-dollar navel orange industry. The first navel orange tree ever grown in California stands on the corner of Magnolia and Arlington Streets. Brought from Brazil in 1873, it still bears fruit!

Redlands was California's major producer of navel oranges in the 1890s. Many Victorian homes from that period line the city streets, and are open to the public. Among them are the **Edwards Mansion,** 2064 Orange Tree Lane, the **Morey Mansion,** 190 Terracina Blvd., and the **Kimberly Crest House,** 1325 Prospect Drive. History buffs will enjoy a visit to the **San Bernardino County Museum,** 2024 Orange Tree Lane, as

Above: Up, up and away in a balloon over the San Bernardino Valley.

well as the nearby **University of Redlands.** Each summer, the city hosts the **Redlands Bowl Music Festival.**

Ontario not only has an interesting local heritage, but its ties with the Cucamonga Wine District give it a distinctive vintage. California's oldest wine-producing region dates to 1839, when Tiburcio Tapia built an adobe home and planted his vines. The **San Antonio Winery,** 2801 Milliken St., and the **Cucamonga Vineyard,** 10013 8th St. in neighboring Cucamonga, carry on the tradition. Martini lovers may also be fascinated by the **Graber Olive House,** 315 E. 4th St., Ontario, where olives have been processed and shipped since 1894.

Rancho/California/Temecula lies only 56 miles (90 km) south of Ontario and boasts prize-winning wineries and balloon fests. Temecula has an authentic Western atmosphere with antique and art shops. The six-block Old Town area has unpaved roads and wooden sidewalks.

The **San Bernardino Mountains** offer year-round recreational options in San Bernardino National Forest. Eight ski areas assure runs for skiers of every skill level. The most extensive facilities are at **Bear Mountain,** which stretches across four peaks to an elevation of 8,800 feet. Like other Southern California ski areas, Bear uses snow machines to insure its slopes are covered.

In summer, water sports abound at the three major mountain lakes – **Silverwood, Arrowhead,** and **Big Bear.** And about 55 miles (88 km) southeast of Riverside, **Idyllwild,** a sleepy country resort town, comes alive every summer with the exciting summer arts program of the University of Southern California.

Beaumont and **Yucaipa** are in the high desert, a short drive east of San Bernardino and Riverside. Yucaipa is considered California's apple capital, along with adjacent Oak Glen. Fall is the best time to visit, while June sees the cherry festival in Beaumont.

ONTARIO
(All local phone numbers have 714 area code.)
Accommodation
LUXURY: **Red Lion Inn**, 222 N. Vineyard Ave., 91764 (Tel. 983-0909, 800-547-8010).
MODERATE: **Clarion**, 2220 E. Holt Blvd., 91764 (Tel. 986-8811, 800-252-7466); **Compri**, 429 N. Vineyard Ave., 91764 (Tel. 391-6411, 800-426-6774); **Griswold's Inn**, 555 W. Foothill Blvd., Claremont 91711 (Tel. 626-4211, 800-854-5733). *BUDGET:* **Lexington Suites**, 231 N. Vineyard Ave., 91764 (Tel. 983-8484, 800-527-1877); **Quality Inn**, 1818 E. Holt Blvd., 91764 (Tel. 988-8466, 800-228-5151); **Super 8 Lodge**, 514 N. Vineyard Ave., 91764 (Tel. 983-2886, 800-843-1991).
Restaurants
AMERICAN: **Bengie's**, 652 N. Central Ave., Upland; **Magnolia's Peach Rest. and Saloon**, 530 N. Mountain Ave., Upland.
Attractions
Graber Olive House, 315 E. 4th St. (Tel. 983-1761), daily; **Kenneth G. Fisk Musical Instrument Museum**, 450 N. College Way, Claremont (Tel. 621-8307); **Museum of History and Art**, 225 S. Euclid Ave. (Tel. 983-3198). 12-4pm Thu-Sun, free; **Plane of Fame Museum**, 7000 Merrill Ave., Chino Airport (Tel. 597-3722), 9am-5pm daily; **Rancho Santa Ana Botanic Garden**, 1500 N. College Ave., Claremont (Tel. 626-1917), 8am-5pm daily, free.
Tourist Information
Greater Ontario Visitors and Convention Bureau, 421 N. Euclid Ave., Ontario 91762 (Tel. 984-2450); **Claremont Convention and Visitors Bureau**, 205 Yale Ave., Claremont 91711 (Tel. 621-9644).
Transportation
Ontario Intern. Airport (ONT) (Tel. 984-1207) is served by foreign and domestic airlines.

RIVERSIDE
Accommodation
MODERATE: **Sheraton**, 3400 Market St., 92501 (Tel. 784-8000, 800-325-3535).
BUDGET: **Hampton Inn**, 1590 University Ave., 92507 (Tel. 683-6000, 800-426-7866); **Holiday Inn**, 1200 University Ave., 92507 (Tel. 682-8000); **Howard Johnson's**, 1199 University Ave., 92507 (Tel. 682-9011, 800-654-2000).
Attractions
California Museum of Photography, 3824 Main St. (Tel. 787-4787), 10am-5pm Tue-Sat, 12-5pm Sun, free; **Glen Ivy Hot Springs**, 25000 Glen Ivy Rd., Corona (Tel. 737-4723); **Heritage House**, 8193 Magnolia Ave. (Tel. 689-1333),

open 12-3:30pm Tue and Thu, 12-3:30pm Sun; **Jurupa Cultural Center**, 7621 Granite Hill Dr. (Tel. 685-5818), 9am-5pm Tue-Sat; **Lake Perris State Recreational Area**, 17801 Lake Perris Dr., Perris (Tel. 657-0676 or 657-9000); **March Field Museum**, March Air Force Base (Tel. 655-3725), 10am-4pm Mon-Fri, 12-4pm Sat-Sun, free; **Orange Empire Railway Museum**, 2201 South A St., Perris (Tel. 657-2605), weekends and holidays; **Riverside Art Museum**, 3425 7th St. (Tel. 684-7111); **Riverside Botanic Gardens**, University of California-Riverside (Tel. 787-4650), 8am-5pm daily, free; **Riverside Municipal Museum**, 3720 Orange St. (Tel. 782-5273), 9am-5pm Tue-Sat, 1-5pm Sun.
Tourist Information
Riverside Visitors and Conv. Bureau, 3443 Orange St., Riverside 92501 (Tel. 787-7950).

SAN BERNARDINO
Accommodation
LUXURY: **Arrowhead Hilton Lodge**, P.O. Box 1699, Lake Arrowhead Village 92352 (Tel. 336-1511, 800-223-3307). *MODERATE:* **Big Bear Inn**, 42200 Moonridge Road, Big Bear Lake 92315 (Tel. 866-3471, 800-232-7466); **Inland Empire Hilton**, 285 E. Hospitality Lane, 92408 (Tel. 889-0133, 800-445-8667); **Maruko**, 295 North E St., 92401 (Tel. 381-6181, 800-472-3353). *BUDGET:* **Econo Lodge**, 668 Fairway Dr., 92408 (Tel. 825-7750); **Thunder Cloud Inn**, 20498 Lakeview Dr., Big Bear Lake 92315 (Tel. 866-7594); **Villa Viejo Motel**, 777 W. 6th St., 92410 (Tel. 889-3561, 800-228-9669).
Restaurants
AMERICAN: **Jeremiah's Steak House**, 205 E. Valley Blvd., Colton.
CONTINENTAL: **Cliffhanger**, 25187 Highway 18, Arrowhead Highlands; **Edwards Mansion**, 2064 Orange Tree Lane, Redlands. *ITALIAN:* **Salvatore's**, 16689 Foothill Blvd., Fontana.
Attractions
Big Bear Lake, Fawnskin (tel. 866-3437); **Kimberly Crest House and Gardens**, 1325 Prospect Dr., Redlands (Tel. 792- 2111). 1-4pm Sun and Thu; **Lake Arrowhead Village**, Lake Arrowhead (Tel. 337-3715); **Morey Mansion**, 190 Terracina Blvd., Redlands (Tel. 793-7970); **San Bernardino County Museum**, 2024 Orange Tree Lane, Redlands (tel. 825-4825). 9am-5pm Tue-Sat, 1-5pm Sun.
Tourist Information
Inland Empire Tourism Council, P.O. Box 638, Skyforest 92385 (Tel. 336-3661); **San Bernardino Conv. and Visitor Bureau**, 546 W. 6th St., San Bernardino 92402 (Tel. 889- 3980).

SAN DIEGO

Like a beautiful gem on the south-western rim of America's Sun Belt, the city of San Diego sparkles on the edge of a sun- drenched harbor. Cruise ships, navy vessels, and tuna seiners glide across the water, while all sizes of sail-boats use the prevailing offshore breeze to their best advantage. Nearby, sleek office towers dominate the skyline, dwarfing low-rise buildings which reflect the community's Hispanic heritage.

Palm trees, as well as colorful bougain-villeas and birds of paradise, thrive in the Mediterranean climate where the average annual daytime temperature is 70 °F (21 °C) and the yearly rainfall is less than 10 inches (25 cm). Outside the downtown area, the blue Pacific Ocean rolls up on 70 miles (112 km) of sandy beaches.

San Diego has long been known as one of California's most pleasant play-grounds. The region boasts more golf courses per capita than anywhere else, and the best surfing east of Hawaii.

Recently, it has emerged as a major center for the performing arts and other cultural endeavors. No longer "just another pretty place", the city offers a great variety of sophisticated dining, shopping, and many artistic experiences. Today, San Diego's theaters, museums, and research institutes receive as much attention as its world-class zoo.

This wide range of things to do, and the picturesque backdrop against which to do them, attracts more than 30 million out-of-towners each year. (Tourism is the third largest revenue generator in San Diego, after manufacturing and the military.) At the same time, the permanent population has swelled – by 25 per cent in a recent decade – to over one million. San Diego, called "America's finest city" by its inhabitants, is now the sixth largest metropolis in the United States; within California, only Los Angeles, 120 miles (192 km) north, has more people.

Above: Point Loma in San Diego county.
Right: Mission San Diego del Alcala.

Hispanic Beginnings

Until 1542, the corner of the continent now known as San Diego County was inhabited solely by native Indians. Then Portuguese explorer Juan Rodriguez Cabrillo sailed into what he described as "a very good enclosed port" and claimed it for Spain. He did not stay long. The locals were left undisturbed again until 1602, when Sebastian Vizcaino led three ships into the harbor. The Spaniard named the bay "San Diego" after a priest from the town of Alcala.

The Cabrillo National Monument, a park-like place on a lofty summit at the tip of **Point Loma**, commemorates the first European discovery and provides visitors with an opportunity to learn about this early period of history. The spot also provides one of the best views of San Diego and its surrounding blue waters. During the winter months, December through February, Point Loma is an excellent vantage point for sighting California gray whales. These giants of the sea make their way to breeding grounds off the coast of Baja California, Mexico, at the same time each year.

As the displays at Cabrillo National Monument explain, the Spanish ignored San Diego Bay until the 1760s, when they became worried about the possibility of colonizing efforts by other nations. To protect their interests, they dispatched an overland expedition, which met a group that arrived by sea. Together they established a mission, and when it was blessed on July 16, 1769, by a priest named Junipero Serra, the birth of the new community was official.

In addition to being home to **Mission San Diego de Alcala**, "the birthplace of California", San Diego County is blessed with a second sanctuary – **Mission San Luis Rey de Francia,** 40 miles (64 km) north near the city of Oceanside. Both missions still house active parishes, and Roman Catholic services are held regularly. Each has a museum open to the public. The missions also present an excellent opportunity for visitors to admire

to Los Angeles

Escondido

San Diego
Wild Animal Park ★

*Batiquitos
Lagoon*

78

Leucadia

Encinitas

Cardiff-
by-the-Sea

5

Rancho Santa Fe

*Lake
Hodges*

Woodson Mt.
2893 ft•
(882 m)

Ramona

67

Solana Beach

Del Mar

15

Poway

*San Vicente
Lake*

Torrey Pines
State Res.

Univ. of Calif.
San Diego

Scripps Aquarium ★

Pt. La Jolla
The Cove ★

Mus. of
Contemp. Art

La Jolla

Pacific Beach

805

52

274

163

MURPHY CANON RD.

CABRILLO

L. Miramar

GORGE RD.

MISSION

Cowles Mt.
1588 ft
(484 m)

Murray

Mission
San Diego
de Alcala

ALVARADO

8

La Mesa

Lakeside

67

*Loveland
Res.*

to
Mexicali

8

Santee

El Cajon

125

54

Spring Valley

Mission Beach

Mission Bay Park
Sea World

Ocean Beach

Old Town
State Hist. Park

SAN DIEGO

15

5

Balboa Park,
Zoo, Museums

HELIX

94

Lemon Grove

94

Jamul

San Miguel Mt.
2565 ft (782 m)

San Diego
Intl. Airp.

209

Coronado

Cabrillo
Nat. Monument ★
Pt. Loma

Zuniga Pt.

Hotel
del Coronado

National City

54 BAY

*Sweetwater
Res.*

Nature
Interpretive C.

Chula Vista

805

*Upper
Otay Res.*

*Lower
Otay Res.*

P A C I F I C

SILVER STRAND

MONTGOMERY BLVD.

75

Imperial Beach

Otay

O C E A N

Border Field
State Pk.

5

905

San Ysidro

U.S.A.

MEXICO

METROPOLITAN SAN DIEGO

1

0   5   10   15 km

0   2,5   5   7,5 miles

TIJUANA

to Ensenada

1

122

the graceful arches, thick adobe walls, bell towers, whitewashed facades, and other features typical of California mission architecture.

This early era of history accounts for many local place names: Mission Bay, Mission Beach, Friars Road, Junipero Serra Highway, the Serra Museum, and Spanish Landing, to name just a few. Even the city's professional baseball team, the *San Diego Padres*, is named in honor of the humble priest.

Old Town, New Town

In 1822, San Diego became a Mexican possession following that country's successful revolution against Spain. In 1846, the town, which by then had several hundred inhabitants, was claimed by the United States.

As an American community, San Diego began to trade actively by sea with other nations. The town grew rapidly. Warehouses, hotels, saloons, boarding houses, and other necessary buildings were constructed. However, a major problem became apparent: The Old Town site was too far from the harbor.

During the 1850s, several attempts to build a New Town closer to the water failed. However, the U.S. government succeeded in building a lighthouse on Point Loma. The original lighthouse and its modern successor are now part of the acreage of Cabrillo National Monument.

The arrival of Alonzo Horton in 1867 started a new era. Horton had made a lot of money in San Francisco during the 1848-50 California gold rush, and he was determined to turn San Diego into a great city. He bought a large plot of land near the water, sold off lots, and constructed buildings. The city government moved to New Town in 1871. The arrival of the railroad in 1885 and the discovery of gold

Above: Downtown San Diego has never entirely shaken its past, Horton Plaza.

in the back country in 1869 further aided the community's growth. In 1888 the population hit 40,000; by 1890, Old Town had withered.

Today, **Old Town** lives again, urban revitalization having turned many of the old Spanish buildings into shops and restaurants. In 1967, the state of California bought six blocks of early San Diego buildings for $2.5 million and turned them into **Old Town State Historic Park.** Some of the adobes date all the way back to 1821, although most were built in the late nineteenth century. Narrated walking tours, offered daily, are the preferred introduction to the area. Old Town's centerpiece is the **Bazaar del Mundo,** a courtyard surrounded by 16 Hispanic crafts shops and four restaurants. **Casa de Bandini** and **Casa de Pico** feature Mexican fare, mariachis and, sometimes, flamenco dancers.

Even forward-thinking Alonzo Horton would be surprised to see the avant-garde shopping complex that now graces his New Town site. Named in his honor,

Horton Plaza covers six and a half city blocks and includes 150 specialty shops and restaurants as well as four major department stores. The multi-level mall is best known for its colorful, fanciful, quasi-Moorish architecture.

Since it opened in 1985, Horton Plaza has become the focal point of a re-development effort in the oldest part of downtown San Diego. Nearby, in the **Gaslamp Quarter,** handsome Victorian buildings have been restored and now house art galleries, antique shops, restaurants, and two theaters. Both Horton Plaza and the Gaslamp Quarter start on the south side of Broadway, San Diego's main thoroughfare. The central business district is to the north.

Navy Town, USA

San Diego continued to grow steadily during the latter part of the nineteenth

Above: Victorian façades in the Gaslamp Quarter. Right: Concert hall in Balboa Park.

century and the early part of the twentieth. The harbor was dredged to facilitate ship movement. World War I placed additional emphasis on the city's role as a navy base. The now world-famous **San Diego Zoo** was started in 1910, and the Panama California Exposition of 1915, acclaiming the opening of the Panama Canal, was highly successful. Some of the magnificent Spanish colonial buildings constructed in Balboa Park for the exposition still house museums and contribute to the park's atmosphere.

In the 1920s, San Diego became known as an aviation center. This talent was recognized by Charles Lindbergh, who chose the city's Ryan Corporation to manufacture the *Spirit of St. Louis,* in which he made his historic transatlantic solo flight. San Diego responded in kind and, in 1928, named its new airport Lindbergh Field. A full-scale replica of the famous plane, and various memorabilia of Lindbergh himself, are kept in Balboa Park at the **San Diego Aerospace Museum**, one of the nation's finest.

The city's population jumped dramatically after the United States entered World War II. The metropolitan area had 256,000 residents in 1940; by 1950, that number had risen to 556,000. This "boom town era" was dominated by the navy, which expanded its existing bases and built new ones. A constant influx of military personnel and their families helped to create a thriving economy. After the war, the navy and Marine Corps continued to use the bases. Today, San Diego is the home of the largest concentration of naval power in the U.S. Military installations are closed to the public, but on weekend afternoons, the navy moves one of its ships to **Broadway Pier,** and visitors are welcome aboard.

San Diego Today

Once called "the unconventional city" because it lacked a hall big enough to accommodate large meetings, San Diego now boasts a commodious **Convention Center** overlooking the harbor. It also has expanded its economic base by luring non-polluting high-tech industries to the area, and encouraging the establishment of scientific and medical research facilities. Three major universities and several colleges are scattered around the city.

A beautiful bridge arches across the bay, connecting San Diego with neighboring **Coronado**. Modern freeways make life in many suburbs an attractive option. A bright red trolley carries residents and visitors alike 20 miles (32 km) south, through various seaside communities, to the U.S.-Mexican border. The population of the metropolitan area today exceeds 2.3 million.

Besides Cabrillo National Monument, the missions, Horton Plaza, Old Town, and the Gaslamp Quarter, San Diego has many other points of interest.

It is not hard to find your way around downtown San Diego, but a short lesson might be in order. Most north-south streets are numbered; east-west streets bear the names of trees, in alphabetical order: Ash, Beech, Cedar, Date, etc. Most

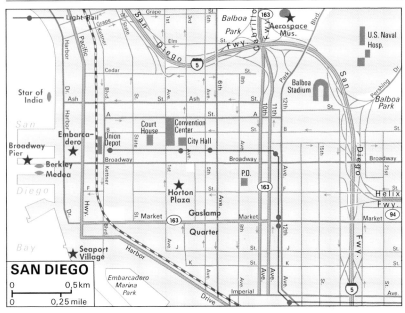

folks start their exploration at **Balboa Park,** known for its zoo. The tree-clad park, which sprawls over 1,074 acres (2,653 hectare), lies slightly northeast of the city center, with its main entrance at 6th and Laurel streets. It is home to five gardens, four restaurants, a miniature train and puppet theater for children, and no fewer than 10 museums, among them the **Aerospace Museum**, the **Museum of San Diego History,** the **San Diego Natural History Museum,** the **Museum of Photographic Arts,** the **House of Pacific Relations** international cottages, the **Hall of Champions** sports museum, and the **Model Railroad Museum.**

Especially noteworthy attractions include the **San Diego Museum of Art,** with permanent collections of great Dutch, Flemish, Italian, and Spanish Renaissance painters; the **Timken Art Gallery,** featuring European old masters, American painters and Russian icons; the

Right: The Del Coronado Hotel offers luxury to its guests.

San Diego **Museum of Man,** an anthropological museum focusing on the native culture of the Western Americas, with traveling exhibits covering the globe; the **San Diego Automotive Museum,** with a superb display of vintage and historically significant cars and an active restoration program; and the **Reuben H. Fleet Space Theater and Science Center,** an enormous planetarium with adjoining hands-on exhibition hall.

The park's **Old Globe Theater**, which, with the Festival Theater and the Cassius Carter Center Stage, make up the **Simon Edison Center** for the Performing Arts, is acknowledged to be one of the finest regional theaters in the country. The winner of several Tony Awards, the Old Globe stages 12 productions a year, from Shakespeare and the classics to world premieres of contemporary works.

The **San Diego Zoo** covers more than 100 acres (40 hectares) and houses over 3,400 exotic animals of 800 different species. Of these, koalas are a popular favorite, followed closely by wild Przewalski's horses from Mongolia, sun bears from Malaysia, and long-billed kiwis from New Zealand. Other highlights include a walk-through aviary, a simulated rainforest, and moving sidewalks which stretch from canyons to upper levels. The garden-like grounds contain innumerable trees and shrubs, some of which find their way onto the animals' dinner plates. Guided bus tours provide the best introduction; lofty aerial tramway trips lend a new perspective. The **Children's Zoo**, built to scale for youngsters, is another popular feature for smaller visitors.

While the zoo's animals are confined to moats and other unobtrusive methods, their counterparts can be seen roaming in more natural settings at the **San Diego Wild Animal Park** 30 miles (48 km) north of the city. In terms of both flora and fauna, the 1,800-acre (725-hectare) preserve closely resembles areas of Africa and Asia. A monorail excursion, narrated by a guide, offers a good survey of the park.

In addition to land animals, San Diego has a special place for ocean dwellers: **Sea World,** located on Mission Bay just a few miles northwest of downtown. Marine life from around the world is featured in exhibits and shows at the 135-acre (54-hectare) park. The Penguin Encounter and the killer whale show are two of the most popular features. Other favorites are the world's largest live shark exhibit, a dolphin petting pool, and the Places of Learning educational exhibit.

Sea World is located in **Mission Bay Park,** a 4,600-acre (1,860-hectare) area consisting of a large calm-water inlet with many coves, two islands, and a convoluted sandy shoreline. This aquatic playground is popular for water-skiing, sailing, and windsurfing. Grassy expanses along the water's edge provide a picturesque setting for kite-flying and picnicking, cycling and jogging. Deep-sea sportfishing boats leave daily from the park's Quivira Basin.

Coastal Communities

Those who prefer ocean beaches should head to one of the seaside suburbs: **Ocean Beach, Mission Beach, Pacific Beach,** or **La Jolla.** Surfers seem to prefer La Jolla's Windansea Beach; families flock to La Jolla Shores.

La Jolla is also home to **The Cove,** an underwater marine park, where sea creatures can be observed but not taken from the water. **Scripps Aquarium,** located on the grounds of the Scripps Institution of Oceanography, is another good place for viewing marine life. Nearby, the campus of the **University of California-San Diego** is a pleasant place for strolling, though serious walkers prefer the many trails and wonderful viewpoints in **Torrey Pines State Reserve.**

In addition to marine life, La Jolla provides some of San Diego's best nightlife. The **Hard Rock Café**, featuring music and memorabilia of the 1950s and 1960s, is the focal point; other hot spots are interspersed with dining venues along Pro-

spect Street. La Jolla also attracts an affluent set to shop in posh boutiques, meander among million-dollar homes, and rub elbows with the rich and famous.

Just north of La Jolla, the community of **Del Mar** has its own beautiful beaches and the **Del Mar Fair Grounds.** A lively county fair, the third largest in the state, takes place on this site in late June every year, ending with Fourth of July fireworks. From late July to mid September, the Del Mar Thoroughbred Club hosts horse races six days a week; in October, the fairgrounds are transformed into a racetrack for the Del Mar Grand Prix, a major auto-racing event.

Further up the coast at **Carlsbad,** a framework house recalls the Bohemian origin of the town's name, which it owes to its therapeutic springs. The **La Costa Hotel and Spa** is a well-known "fitness factory" for the rich and famous. The resort features eight restaurants, two golf

Above: Painters on La Jolla beach. Right: In the Anza Borrega Desert State Park.

courses, 23 tennis courts, and complete club facilities for anyone wanting to lose prounds or tone muscles.

Coronado and the Embarcadero

Coronado, located across the harbor from downtown San Diego, is another interesting place to explore. Access is either by car across the graceful San Diego-Coronado Bay Bridge, or by pedestrian ferry. The community feels like an island, but in fact is connected to the mainland by a long, narrow stretch of land known as the **Silver Strand**.

A highlight of any visit to Coronado is a stop at the **Hotel del Coronado.** Built in 1888, the hotel has been designated a National Historic Landmark. The enchanting wooden structure features turrets, tall cupolas, hand-carved wooden pillars, and Victorian filigree. L. Frank Baum stayed at "The Del" while he wrote *The Wizard of Oz*, and it is easy to see that the hotel provided inspiration for the castle in the Emerald City.

As well as having a storybook atmosphere, the hotel provides first-rate accommodation in 700 rooms, and dining in several different restaurants and cafes. The Duke of Windsor, Thomas Edison, and a dozen US presidents are just a sampling of the prominent personalities who have been guests at the hotel. Marilyn Monroe also stayed at "The Del" during the filming of *Some Like It Hot,* just one of the many movies and television shows filmed on the site.

Ferries to Coronado leave from San Diego's Broadway Pier, one of several wharves located along the **Embarcadero.** This is a colorful area to explore on foot. The *Star of India,* the oldest iron-hulled merchant vessel afloat, is moored at the west end of Ash Street. Built in the Isle of Man in 1863, the ship is sailed on San Diego Bay on very special occasions. The *Star of India,* along with the *Medea,* a 1904 Scottish steamer, and the *Berkeley,* a San Francisco ferry boat dating from 1898, comprise the attractive **Maritime Museum.**

Back Country Excursions

San Diego's back country has a beauty of its own. Many worthwhile destinations are within two hours of the city by car.

For example, America's second largest telescope is located atop **Mount Palomar,** 66 miles (106 km) north of San Diego. The 200-inch (508-cm) Hale telescope has an optical range of approximately 1 billion light years. The observatory is open to visitors daily.

Gold was discovered at **Julian,** 60 miles (96 km) northeast of San Diego, in 1869. Relics of this area are on display in the quaint mountain town, which today is more famous for its delicious apples.

Anza-Borrego Desert State Park, 20 miles (32 km) beyond Julian, is the largest state park in the United States. Within its 600,000 acres (242,000 hectares) are geological formations, plants, and animals found nowhere else on earth. The best time to visit is during the spring, February through April, when the wildflowers are in bloom.

SAN DIEGO
Accommodation

All telephone numbers have 619 area codes; toll-free numbers are indicated by 800 prefix.

LUXURY: **Del Coronado**, 1500 Orange Ave., Coronado 92118 (Tel. 435-6611); **Embassy Suites**, 601 Pacific Hwy., 92101 (Tel. 239-2400, 800-362-2779); **La Valencia**, 1132 Prospect St., La Jolla 92037 (Tel. 454-0771, 800- 451-0772); **Le Meridien**, 2000 Second St., Coronado 92118 (Tel. 435-3000, 800-543-4300); **Marriott Hotel & Marina**, 333 W. Harbor Dr., 92101 (Tel. 234-1500, 800-228-9290); **Omni**, 910 Broadway Circle, 92101 (Tel. 239-2200, 800-843-6664); **Princess Resort**, 1404 W. Vacation Rd., 92109 (Tel. 274-4630, 800-542-6275); **U.S. Grant**, 326 Broadway, 92101 (Tel. 232-3121, 800-237-5029). *MODERATE:* **Balboa Park Inn,** 3402 Park Blvd., 92103 (Tel. 298-0823); **Dana Inn & Marina,**1710 W. Mission Bay Dr., 92109 (Tel. 222-6640, 800-345-9995); **Horton Grand**, 311 Island Ave., 92101 (Tel. 544-1886, 800-544-1886); **Horton Park Plaza**, 901 Fifth Ave., 92101 (Tel. 232-9500, 800-443-8012); **Ramada**, 660 K St., 92101 (Tel. 696-0234, 800-272-6232); **Sommerset Hillcrest**, 606 Washington St., 92103 (Tel. 692-5200, 800-962-9665); **Town & Country**, 500 Hotel Circle N., 92108 (Tel. 291-7131, 800-854-2608); **Vacation Inn Old Town**, 3900 Old Town Ave., 92110 (Tel. 299-7400, 800-451-9846). *BUDGET:* **Armed Services YMCA**, 500 W. Broadway, 92139 (Tel. 232-1133); **Budget Motels**, 3880 Greenwood Dr., 92110 (Tel. 543-9944, 800-824-5317); **Clarke's Lodge**, 1765 Union St., 92101 (Tel. 234-6787, 800-822-0133); **Comfort Suites**, 631 Camino del Rio S., 92108 (Tel. 294-3444, 800-221-2222); **Coronado Village Inn**, 1017 Park Place, Coronado 92118 (Tel. 435-9934); **Image Inn at Mission Bay**, 2575 Clairemont Dr., 92117 (Tel. 275-5700, 800-828-8111).

Bookstores and Libraries

Doubleday Books (general), 367 Horton Plaza (Tel. 696-9616); **Le Travel Store**, 241 Horton Plaza (Tel. 544-0005). *LIBRARY:* **San Diego Public Library**, 820 E St. (Tel. 236-6278).

Museums and Art Galleries

Aerospace Historical Center, 2001 Pan American Plaza, Balboa Park (Tel. 234-8291), 10am-4:30pm daily; **Automotive Museum**, 2080 Pan American Plaza, Balboa Park (Tel. 231-2886), 10am-4pm daily; **Junipero Serra Museum**, 2727 Presidio Dr. (Tel. 297-3258), 10am-4:30pm Tue-Sat; **La Jolla Museum of Contemporary Art**, 700 Prospect St., La Jolla (Tel. 454-3541), 10am-5pm Tue-Sun; **Maritime Museum**, 1306 N. Harbor Dr. (Tel. 234-9153), 9am-8pm daily; **Mingei International Museum of World Folk Art,** 4405 La Jolla Village Dr., La Jolla (Tel. 453-5300), 11am-5pm Tue-Sat, 2-5pm Sun; **Museum of Art**, 1450 El Prado, Balboa Park (Tel. 232-7931), 10am-4:30pm Tue-Sun; **Museum of Man**, 1350 El Prado, Balboa Park (Tel. 239-2001), 10am-4:30pm daily; **Natural History Museum**, 1788 El Prado, Balboa Park (Tel. 232-3821), 10am-4:30pm daily; **Reuben H. Fleet Space Theater/ Science Center**, 1875 El Prado, Balboa Park (Tel. 238-1233), 9:30am-9:30pm daily; **Timken Art Gallery**, 1500 El Prado, Balboa Park (Tel. 239-5548), 10am-4:30pm Tue-Sat, 1:30- 4:30pm Sun, free.

Other Attractions

Balboa Park, Park Blvd. (Tel. 239-0512); **Cabrillo National Monument**, Cabrillo Memorial Drive, Point Loma (Tel. 557-5450), 9am-sunset daily; **Chula Vista Nature Interpretive Center**, 1000 Gunpowder Point Rd., Chula Vista (Tel. 422-2473), 10am-5pm Tue-Sun, free; **Gaslamp Quarter** (Tel. 233-5227), historic tours 10am and 1pm Sat, from 410 Island Ave.; **Heritage Park**, 2455 Heritage Park Row, Juan and Harney streets (Tel. 565-5928); **Mission Basilica San Diego de Alcala**, 10818 San Diego Mission Rd. (Tel. 281-8449), 9am-5pm daily; **Old Town State Historic Park**, 2645 San Diego Ave. (Tel. 237-6770), walking tours; **San Diego Zoo**, Zoo Drive, Balboa Park (Tel. 234-3153 or 231-1515), 9am-4pm daily; **Scripps Aquarium**, 8602 La Jolla Shores Dr., La Jolla (Tel. 534-6933), 9am-5pm daily; **Sea World of California**, 1720 S. Shores Rd., Mission Bay (Tel. 222-6363), 9am-5:30pm daily; **Simon Edison Centre for the Performing Arts**, Balboa Park (Tel. 239-2255).

Postal Services

Main Post Office, 2535 Midway Dr. (Tel. 574-0477), between Old Town and Mission Bay; downtown station on E St. between 8th and 9th avenues. Dozens of other stations are in the metropolitan area.

Restaurants

AMERICAN: **Bully's**, 5755 La Jolla Blvd. **Hob Nob Hill**, 2271 First Ave. (Tel. 239-8176). *CALIFORNIA:* **Chez Loma**, 1132 Loma Ave., Coronad; **Fat City**, 2137 Pacific Hwy *CHINESE:* **North China**, 5043 N. Harbor Dr. *CONTINENTAL:* **Dobson's**, 956 Broadway Circle. **Sky Room**, La Valencia Hotel, 1132 Prospect St., La Jolla; **Top o' the Cove**, 1216 Prospect St., La Jolla . *FRENCH:* **L'Escargot**, 5662 La Jolla Blvd., La Jolla. *ITALIAN:* **Issimo**, 5634 La Jolla Blvd., La Jolla; **Old Spaghetti Factory**, 275 Fifth Ave. *JAPANESE:* **Yakitori II**, 1533

Pacific Hwy. *MEXICAN:* **Casa de Bandini**, 2754 Calhoun St., Old Town. *SEAFOOD:* **Anthony's Harborside**, 1355 Harbor Dr.; **Cafe Pacifica**, 2414 San Diego Ave., Old Town. *THAI:* **Bangkok Palace**, 9248 Grammercy Dr.

Shopping

Horton Plaza, 1st Ave. to 4th Ave., E St. to G St., downtown (Tel. 239-8180), is a $140 million shopping, dining, and entertainment complex completed in 1985. Colorful and multi-level, it includes 150 shops and four major department stores. On San Diego Bay adjacent to downtown is **Seaport Village**, 849 W. Harbor Dr. (Tel. 235-4014), an imaginative 14-acre complex that emulates late 19th century San Diego.; Bazaar del Mundo, in Old Town (Tel. 296-3161), has 16 shops and four restaurants offering authentic Mexican crafts and cuisine.

Tourist Information

San Diego Convention and Visitors Bureau, 1200 3rd Ave., Suite 824, San Diego 92101 (Tel. 232-3101); **International Visitor Info Center**, 11 Horton Plaza, 1st Ave. and F St. (Tel. 236-1212), 8:30am-5pm daily. Recorded info 239-9696; **Visitor Info Center**, 2688 E. Mission Bay Dr. (Tel. 276-8200).

Transportation

San Diego International Airport (Lindbergh Field), 3165 Pacific Hwy. (Tel. 231-5220), is three miles west of downtown. Major carriers link it to Europe, Asia, and cities throughout North America. The **Metropolitan Transit System**, 449 Broadway (Tel. 234-1060), has 90 bus routes; one-day passes cost $3. The **San Diego Trolley**, 1255 Imperial Ave. (Tel. 231-1466), operates 5am-1am from downtown to near the Mexican border crossing; fares are 50 cents to $1.50. The **Molly Trolley**, a tourist bus system, plies four routes between hotels and various attractions 9am-7pm daily; an all-day pass is $6.

NORTHERN BEACHES
Accommodation

LUXURY: **La Costa Hotel & Spa**, Costa del Mar Rd., Carlsbad 92009 (Tel. 438-6111, 800-854-5000); **Tamarack Beach Resort**, 3200 Carlsbad Blvd., Carlsbad 92008 (Tel. 729-3500, 800-237-3812). *MODERATE:* **Pea Soup Andersen's Inn**, 850 Palomar Airport Rd., Carlsbad 92008 (Tel. 438-7880, 800-874-1421); **Sanderling Place**, 85 Encinitas Blvd., Encinitas 92024 (Tel. 942-7455, 800-367-6467). *BUDGET:* **Moonlight Beach**, 233 Second St., Encinitas 92024 (Tel. 753-0623); **Sandman Motel**, 1501 Carmelo Dr., Oceanside 92054 (Tel. 722-7661).

Restaurants

AMERICAN: **Remington's**, 2010 Jimmy Durante Blvd., Del Mar. *CONTINENTAL:* **Frederick's**, 128 S. Acacia St., Solana Beach. *FRENCH:* **La Bonne Bouffe**, 471 Encinitas Blvd., Encinitas.

Attractions

Antique Gas & Steam Engine Museum, 2040 N. Sante Fe Dr., Vista (Tel. 941-1791), 10am-4pm daily, free; **Mission San Luis Rey de Francia**, 4040 Mission Ave., Oceanside (Tel. 757-3651), 10am-4pm Mon-Sat, 12-4pm Sun; Torrey Pines State Reserve, Del Mar (Tel. 755-2063).

Tourist Information

Carlsbad Conv. & Visitors Bureau, 5411 Avenida Encinas, Suite 100, Carlsbad 92008 (Tel. 729-1786).

INLAND COMMUNITIES
Accommodation

LUXURY: **Rancho Bernardo Inn**, 17550 Bernardo Oaks Dr., San Diego 92128 (Tel. 487-1611, 800-854-1065). *MODERATE:* **Compri Hotel at Rancho Bernardo**, 11611 Bernardo Plaza Court, San Diego 92128 (Tel. 485-9520, 800-426-6774); **Inn at Rancho Santa Fe**, Paseo Delicias and Linea del Cielo, Rancho Santa Fe 92067 (Tel. 756-1131); **Lawrence Welk Resort**, 8860 Lawrence Welk Dr., Escondido 92026 (Tel. 749-3000, 800-932-9355). *BUDGET:* **Hacienda TraveLodge**, 588 N. Mollison Ave., El Cajon 92021 (Tel. 579-1144, 800-255-3050); **Pine Hills Lodge**, 2960 La Posada Way, Julian 92036 (Tel. 765-1100).

Restaurants

AMERICAN: **Bread Basket**, 1347 Tavern Road, Alpine. *CONTINENTAL:* **El Bizcocho**, Rancho Bernardo Inn, 17550 Bernardo Oaks Dr. *FRENCH:* **Mille Fleurs**, 6009 Paseo Delicias, Rancho Sante Fe.

Attractions

Mission San Antonio de Pala, Pala (Tel. 742-3317), 10am-3pm Tue-Sun; **Mission Santa Ysabel**, Santa Ysabel (Tel. 765-0810), 7am-dusk daily; **Palomar Observatory**, Palomar Mountain (Tel. 742-3476), 9am-4pm daily, free; Railroad Museum, 916 Sheridan Rd., Campo (Tel. 478-9937), 9am-5pm Sat-Sun, train ride; **San Diego Wild Animal Park**, 15500 San Pasqual Valley Rd., Escondido (Tel. 747-8702 or 231-1515), 9am-4pm daily

Tourist Information

Escondido Convention & Visitors Bureau, 720 N. Broadway, Escondido 92025 (Tel. 745-4741); **Julian Chamber of Commerce** (Tel. 765-1857).

THE CENTRAL COAST

Even without its famous castle, the Central Coast would still be a region fit for a king. Treasures abound up and down this gentle 150 miles (240 km) of coastline. There are charming seaside villages, romantic old missions, and vineyard-covered hills. Happily existing in a time warp, this is a California characterized more by antique shops, sea breezes and country lanes than by malls, smog, and freeway interchanges.

Despite its remoteness, newspaper publisher William Randolph Hearst knew a hilltop site overlooking the sea near **San Simeon** would make a majestic backdrop for his Spanish-Moorish palace, complete with private zoo and enough art objects to fill a dozen museums. Hollywood stars and heads of state were frequent callers at the estate during the 1930s and 1940s, making the long train and car journey up the coast to attend parties given by Hearst and his vivacious mistress, Marion Davies.

Today, visitors to **Hearst Castle**, now a state historical monument, must make advance reservations for one of several different guided tours that leave from the visitor center at the foot of the hill. Most first-time visitors choose Tour One, which includes the gardens, pools, a guest house, and the main floor of the castle.

Hearst's acquisitions were once said to represent one-fourth of all sales of *objets d'art* in the world. The result of his insatiable collecting, which sometimes involved having entire ancient European buildings dismantled and shipped to California, is an incredible hodgepodge of furnishings and architectural detail that somehow forms a pleasing whole.

Perhaps the most photographed room is the dining hall, with its Flemish tapestries, sixteenth-century monastic ceiling, and fifteenth-century choir stalls lining the walls. Despite the room's grandeur, the central table is set with paper napkins and bottles of ketchup and mustard, a reminder that Hearst regarded the castle as a rustic retreat from city life. Far from rustic, however, is the 104-foot (31.6-m) outdoor Neptune Pool with its Greco-Roman façade and white marble statues surrounding the sparkling blue waters. Hearst had an indoor pool as well, this one a masterwork of tiny mosaic tiles.

In contrast to the magnificence of Hearst Castle, the pleasures offered by nearby coastal villages are of a simpler variety: pottery galleries, antique shops housed in tiny Victorian cottages, and picnic spots by the sea. All of these things are available in **Cambria,** in pine forests south of the castle along Highway 1. The most famous of Cambria's quaint shops is the **Soldier Factory** on Main Street. Originally specializing in tin soldiers, the gallery makes thousands of pewter figurines, ranging from medieval jesters to chess sets inspired by the *Arabian Nights.* Another popular spot is the **School House Gallery:** the works of local artists are displayed in a one-room schoolhouse built in 1881. You can picnic at **Leffingwell's Landing,** on a rocky promontory overlooking the ocean.

Just south of Cambria, Highway 1 leads to the tiny hamlet of **Harmony,** a picturesque jumble of old barnyard buildings in the midst of rolling ranchland. Hearst himself often stopped in this one-time dairy community to buy butter and cheese. Today the dairies have been replaced by craft shops and pottery works.

The next coastal charmer is **Cayucos,** a sprawling community with wide swimming beaches and a main street crowded with antique shops. The town's focus is its 940-foot (286-m) fishing pier, first built in 1874. Boats can be chartered here for fishing trips; otters can be observed swimming in the waters below.

Left: An indubitable taste for luxury, the Hearst castle on the central coast.

A few miles south, **Morro Bay** has been attracting explorers ever since Portuguese navigator Juan Rodriguez Cabrillo spotted it in 1542 while making his way up the uncharted coast. The distinctive landmark he saw was **Morro Rock,** the remnant of an extinct volcanic cone which guards the harbor at its north end. Now a historical site, the rock is home to rare peregrine falcons, brown pelicans, and cormorants. The heart of town is centered along the **Embarcadero,** a waterfront street lined with galleries and an aquarium. At the town's southern end **Morro Bay State Park** invites with campsites, hiking trails, and a museum of natural history with exhibits on the great blue herons native to the area.

A little way inland is **San Luis Obispo,** a small city with roots that go back to 1772, the year the **Mission San Luis Obispo de Tolusa** was founded. Although a lively downtown area has long

since grown up around it, the mission remains the town's centerpiece, a handsomely restored whitewashed adobe structure with a small museum and a church. Services are still held here.

Downhill from the mission, tree-lined San Luis Creek runs through the downtown district. Numerous wooden footbridges cross it. The creek is an attractive area of outdoor restaurant patios and walkways where strollers can often hear live music.

Another worthwhile attraction is the **San Luis Obispo County Historical Museum,** housed in a Romanesque sandstone structure built in 1905 as a Carnegie library. Inside are exhibits that include a Victorian parlor with costumed mannequins and artifacts from the town's early days. Without a doubt San Luis Obispo's most unusual attraction is the **Madonna Inn,** a hotel with a bizarre assortment of architectural features such as pink turrets and gables, terrace railings fashioned from wagon wheels, and even a waterfall in the men's room.

To the north and south of "SLO" are vineyards that support nearly 30 small wineries. Some, such as **York Mountain,** a rustic winery in an 1882 brick building near **Paso Robles,** and **Maison Deutz,** the American headquarters of a French champagne maker near **Arroyo Grande,** have tasting rooms.

Of all the 21 missions in the California chain, perhaps none gives the feeling of typical eighteenth-century mission life as strongly as La Purisima Concepcion, 4 miles (6 km) northeast of **Lompoc.** Now a part of **La Purisima Mission State Historic Park,** the mission is one of California's longest ongoing restoration projects, one that began in the 1930s when the Civilian Conservation Corps began work on structures ravaged by 150 years of earthquake, weather, and neglect. Along with its restored chapel, kitchen, and bedchambers, the mission compound recalls its early days with vegetable and

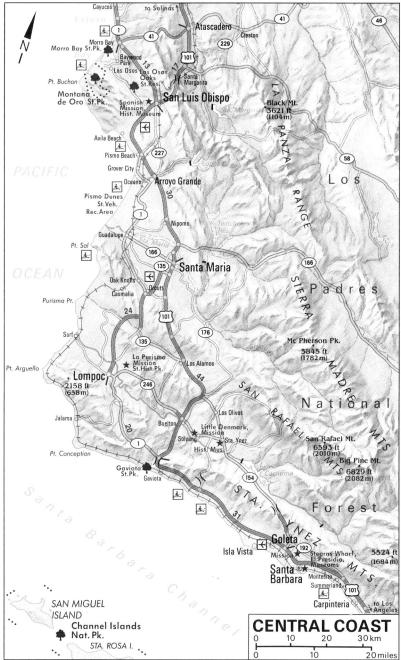

CENTRAL COAST

| 0 | 10 | 20 | 30 km |

| 0 | 10 | 20 miles |

135

flower gardens, livestock, and working aqueducts. During the summer Mission Life Days, the past is further recalled with volunteers dressed as padres, soldiers, and native converts.

The valleys just west of Lompoc produce more flower seed than anywhere else in the nation, resulting in a vivid patchwork quilt of flower fields that bloom from June to mid July. During the last weekend of June, the blooms are celebrated with a parade during Lompoc's annual Flower Festival. It is well attended by military men and their families, many of whom are stationed at adjacent **Vandenberg Air Force Base.**

A few miles southeast of Lompoc, off U.S. Highway 101, is **Solvang,** a town sometimes referred to as "Little Denmark" because of its architecture, windmills, and gas street lamps. Founded in 1910 by a group of Danes from the Mid-

Above: Poetic landscape in Ynez Valley. Right: The flowering mission of Santa Barbara.

west, Solvang has mushroomed into a major tourist attraction during the last two decades. Hundreds of shops sell gift items of all kinds, by no means exclusively Danish imports. Not surprisingly, the town also boasts an unusually high number of bakeries producing flaky pastries and rich butter cookies.

Surrounding Solvang is the **Santa Ynez Valley,** a verdant area of small ranches and orchards. A pleasant drive can be taken through such quaint small towns as **Los Olivos** and **Santa Ynez,** which boast a number of antique shops and art galleries. The valley is also a wine-growing region, with the **Ballad Winery** in Solvang among those that offer tastings.

Few places, even in California, can rival **Santa Barbara** for its climate, setting, and superb examples of tile-roofed Spanish Mission-style architecture. Lying between a backdrop of mountains to the east and palm-fringed beaches to the west, Santa Barbara owes much of its present look to a severe earthquake that

destroyed many of its existing buildings in 1925. When the city was rebuilt, local ordinances called for the white walls, red-tiled roofs, and subtropical landscaping of early California.

Many of the lovely civic buildings can be explored in the "Red Tile Walking Tour" outlined in a chamber of commerce brochure. Starting point for the walk is the **Santa Barbara County Courthouse,** a magnificent structure with hand-painted ceilings and giant murals built around a sunken garden. The top of its 70-foot (21-m) clock tower offers panoramic views of the entire city. Another treasure from the post-earthquake period is **El Paseo,** an old-fashioned shopping arcade with specialty shops, galleries, and a sidewalk café. Here a huge outdoor breakfast is held every August, when the town celebrates its "Old Spanish Days".

Within its compact downtown, Santa Barbara offers several museums and historic buildings that detail its beginnings. Among them is the **Santa Barbara Historical Museum,** which includes two adobe homes dating from 1817 and 1936. The museum also features numerous relics of the Chumash Indians, including objects used by them in daily life such as tools and baskets, as well as beads that were used by them as money.

More early structures can be visited at **El Presidio de Santa Barbara State Historic Park;** they include a chapel, a guard's house, and other edifices from what was the last Spanish military outpost in North America.

Considered by some the loveliest of all the California missions is **Mission Santa Barbara,** just north of the downtown district. Founded in 1786, the pink-and-white mission is distinguished by a twin bell tower. It contains an exquisite church with an interior painted to emulate the marble cathedrals of Europe.

Although Santa Barbara's waterfront is alive with such contemporary sights as roller skaters and street artists, it too has a historical monument, **Stearns Wharf.** Built in 1872, the wharf is the oldest in operation on the West Coast, and offers

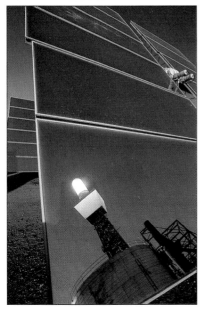

everything from wine-tasting rooms to seafood stands. A recent addition to the old wharf is the **Sea Center,** presenting exhibits on marine life as a branch of the **Santa Barbara Museum of Natural History.**

Inland from Santa Barbara is **Ojai**, a town most scenically reached by taking the Highway 150 exit off U.S. 101. Ojai is the Chumash Indian word for "nest", which may refer to the town's nest-like location in the midst of oak-shrouded mountains. Locals look forward to sunset's "Pink Moment", when the mountains are bathed in a rose-violet glow. The prime spot to savor the phenomenon is the **Valley of Shangri-La Overlook**, reached by heading east on Ojai Avenue. The view of the valley spread below you was filmed as Shangri-La in Frank Capra's 1937 movie, *Lost Horizon*.

Much of downtown Ojai is sheltered by a long Spanish-style covered veranda

Above: Californian sun not only tans tourists: The first solar energy plant at Daggett.

138

that runs along the north side of Ojai Avenue. Beneath **The Arcade** are boutiques, specialty shops, and art galleries, including **Massarella Pottery,** where visitors can watch the works in progress. East of town is the **Beatrice Wood Studio,** where the ceramicist – whose works are exhibited at museums around the world – has numerous ceramics on display and for sale.

Other treasures of the Central Coast lie not on the shoreline but some 25 miles (40 km) out to sea. **Channel Islands National Park** is made up of five islands: Anacapa, Santa Cruz, Santa Rosa, San Miguel and Santa Barbara. Two of these, Anacapa and Santa Cruz, can be seen from an observation tower located at the park's visitors center in Ventura, where a museum is also housed. Trips to the islands are available all year round through Island Packers in Ventura or Channel Island Adventures in Camarillo.

The Channel Islands were inhabited by seafaring Chumash Indians when the first European, Juan Cabrillo, arrived there in 1542. One can still see the large mounds of mollusk shells they left behind.

Due to their relatively isolated position, the islands are a haven for several species of sea birds and mammals. The waters surrounding them for six nautical miles form the **Channel Islands National Marine Sanctuary**.

Giant kelp forests line the ocean's floor here, as they do from Alaska to Baja California, and provide scuba divers or snorkelers with interesting diving sites. A perfect time to visit the park is when herds of gray whales make their way south past the islands in December-January, or head back north to the icy arctic waters in March-April. But with some luck one might also encounter minke whales, pilot whales, killer whales, several species of dolphin as well as California seals and sea lions.

Bring a lunch bag as there are no eating facilities on the islands.

(All local phone numbers have 805 area code)

SAN LUIS OBISPO AREA
Accommodation
LUXURY: **San Luis Bay Inn,** Avila Road (P.O. Box 189), Avila Beach 93424 (Tel. 595-2333, 800-592-5928).
MODERATE: **Apple Farm Inn,** 2015 Monterey St., San Luis Obispo 93401 (Tel. 544-2040, 800-255-2040).
BUDGET: **Budget Motel,** 345 Marsh St., San Luis Obispo 93401 (Tel. 543-6443, 800-458-8848).

Attractions
County Historical Museum, 696 Monterey St., San Luis Obispo (Tel. 543-0638), 10am-4pm Wed-Sun.
Mission San Luis Obispo de Tolosa, 782 Monterey St., San Luis Obispo (Tel. 543-6850), 9am-5pm daily.

Tourist Information
San Luis Obispo County Visitors and Conference Bureau, 1041 Chorro St., Suite E, San Luis Obispo 93401 (Tel. 541-8000, 800-634-1414).

SAN SIMEON AREA
Accommodation
LUXURY: **Carriage Inn,** 9280 Castillo Dr., San Simeon 93452 (Tel. 927-8659, 800-556-0400).
MODERATE: **Cambria Pines Lodge,** 2905 Burton Dr., Cambria 93428 (Tel. 927-4200).
BUDGET: **San Simeon Lodge,** 9520 Castillo Dr., San Simeon 93452 (Tel. 927-4601).

Attractions
Hearst San Simeon Historical Monument, P.O. Box 8, San Simeon (Tel. 800-444-7275), daily except major holidays. Reserve ahead for tours.

Tourist Information
San Simeon Chamber of Commerce, 9190 Castillo St., San Simeon 93452 (Tel. 927-3500).

SANTA BARBARA AREA
Accommodation
LUXURY: **Four Seasons Biltmore,** 1260 Channel Dr., 93108 (Tel. 969-2261, 800-332-3442).
MODERATE: **El Escorial,** 625 Por La Mar Circle, 93103 (Tel. 963-9302, 800-966-7414).
BUDGET: **Goleta Valley Inn,** 6021 Hollister Ave., Goleta 93117 (Tel. 967-5591).

Attractions
County Courthouse, Anapamu/Anacapa streets (Tel. 962-6464), 9am-5pm daily.
El Presidio de Santa Barbara State Historic Park, 122 E. Canon Perdido St. (Tel. 966-9719), 10:30am-4pm daily.

Historical Museum, 136 E. De la Guerra St. (Tel. 966-1601), 10am-5pm Tue-Sat, 12-5pm Sun. **Museum of Art,** 1130 State St. (Tel. 963-4364), 12-5pm Tue-Sun.
Sea Center, 211 Stearns Wharf (Tel. 962-0885).

Tourist Information
Santa Barbara Conference and Visitors Bureau, 222 E. Anapamu St., Santa Barbara (Tel. 966-9222).

SANTA YNEZ VALLEY
Accommodation
LUXURY: **Alisal Guest Ranch,** 1054 Alisal Rd., Solvang 93463 (Tel. 688-6411).
MODERATE: **Sheraton Royal Scandinavian,** 400 Alisal Rd., Solvang 93463 (Tel. 688-8000, 800-325-3535).
BUDGET: **Rodeway Inn,** 1621 N. H St., Lompoc 93436 (Tel. 735-8555).

Attractions
La Purisima Mission, 2295 Purisima Rd., Lompoc (Tel. 733-3713), 9am-4:30pm daily.
Mission Santa Ines, 1760 Mission Dr., Solvang (Tel. 688-4815), 9:30am-4:30pm Mon-Sat, 12-4:30pm Sun.
Santa Ynez Valley Historical Museum, Santa Ynez (Tel. 688-7889), 10am-4pm Tue-Thu, 1-4pm Fri-Sun.

Tourist Information
Solvang Visitors Bureau, 1571 Mission Dr., Solvang 93463 (Tel. 688-6144, 800-468-6765).

VENTURA-OXNARD AREA
Accommodation
LUXURY: **Ojai Valley Inn,** Country Club Rd., Ojai 93023 (Tel. 646-5511, 800-422-6524).
MODERATE: **Casa Sirena,** 3605 Peninsula Rd., Oxnard 93035 (Tel. 985-6311).
BUDGET: **La Quinta Inn,** U.S. Hwy. 101 at Victoria St., Ventura 93001 (Tel. 800-531-5900).

Attractions
Channel Islands National Park, Visitor Center, 1901 Spinnaker Dr., Ventura (Tel. 644-8262), 8am-5pm daily; **Mission San Buenaventura,** 211 E. Main St., Ventura (Tel. 643-4318), 10am-5pm Mon-Sat, 10am-4pm Sun; **Ojai Valley Museum,** 109 S. Montgomery St., Ojai (Tel. 646-2290), 1-5pm Wed-Mon; **Ventura County Museum of History and Art,** 100 E. Main St., Ventura (Tel. 653-0323), 10am-5pm Tue-Sun.

Tourist Information
Oxnard Convention and Visitors Bureau, 400 Esplanade Drive, Oxnard 93030 (Tel. 485-8833); **Ventura Visitors and Convention Bureau,** 89-C S. California St., Ventura 93001 (Tel. 648-2075).

THE DESERT

PALM SPRINGS
LOW DESERT
DEATH VALLEY
HIGH DESERT

California visitors are fortunate in having not one, but two vast deserts to explore: the Mojave and the Colorado. The Mojave is referred to as a high desert, for reasons of latitude and altitude. There is (relatively) more rainfall in this region, and the hot season is not so hot and severe as it is in the lower desert.

The **Colorado Desert**, in the extreme southeastern portion of California, is only a small part of the larger Sonoran Desert, which covers 120,000 square miles (310,000 sq km) of the American Southwest. Lower in elevation and altitude than the Mojave Desert, it is therefore hotter and drier.

During the 1920s, there was a worldwide fascination with the desert, and cactus gardens were very much in vogue. Entrepreneurs hauled truckloads of desert plants into Los Angeles for quick sale or export. The Mojave was in danger of being picked clean of its cacti, yucca, and ocotillo. A wealthy socialite, Mrs. Minerva Hoyt, organized the International Desert Conservation League to halt this destructive practice. Through her lobbying efforts and crusade in Washington, D.C., **Joshua Tree National Monument** was established in 1936.

Previous pages: Its name tells the whole story: sand dune in Death Valley.

Today, the desert desolation seems to attract rather than repel visitors. In places the Colorado Desert appears too civilized. Extensive irrigation for agriculture and a host of water reclamation projects have turned parts of the Colorado Desert an unnatural green. In Palm Springs, imported water, land speculators, and eager developers have created a renowned resort area in what was once considered the middle of nowhere.

PALM SPRINGS

In the early years of this century, it was called a "Desert Eden", "Our Araby", and "Garden in the Sun". Now, it is "Desert Hollywood", "Fairway Living", and "Rodeo Drive East".

Prior to the 1930s, **Palm Springs** had successively been the domain of Cahuilla Indians, a stagecoach stop, and a healing place for the convalescent and tubercular. When a paved road linked Palm Springs to Los Angeles, actors and directors began wintering in the desert.

Sixty years of growth have brought enormous changes to the resort, but it remains the most popular and widely known desert recreation center in the world. Here you may laze away long sunny days, swim, golf, play tennis, bicycle, hike, and shop till you drop.

Palm Springs and its wealthy "suburbs" of **Indian Wells, Palm Desert,** and **Rancho Mirage** attract a variety of famous visitors. Entertainers Bob Hope and Frank Sinatra have streets named for them. Former presidents Dwight Eisenhower and Gerald Ford retired to Palm Springs. The stars still drive in from Los Angeles and continue to be a part of the scene; 1960s pop star Sonny Bono was elected mayor in 1988. And each spring, between semesters, thousands of college students descend on Palm Canyon Drive, to the consternation of older and more conservative residents and visitors.

A visit to **Moorten's Botanical Garden** is an introduction not only to the Palm Springs of the past, but to the botanical diversity found in deserts all over the world. A self-guided tour takes visitors through the environments of the Sonoran, Coloradan, Chihuahuan, and Mojave Deserts, as well as the deserts of Africa and South America. Other attractions include the world's first Cactarium, a hothouse where unique cactus species flourish; the Tortoise Terrace, where several desert tortoises lumber about and bask in the sun; and an S-shaped palm tree that was hit by lightning years ago. Desert plants of all sizes may be purchased at the nursery.

The garden reflects the personality of its owner, Patricia Moorten, who created it more than 50 years ago with her husband, Chester "Cactus Slim" Moorten. A well-read botanist who consults with cactus lovers the world over, she frequently inspects her garden paths. To Patricia Moorten, and to visitors who step off the commercial path, Moorten's Botanical Garden is a place that celebrates the diversity of desert life – there are 3,000 species of cactus here! – and is living proof that the desert is not a barren wasteland.

About 3.5 miles (5.6 km) southwest of Palm Springs, the **Palm Springs Aerial Tramway** rises 5,873 feet (1,790 m) from a desert canyon to the edge of the cool, forested **Mount San Jacinto State Wilderness Area.** The Swiss-made gondola carries visitors over one of the most abrupt mountain faces in the world, over cliffs only a bighorn sheep can scale, over several life zones from palms to pines. In just minutes tram riders can witness changes in flora and fauna equivalent to those viewed on a motor trip from the Sahara Desert to the Arctic Circle.

The hills and canyons bordering Palm Springs have the greatest concentration of palm trees in North America, and **Palm Canyon,** 4 miles (6.4 km) south of the city in the **Agua Caliente Indian Reservation,** has more trees than any other desert oasis. A meandering stream and lush undergrowth complement more than 3,000 palms, creating a jungle-like atmosphere in some places. Tree lovers enjoy the California fan palms, some of them estimated to be 2,000 years old.

Andreas and Murray canyons are two tributaries of 15-mile (24 km) Palm Canyon. Both have hundreds of palms, crystalline streams, and dramatic rock walls. Adding to the lush scene are alders, willows, cottonwoods and sycamores.

The Living Desert, near the town of Palm Desert, is a combination zoo, botanical gardens, and hiking area. Gardens represent major deserts throughout the world, with emphasis on the American Southwest. Wildlife watchers can observe coyotes in their burrows and bighorn sheep atop a mountain peak. It has a walk-through aviary and a pond inhabited by the rare desert pupfish.

Back in Palm Springs, the **Palm Springs Desert Museum** is a thoroughly modern building that hides behind a somewhat old-fashioned stone façade. It is a perfect place to visit at high noon, when the desert sun slows down outdoor pursuits. Natural science exhibits recreate the unique ecology of Palm Springs and the surrounding Colorado Desert. Other displays portray the original inhabitants

143

of the area, people who managed to live in what seems to be a harsh and unforgiving land. The museum also has an impressive collection of modern and contemporary art.

Joshua Tree National Monument

Located just east of Palm Springs, 467,000-acre (189,000-hectare) **Joshua Tree National Monument** is a natural desert oasis that leaves glitz and glitter far behind. Well known for its incredible granite boulders that attract rock climbers, and for its forests of Joshua trees, the reserve lures visitors as a year-round destination for many outdoor activities, including hiking and camping.

The Joshua tree is said to have been named by early Mormon settlers traveling west. The tree's upraised limbs and bearded appearance reminded them of the prophet Joshua leading them to the

Above: A Joshua tree looks like the prophet and raises its hands like the prophet.

promised land. Despite its harsh appearance, the tree, which is pollinated by the Tegeticula moth, belongs to the lily family. One of the many fascinations of the national monument is the **Wonderland of Rocks**, 12 square miles (31 sq km) of massive jumbled granite. This curious maze of stone hides groves of Joshua trees, trackless washes, and several small pools of water.

California's largest state park with 763 square miles (1,975 sq km), **Anza-Borrego Desert State Park**, is named for the Mexican explorer de Anza and a bighorn sheep. De Anza traveled through the region in 1774, and the sheep still graze some parts of the park. This diverse desert park boasts more than 20 palm groves and year-round creeks, great stands of cholla and elephant trees, slot canyons and badland formations. Numerous self-guided nature trails and automobile tours allow visitors to set their own pace. A natural history association and foundation sponsors regularly scheduled ranger and naturalist-led activities.

(All local phone numbers have 619 area code)

COACHELLA VALLEY
Accommodation
LUXURY: **Hilton,** 400 E. Tahquitz Way, Palm Springs 92260 (Tel. 320-6868, 800-522-6900); **La Mancha Private Villas,** 444 Avenida Caballeros, Palm Springs 92262 (Tel. 323-1773, 800-854-1298); **Marriott's Rancho Las Palmas Resort,** 41000 Bob Hope Dr., Rancho Mirage 92270 (Tel. 568-2727, 800-228-9290); **Oasis Water Resort Villa**, 2345 Cherokee Way, Palm Springs 92264 (Tel. 328-1499, 800-543-5160); **Ritz Carlton**, 69-900 Frank Sinatra Dr., Rancho Mirage 92270 (Tel. 321-8282, 800-241-3333). *MODERATE:* **Cathedral Canyon Resort,** 34567 Cathedral Canyon Dr., Cathedral City 92264 (Tel. 32-9000, 800-824-8224); **Hyatt Grand Champions Resort,** 44-600 Indian Wells Lane, Indian Wells 92210 (Tel. 341-1000, 233-1234); **Shadow Mountain Resort**, 45-750 San Luis Rey, Palm Desert 92260 (Tel. 346-6123, 800-472-3713). *BUDGET:* **Best Western Ponce de Leon Spa Hotel,** 11000 Palm Dr., Desert Hot Springs 92240 (Tel. 329-6484, 800-528-1234); **The Dunes,** 390 S. Indian Ave., Palm Springs 92262 (Tel. 325-1172); **Indian Palms Resort**, 48-630 Monroe St., Indio 92201 (Tel. 347-0688).
Restaurants
AMERICAN: **Cunard's Sandbar,** 78120 Calle Tampico, La Quinta; **Cafe St. James,** 254 N. Palm Canyon Dr., Palm Springs. *CONTINENTAL:* **Wally's Desert Turtle,** 71775 Hwy. 111, Rancho Mirage. *FRENCH:* **Cunard's,** 78045 Calle Cadiz, La Quinta. *ITALIAN:* **Banducci's,** 1260 S. Palm Canyon Dr., Palm Springs. *JAPANESE:* **Otani,** 1000 Tahquitz Way, Palm Springs. *MEXICAN:* **Las Casuelas Terraza,** 222 S. Palm Canyon Dr., Palm Springs. *SEAFOOD:* **Rusty Pelican,** 72191 Hwy. 111, Palm Desert.
Attractions
Agua Caliente Indian Canyons, South Palm Canyon Dr., Palm Springs (Tel. 325-5673), 8:30am-4:30pm Oct-May; **Cabot's Old Indian Pueblo Museum,** 67-616 E. Desert View, Desert Hot Springs (Tel. 329-7610), 9:30am-4:30pm Wed-Mon; **Joshua Tree National Monument,** 74485 National Monument Dr., Twentynine Palms 92277 (Tel. 367-7511); **Living Desert,** 47-900 Portola Ave., Palm Desert 92260 (Tel. 346-5694), 9am-5pm Sept-mid June; **Moorten's Botanical Garden,** 1701 S. Palm Canyon Dr., Palm Springs (Tel. 327-6555), 9am-5pm daily; **Oasis Water Resort,** 1500 Gene Autry Trail, Palm Springs (Tel. 325-7873); **Palm Springs Aerial Tramway,** 1 Tramway Rd., Palm Springs

(Tel. 325-1391), from 10am Mon-Fri, 8am Sat-Sun; **Palm Springs Desert Museum,** 101 Museum Dr., Palm Springs (Tel. 325-7186), 10am-4pm Tue-Fri, 10am-5pm Sat-Sun, closed in summer; **Ruddy's General Store Museum,** 221 S. Palm Canyon Dr., Palm Springs (Tel. 327-2156), 10am-4pm Thu-Sun Oct-June, 12-6pm Sat-Sun July-Sept.
Tourist Information
Palm Springs Desert Resorts Convention and Visitors Bureau, 255 N. El Cielo Rd., Suite 315, Palm Springs 92262 (Tel. 327-8411, 800-333-7232); **California Deserts Tourism Association,** 37-115 Palm View Dr. (P.O. Box 364), Rancho Mirage 92270 (Tel. 256-8617).

IMPERIAL VALLEY REGION
Accommodation
MODERATE: **La Casa del Zorro Resort,** 3845 Yaqui Pass, Borrego Springs 92004 (Tel. 800-824-1884). *BUDGET:* **Barbara Worth Country Club,** 2050 Country Club Dr., Holtville 92250 (Tel. 356-2806); **Vacation Inn TraveLodge,** 2000 Cottonwood Circle, El Centro 92243 (Tel. 352-9523, 800-255-2050).
Attractions
Anza-Borrego Desert State Park, Borrego Springs (Tel. 767-4684); **Imperial Sand Dunes,** near Glamis (Tel. 352-5842); **Imperial Wildlife Area,** 5 miles north of Niland on Hwy. 111 (Tel. 348-0577); **Salton Sea,** between state highways 86 and 111 south of Palm Springs (Tel. 393-3052), includes state recreation area and national wildlife refuge.
Tourist Information
Borrego Springs Chamber of Commerce, 622 Palm Canyon Dr., Borrego Springs 92004 (Tel. 767-5555); **El Centro Chamber of Commerce,** 1100 Main St., El Centro 92244 (Tel. 352-3681).

COLORADO RIVER AREA
Accommodation
BUDGET: **Best Western Tropics Motor Hotel,** 9274 E. Hobson Way, Blythe 92225 (Tel. 922-5101, 800-528-1234); **Rodeway Inn,** 401 E. Hobson Way, Blythe 92225 (Tel. 922-2184, 800-228-2000).
Attractions
Cibola National Wildlife Refuge, 28 miles south of Blythe on the Colorado River. **Picacho State Recreation Area,** 25 miles north of Winterhaven on the Colorado River.
Tourist Information
Blythe Chamber of Commerce, 201 S. Broadway, Blythe 92225 (Tel. 922-8166, 800-443-5513).

DEATH VALLEY
AND THE HIGH DESERT

There is something about the desert, and especially this desert that at first glance seems the antithesis of all that park-goers find desirable. To their needs – shade, water, and easy-to-follow self-guided nature trails – Death Valley answers with a resounding "No".

And the word "park" suggests a landscape under man's control. In this great land of extremes, nothing could be further from the truth. A bighorn sheep standing watch atop painted cliffs, sun light and shadow playing on the salt-and-soda floor, a blue-gray cascade of gravel pouring down a gorge to a land below the level of the sea: This territory is as ungovernable as its flaming sunsets.

Officially designated Death Valley National Monument, it is slated to become a national park if environmentally concerned legislators have their way. Park status would give a little more ecological protection. In Death Valley, the forces of the earth are exposed to view with dramatic clarity. In fact, geologists tell us it is not even a valley – it is a "graben". Valleys are carved by rivers; here, a block of the earth's crust dropped along fault lines, in relation to its mountain walls. The sink became a lake, and when the water evaporated, it left behind borax and, above all, fantastic scenery.

At **Racetrack Playa,** a dry lake bed, visitors puzzle over rocks that weigh as much as 5,000 pounds (2,270 kg), yet move mysteriously across the mud floor, leaving trails as a record of their movement. Research suggests that a combination of powerful winds and rain may skid the rocks over the slick clay.

Badwater, the lowest point in the Western Hemisphere at 282 feet (86 m) below sea level, is also one of the hottest

Left: One of the great sights in Death Valley: the Ubahebe Crater.

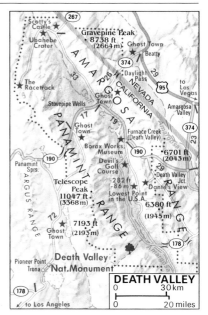

DEATH VALLEY

0	30km
0	20 miles

places in the world. It is not uncommon for air temperature readings of over 120 °F (49 °C) to be recorded in the summer months, and ground temperatures are usually 50 per cent higher. You really *can* fry an egg on the ground here. Temperatures from November to March are mild, however, with highs averaging in the 60s and 70s Fahrenheit (15-25 °C) and lows in the 40s (7-10 °C). Very little rain falls in the valley, but melting snow cascading from higher elevations can cause flash-flooding conditions in spring.

Looking west from Badwater, the eye is drawn to what appears to be a shallow stream of water flowing across the floor of the valley. But this flow is a mirage, caused by the strange terrain and deceptive colorings. As light plays upon the valley floor, the mind spins as though caught in a color wheel, from the gray and gold of sunrise, to the lavender and purple of sunset, to the star-flecked ebony of night.

"Spacing out on the landscape: that's what causes accidents," relates Highway

147

Patrolman David Flegel. "Motorists get to stargazing, moongazing, or just plain gazing at the mirages, and run themselves off the road. Most accidents here involve only one vehicle." Flegel has the largest police patrol area in California. He drives 250 to 400 miles (400-650 km) a day; even so, he cannot cover all of Death Valley in one day. He is the only law in this territory for 100 miles in any direction.

Sometimes Flegel stops his patrol car and gazes out at the far horizon. "**Mushroom Rock, Zabriskie Point** – I never get tired of the scenery. And Dante's View: Wow!"

From the crest of the Black Mountains at **Dante's View** unfolds a panorama never to be forgotten. A vertical mile down lies the lowest spot on the continent. Opposite the overlooks, across the valley, rises **Telescope Peak** and the snow-clad summits of the **Panamints.** Farther still, on the western horizon,

Above: Joshua trees can survive the climate. Right: Zabriskie Point in Death Valley.

loom the granite ramparts of the Sierra Nevada. North and south from Dante's View rise the **Funeral Mountains.** And from here, too, you see the glimmer of that alkaline pool known as Badwater ... or is that just a mirage, too?

Americans looking for gold in California's mountains in 1849 were forced to cross the burning sands to avoid severe snowstorms in the nearby Sierra Nevada. Many a man and beast perished along the way, and the land became known as Death Valley. Many of Death Valley's topographical features are associated with hellish images – Funeral Mountains, Furnace Creek, Dante's View, **Coffin Peak, Devil's Golf Course** – but the national monument is a place of serenity.

A multitude of living things have miraculously adapted to living in this land of little water, extreme heat, and high winds. Two dozen Death Valley plant species grow nowhere else on earth.

In spring, even this most forbidding of deserts breaks into bloom. The deep-blue pea-shaped flowers of the indigo bush brighten **Daylight Pass.** Lupine, paintbrush, and Panamint daisies grow on the lower slopes of the Panamint Mountains, while Mojave wild rose and Mariposa lily dot the higher slopes.

Two hundred species of birds are found in Death Valley. The brown whiplike stems of the creosote bush help shelter the movements of the kangaroo rat, desert tortoise, and antelope ground squirrel. Night covers the movements of the bobcat, fox, and coyote. Small bands of bighorn sheep roam remote slopes and peaks. Three species of desert pupfish, survivors from the Ice Age, are found in the valley's saline creeks and pools.

The community of **Furnace Creek** serves as headquarters for the national monument. There are two hotels – the four-star Furnace Creek Inn and the older Furnace Creek Ranch – as well as three campgrounds with some 1,300 spaces for tents or vehicles. The interesting **Borax**

Museum at Furnace Creek displays large mining machinery and historical exhibits; get directions here to the **Harmony Borax Works,** where the ruins of a late nineteenth-century refinery can be seen. The only other community within the park is **Stovepipe Wells,** named for a waterhole that meant life for early travelers. Stove Pipe Wells Village and a 200-unit campground are located here, along with a ranger station.

One of Death Valley's more astounding sights is **Scotty's Castle,** at the park's northern edge. This Spanish-Moorish mansion was begun in 1924 at the behest of Chicago millionaire Albert Johnson, and named for (and by) his prospecting friend Walter Scott. The $2.5-million house, though never completed, is open to public tours.

Numerous ghost towns are located throughout the monument, reminders of mining days of yore. Among them are **Ballarat,** active from 1890 to 1915 in the Panamint Valley; **Chloride City,** which flourished in the 1870s and again from 1905 to 1916; **Greenwater,** which boasted a bank, a post office, two newspapers, and 1,000 residents in 1905 to 1908; and **Skidoo,** where 700 people lived between 1906 and 1917.

Death Valley celebrates life. Despite the outward harshness of this land, those who get to know the valley see it in a different light. As naturalist Joseph Wood Krutch put it: "Hardship looks attractive, scarcity becomes desirable, starkness takes on an unexpected beauty."

Antelope Valley

The California poppy blooms on many a grassy slope in California, but only in the Antelope Valley does the showy flower blanket whole hillsides in such brilliant orange sheets. Surely the finest concentration of California's state flower is preserved at the **California State Poppy Reserve** in the Mojave Desert west of Lancaster. The poppy is the star of the flower show, which includes a supporting cast of fiddlenecks, cream-

cups, tidytips and goldfields. March to May is the best time to saunter through this display of desert wildflowers.

The poppy has always been recognized as something special. Early Californios called it *dormidera,* "the drowsy one", because its petals curl up at night. They fashioned a hair tonic and restorer by frying the blossoms in olive oil and adding perfume. Seven miles of gentle trails crisscross the poppy reserve, and there are impressive views of the Mojave Desert and the snow-covered mountains.

East Mojave Desert

Just a few hours' drive from Los Angeles is a virtually undiscovered gem of the desert, sometimes referred to as "The Lonesome Triangle". These 1.5 million acres (607,000 hectares) within that triangle, bounded by Interstate 15 on the north and Interstate 40 to the south, Bar-

Above: "Hardship looks attractive" ,the Salt Flats in Death Valley 200 ft. below sea level.

stow on the west and Needles on the east, are the **East Mojave National Scenic Area.** It is a land of great diversity – of grand mesas and mountain ranges, sand dunes and extinct volcanoes. It is a land that is easy to like, hard to know.

The view from the busy highway on the way to Las Vegas offers little hint of the unique desert environment beyond. But desert explorers are richly rewarded for their efforts. The East Mojave is a mecca for bird watchers and mountain bikers, photographers and rock collectors, amateur astronomers and campers who like the solitude of this unique environment.

This desert land, ranging in elevation from 900 to nearly 8,000 feet (275 m to 2,400 m), is a place of diverse landforms: cinder cones, dry lake beds, mountain ranges, and tabletop mesas. The magnificent 700-foot (213-m) **Kelso Dunes** can be found here, along with the world's largest Joshua tree forest.

An introductory tour of the East Mojave should take in its most popular sights – **Kelso Depot,** a Spanish-style railway station built in 1924 that is the largest building in the East Mojave; **Kelso Dunes,** a 45-square-mile (121-sq-km) formation of marvelously sculpted sand dunes; and **Hole-in-the-Wall,** a red volcanic rock formation where outlaws once hid from sheriffs and their posses. Also interesting are the **Mitchell Caverns,** in the **Providence Mountains State Recreation Area.** Tours of these limestone caverns are offered daily by rangers. West, near Baker, is **Soda Springs,** a former health resort that now houses California State University's Desert Studies Center.

In recent years, the East Mojave has frequently been in the news during controversies over mining and off-road vehicle use. Many conservationists feel that the land is so magnificent and so ecologically significant that Mojave National Park should be designated.

DEATH VALLEY

(Telephone area codes 619)

Accommodation

LUXURY: **Furnace Creek Inn,** Highway 190 (P.O. Box 1), Death Valley 92328 (Tel. 786-2345, 800-528-6367). *MODERATE:* **Furnace Creek Ranch,** Highway 190 (P.O. Box 1), Death Valley 92328 (Tel. 786-2345, 800-528-6367). *BUDGET:* **Stove Pipe Wells Village,** Highway 190, Death Valley 92328 (Tel. 786-2387).

Attractions

Amargosa Opera House, Hwys 127 and 190, Death Valley Junction, performances 8:15pm Fri, Sat and Mon, Oct-Apr.; **Badwater,** 15 miles south of Furnace Creek on Badwater Rd.; **Ballarat Ghost Town,** 23 miles northeast of Trona via Trona-Wildrose Rd.; **Borax Museum,** Furnace Creek, 8am-4pm daily, Nov-Apr.; **Charcoal Kilns,** Mahogany Flat Road, 36 miles south of Stovepipe Wells; **Chloride City Ghost Town,** 25 miles northeast of Stovepipe Wells via Daylight Pass Rd.; **Dante's View,** 21 miles southeast of Furnace Creek via Hwy 190 and Furnace Creek Rd.; **Devil's Golf Course,** 11 miles south of Furnace Creek via Badwater Rd.; **Emigrant Canyon,** 18 miles south of Stovepipe Wells via Wildrose Rd.; **Keane Wonder Mine Ruins,** 20 miles north of Furnace Creek via Daylight Pass Cutoff; **Racetrack Valley,** 33 miles south of Scotty's Castle via Racetrack Valley Rd.; **Rhyolite Ghost Town,** 31 miles northeast of Stovepipe Wells via Hwy 374, in Nevada; **Saratoga Springs,** 77 miles southeast of Furnace Creek via Badwater Rd.; **Scotty's Castle,** 51 miles north of Furnace Creek via North Hwy, 9am-5pm daily; **Skidoo Ghost Town,** 26 miles south of Stovepipe Wells via Wildrose and Skidoo roads; **Tecopa Hot Springs Park,** Tecopa; **Ubahebe Crater,** 5 mi west of Scotty's Castle via Racetrack Valley Rd.

Tourist Information

Death Valley National Monument Visitor Center Museum, Highway 190, Furnace Creek (Tel. 786-2331), 8am-5pm daily; **Grapevine Ranger Station,** Scotty's Castle (Tel. 786-2313); **Stovepipe Wells Ranger Station** (Tel. 786-2342); **Death Valley Chamber of Commerce,** 2 Post Office Row, Tecopa, CA 92389 (Tel. 852-4524).

CHINA LAKE REGION

(Telephone area codes 619)

Accommodation

MODERATE: **Heritage Inn,** 1050 N. Norma St. (P.O. Box 640), Ridgecrest 93555 (Tel. 446-6543). *BUDGET:* **Eldorado Motel,** 410 S. China Lake Blvd., Ridgecrest 93555 (Tel. 375-1354).

Attractions

Desert Tortoise Natural Area, Fremont Valley; P.O. Box 453, Ridgecrest 93555. **Maturango Museum,** Ridgecrest (Tel. 375-6900), 10am-5pm Tue-Sun. **Pinnacles,** 20 miles east of Ridgecrest on Trona Rd. **Randsburg Ghost Town,** 29 miles south of Ridgecrest on U.S. Hwy. 395.

Tourist Information

Ridgecrest Chamber of Commerce, P.O. Box 771, Ridgecrest (Tel. 375-8331).

ANTELOPE VALLEY

(Telephone area codes 805)

Accommodation

MODERATE: **Desert Inn Motor Hotel,** 44219 N. Sierra Hwy., Lancaster 93534 (Tel. 942-8401). *BUDGET:* **Antelope Valley Inn,** 44055 N. Sierra Hwy., Lancaster 93534 (Tel. 948-4651, 800-528-1234).

Attractions

Antelope Valley California Poppy Reserve, 15 miles west of Lancaster on Avenue 1 (Tel. 724-1180); **Antelope Valley Indian Museum,** Lancaster (Tel. 942-0622), open second weekend of month, Oct-June; **Red Rock Canyon State Park,** 25 miles northeast of Mojave on Hwy 14 (Tel. 942-0662).

Tourist Information

Lancaster Chamber of Commerce, 44335 Lowtree St., Lancaster 93534 (Tel. 948-4518).

EAST MOJAVE REGION

(Telephone area code 619)

Accommodation

BUDGET: **Barstow Station Inn,** 1511 E. Main St., Barstow 92311 (Tel. 256-5673, 800-843-1991); **Economy Inn**, 1590 Coolwater Lane, Barstow 92311 (Tel. 256-1737, 800-826-0778).

Attractions

Calico Early Man Archaeological Site, 15 miles south of Barstow via I-15 (Tel. 256-3591), tours Wed-Sun; **Calico Ghost Town,** 10 miles northeast of Barstow via I-15 (Tel. 254-2122); **Mitchell Caverns Natural Preserve,** Providence Mountains State Recreation Area, 17 miles north of I-40 at Essex Road (Tel. 389-2281), tours daily mid Sept-mid June; **Mojave River Valley Museum,** 270 E. Virginia Way, Barstow (Tel. 256-5452), 11am-4pm daily.

Tourist Information

California Desert Information Center, 831 Barstow Rd., Barstow 92311 (Tel. 256-8617); **East Mojave National Scenic Area,** Bureau of Land Management, P.O. Box 888, Needles 92363 (Tel. 326-3896).

THE MOUNTAINS

HIGH SIERRA
LAKE TAHOE
GOLD COUNTRY

HIGH SIERRA

Day begins in the High Sierra an hour before the sun sends its rays to paint the peaks a golden pink. In those early-morning hours, the sky changes from black to purple. Outlines of summits emerge. Their lavender slopes, flecked with snow, are mirrored in dark mountain lakes and streams. It is this time of day that demonstrates why conservationist John Muir felt the Sierra Nevada – literally, the "snowy mountain range" – should have been called "The Range of Light."

Sierran geological history began some 150 million years ago when the earth's oceanic plate began undercutting the continental plate, forming California. About 10 million years ago, along its 390-mile (625-km) length, the Sierra Nevada began to be pushed upward by titanic forces. Towers of granite rock rose along a fault on the eastern border of California; their western flank sloped gently to the San Joaquin Valley. Then, two million years ago, a series of glaciers advanced like great plows, scraping away the older metamorphic rock, revealing granite domes and carving the range into

Preceding pages: Shining gold at sunrise in the High Sierra. A waterfall in the Yosemite National Park.

dramatic sawtooth peaks. The retreating glaciers left behind basins and U-shaped valleys where idyllic alpine meadows formed. California is still rising from the sea, and the Sierra Nevada evidences this. This longest and highest of mountain ranges in the continental U.S. is one of the fastest growing ranges on earth, rising at a rate of two inches (5 cm) per year.

Crossing the Mountains

The Sierra Nevada is so formidable an obstacle that few roads have been constructed across it. Between Route 88 (Carson Pass), just south of Lake Tahoe, and Route 178 (Walker Pass), 225 miles (360 km) to the south, there are only three mountain passes, and not one of them remains open through the winter. The 8,730-foot (2,660-m) **Ebbetts Pass** highway, Route 4, passes through **Murphys,** once a bustling mining camp. Nearby is **Calaveras Big Trees State Park,** one of the finest and few remaining groves of giant sequoias in the High Sierra. The 9,624-foot (2,933-m) **Sonora Pass,** Route 108, cuts from Sonora in the Gold Country to Bridgeport on U.S. 395. Just south of Bridgeport, a dirt road leads to **Bodie,** in the 1870s a rowdy gold-mining town. Today, Bodie is a state historic park and ghost town.

The highest vehicle pass in California is 9,945-foot (3,031-m) **Tioga Pass,** Route 120, which transits Yosemite National Park to Lee Vining on U.S. 395. Scenic jewels along the route include **Tuolumne Meadows,** the largest sub-alpine meadow in the Sierra Nevada; many alpine peaks and lakes surrounding the meadow; **Tenaya Lake;** and the **Tuolumne Grove** of giant old sequoias at Crane Flat.

National Parks

The physical and spiritual heart of the Sierra Nevada is **Yosemite National Park**. This 1,165-square-mile (3,133-sq-km) nature preserve contains spectacular mountain scenery, impressive waterfalls, and colorful plant and animal life.

You may marvel at Ansel Adams' classic photographs of **Yosemite Valley** and read John Muir's poetic descriptions of it. But until you stand at **Discovery View** at the east end of the Wawona Tunnel on Route 41, neither pictures nor words can convey the overwhelming majesty of the Yosemite Valley.

El Capitan's towering rock face rises 3,500 feet (1,060 m), the height of nearly three Empire State Buildings. **Bridalveil Fall** cascades to the right, an ever-flowing lacy ribbon of white. Granite parapets rise along the valley rim. **Half Dome** broods in the background, its sheer granite face beckoning toward discovery of the valley beyond.

Yosemite Valley and the **Mariposa Grove** of giant sequoias were set aside by President Abraham Lincoln in 1864, the first-recorded action by a government to preserve land in its natural state. In 1890, Yosemite became a national park. Today, more than three million people visit the park each year. The park's popularity, limited accommodation, and proximity to large population centers, cause its hotels and campgrounds to be reserved far in advance. Hotels, particularly the four-star

Ahwahnee Hotel, are booked a year ahead. Reservations are also needed in campgrounds; they can be made up to eight weeks in advance.

Yosemite Falls, more than 15 Niagara Falls in height, has the longest drop of any waterfall in North America. Near its base is **Yosemite Village,** containing the park visitor center, museum, art galleries, stores, and restaurants. Exhibits at the visitor center describe geology, botany, and wildlife. Behind the center is a recreation of a **Miwok Indian Village.** The Indians called themselves Uz-u-mati, or "grizzly bear"; which was misinterpreted as "Yosemite" by the first visitors.

Many and varied hiking trails begin from Yosemite Valley. A favorite is the moderate-to-strenuous **Mist Trail,** which leads to **Vernal Falls** and **Nevada Falls.** Rock climbers can be seen scaling El Capitan from spring through fall: Climbing lessons are available for the intrepid. Popular winter activities include downhill skiing, ice skating, snowshoeing and ski touring.

The park's best view is from **Glacier Point,** 17 miles (27 km) from **Chinquapin** on Route 41. From this perch on the rim of Yosemite Valley, you look down 3,214 feet (980 m) to the valley floor, with an eagle's-eye view of Yosemite Falls, Half Dome, and the High Sierra. Near the south entrance to Yosemite are **Wawona**, with its lovely nineteenth-century hotel, and the **Pioneer History Center.** Six miles further is the Mariposa Grove of giant sequoias.

In the late 1800s, trees which had grown for 3,000 years were being cut to provide fenceposts and grape stakes for San Joaquin Valley farmers. A scant few conservationists fought this merciless wasting of the big trees. Important groves were protected, however, when Sequoia and Grant Grove national parks were established in 1890. Today, the **General Grant Grove** is part of Kings Canyon National Park, south of Yosemite and 55

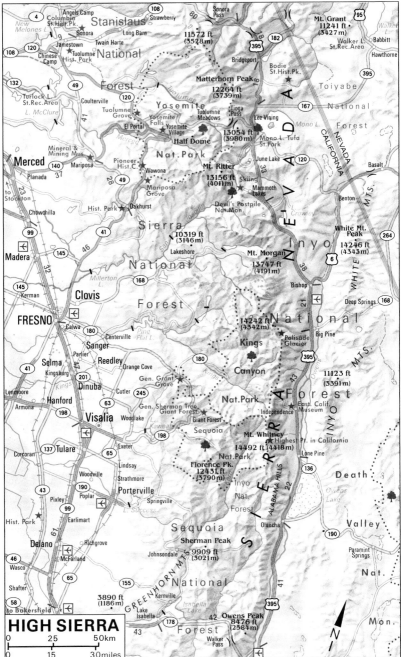

HIGH SIERRA

0   25   50km

0   15   30miles

miles (88 km) east of Fresno on Route 180. It contains the nation's Christmas tree, a remarkably large sequoia.

The road from here descends into **Kings Canyon**'s seemingly endless chasm, winding back and forth until the canyon walls, stained yellow-green with lichen, loom thousands of feet above. Even then, the canyon continues to drop away to water-washed depths. Some call this "the Grander Canyon", and the superlative is deserved. The Kings River cascades through canyons between 4,000 and 8,000 feet (1,200 to 2,400 m) deep, at a rate faster than the Colorado River passes through the Grand Canyon.

The General's Highway, an alternative route from Grant Grove, runs south 33 miles (53 km) to Sequoia National Park. Gem of the park is the **General Sherman Tree,** said to be the world's largest living thing. The base of the tree is so large it could block a three-lane freeway. It continues to grow at an astounding rate, adding 40 cubic feet (1.13 cu m) of wood to its girth each year.

Sequoia has many other incredible sights. There is the **auto log,** a single fallen tree trunk which cars can drive upon; the **tunnel log,** a fallen tree through which cars pass; a granite dome to climb; a crystal cave to explore; sequoia-lined meadows, hiking trails, Indian pictographs, and scores of beautiful groves. Sequoia is also a popular destination of cross-country skiers.

The Eastern Sierra

On the eastern edge of the Sierra, U.S. 395 runs to California's northern border. A worthwhile place to begin exploration is the **Interagency Visitor Center** south of **Lone Pine.** Exhibits, books, and free information describe the many public lands in the **Owens Valley.**

Above right: The towering rock of El Capitan in winter.

Lone Pine is best known as the portal to **Mount Whitney,** the highest peak in the contiguous United States at 14,495 feet (4,418 m). A 10.7-mile (17.2-km) trail leads to the summit from **Whitney Portal,** 13 miles (21 km) from Lone Pine. The strenuous trail is open only from mid July to mid October.

On the way to Whitney Portal are the **Alabama Hills.** In 1861, a bloody war between Indians and settlers was fought here. Hollywood film makers later used the colorful contours as backdrops for movies like *How the West Was Won, Springfield Rifle,* and *Gunga Din.*

Lone Pine is the gateway not only to Mount Whitney, but also to one of the lowest points in American history – the Japanese relocation center of **Manzanar.** During World War II, 10,000 Japanese residents of the United States, many of them citizens, were taken from their homes to Manzanar. Today, little remains of the camp but a monument.

The town of **Big Pine** stands between two contradictory attractions in the state.

159

High in the mountains to the west is **Palisades Glacier,** the southernmost glacier in the United States. To the east, above 10,000 feet (3,000 m) on the arid slopes of the **White Mountains**, survive ancient bristlecone pines, the oldest known living things on earth. The tree called **Methuselah** is some 4,600 years old.

The cool, beautiful **Mammoth Lakes**, with their outstanding fishing, have long attracted vacationers. Today, they are known as the home of **Mammoth Mountain**, America's most-skied area with four million skiers annually. In summer, it mixes trendy events, such as mountain bike races, with laid-back pursuits like fishing, sightseeing by gondola, relaxing in steaming **Hot Creek,** or hiking. Mammoth is also the gateway to **Devil's Postpile National Monument,** a bizarre formation of basalt columns; and to the **Minarets Wilderness,** a dramatic range of peaks and spectacular backcountry.

Above: Not a Hollywood set, but the lunar landscape of Mono Lake.

Like Mammoth, **June Lake** is a ski town. In summer, the June Lake Loop offers travelers a scenic bypass from U.S. 395. It is a picture-perfect scene, with quaint June Lake Village sitting in forests of pine, cottonwood, and aspen.

In stark contrast, pastel-green sagebrush and stunted pinon pine surround desolate **Mono Lake,** one of the oldest bodies of water in North America. A significant migratory bird resting area, Mono Lake provides the nesting grounds for 90 per cent of California's gull population. Along the shores are starkly shaped calcium formations called tufa towers. The best of these is at the **South Tufa Reserve,** 4 miles (6.5 km) east of U.S. 395, south of Lee Vining.

Lee Vining is the eastern entrance to the Tioga Pass highway to Yosemite National Park. It is a good watering spot before starting the steep climb. From the first snowfall of winter until June, the pass is closed; town residents often redirect Yosemite-bound travelers around the High Sierra.

YOSEMITE NATIONAL PARK
(Telephone area code 209)
Accommodation
LUXURY: **The Ahwanee,** Yosemite Village; write Curry Co., address below. *MODERATE:* **Cedar Lodge,** P.O. Box C, El Portal 95318 (Tel. 379-2612, 800-321-5261); **Yosemite Lodge,** Fort Yosemite; write Curry Co., address below. *BUDGET:* **Wawona Lodge,** Mariposa Grove; write Curry Co., address below. *RESERVA-TIONS:* **Yosemite Park and Curry Co.,** 5410 E. Home Ave., Fresno 93727 (Tel. 252-4848).
Restaurants
AMERICAN: **Mountain Room,** Yosemite Lodge; **Yosemite Cafeteria,** Yosemite Lodge. **Four Seasons,** Yosemite Lodge; **The Loft,** Yosemite Village. *CONTINENTAL:* **The Ahwanee,** Yosemite Village (Tel. 372-1489).
Attractions
Badger Pass Ski Area, Glacier Point Road, Yosemite Park (Tel. 372-1330); **Glacier Point,** 30 miles from Valley via Glacier Point Rd.; **Mariposa Grove,** 36 miles from Valley via Wawona Rd. **Tuolumne Grove,** 17 miles from Valley on Big Oak Flat Rd.; **Tuolumne Meadows,** 56 miles from Valley via Tioga Pass Road; **Yosemite Mt. Sugar Pine Railroad,** 56001 Highway 41, Fish Camp (Tel. 683-7273), daily mid Apr-Oct; **Yosemite Museum and Indian Cultural Center,** Yosemite Village; **Yosemite Pioneer History Center,** Wawona.
Tourist Information
Yosemite National Park, National Park Service, Yosemite, CA 95389 (Tel. 372-0264); **Visitor Centers** at Yosemite Village and Tuolumne Meadows.

KINGS CANYON/SEQUOIA NATIONAL PARKS
(Telephone area code 209)
Accommodation
MODERATE: **Giant Forest Lodge,** Sequoia Park; write Guest Services address, below; **Montecito-Sequoia Lodge,** Generals Hwy., Kings Canyon Park; write 1485G Redwood Dr., Los Altos 94022 (Tel. 415-967-8612, 800-227-9900). *BUDGET:* **Grant Grove Lodge,** Kings Canyon Park; **Cedar Grove Lodge,** Kings Canyon Park; **Stony Creek Lodge,** Sequoia Park; write **Kings Canyon/Sequoia Guest Services Inc.,** P.O. Box 789, Three Rivers 93271 (Tel. 561-3314).
Restaurants
AMERICAN: **Giant Forest Lodge,** Sequoia Park; **Irv's River Wharf,** 42323 Sierra Dr., Three Rivers (Tel. 561-4000).

Attractions
Crystal Cave, Sequoia Park, 9 miles from Giant Forest, tours daily 10am-3pm in summer. **General Grant Grove,** Route 180, Kings Canyon Park; **Giant Forest,** Route 180, Sequoia Park; **Mineral King,** Route 198, Sequoia Park, 50 miles from Giant Forest; **Sierra Summit Ski Area,** Route 168 (P.O. Box 236), Lake Shore (Tel. 893-3316).
Tourist Information
Kings Canyon/Sequoia National Parks, National Park Service, Sequoia Park 93262 (Tel. 561-3314); **Grant Grove Visitor Center,** Route 180, Kings Canyon Park (Tel. 335-2315); **Lodgepole Visitor Center,** Route 180, Sequoia Park (Tel. 565-3341).

THE EASTERN SIERRA
(Telephone area code 619)
Accommodation
LUXURY: **Mammoth Ski and Racquet Club,** P.O. Box 1847, Mammoth Lakes 93546 (Tel. 934-6891, 800-367-6684). *MODERATE:* **Mammoth Mountain Inn,** P.O. Box 353, Mammoth Lakes 93546 (Tel. 934-2581, 800-228-4947). *BUDGET:* **Westerner Motel,** 150 E. Elm St., Bishop 93514 (Tel. 873-3564, 800-356-3221).
Attractions
Alabama Hills Recreation Area, office 126 S. Main St., Lone Pine (Tel. 876-4444); **Bodie State Historic Park,** 13 miles east of U.S. Hwy. 395 on Bodie Road, near Bridgeport (Tel. 647-6445), closed winter; **Devil's Postpile National Monument,** Mammoth Lakes (Tel. 934-2289); **Eastern California Museum,** 155 N. Grant St., Independence (Tel. 878-2411); **Inyo National Forest,** office 873 N. Main St., Bishop (Tel. 873-5841); Mount Whitney, Bristlecone Pine Forest Botanical Area; **June Mountain Ski Area,** P.O. Box 146, June Lake 93529 (Tel. 648-7733); **Laws Railroad Museum,** 5 miles northeast of Bishop off Highway 6 (Tel. 873-5950); **Mono Lake and Tufa State Reserve,** 5 miles southeast of Lee Vining off U.S. Hwy. 395 (Tel. 647-6331 or 647-6525); **Mammoth Mountain Ski Area,** P.O. Box 24, Mammoth Lakes 93546; **Paiute Shoshone Indian Cultural Center Museum,** 2300 W. Line St., Bishop (Tel. 873-4478).
Tourist Information
Eastern Sierra Interagency Visitor Center, U.S. Hwy. 395 and Route 190, Lone Pine; **Mammoth Lakes Resort Association,** P.O. Box 48, Mammoth Lakes 93546 (Tel. 934-2712, 800-367-6572); **Mono Lake Committee Visitor Center,** Hwy. 395 (P.O. Box 29), Lee Vining 93541 (Tel. 647-6386).

161

LAKE TAHOE

High in California's Sierra Nevada is a magic water, an island of ocean enclosed by towering peaks, an immense granite basin filled by a celestial storm. Half in California, half in Nevada, Lake Tahoe is one of the world's natural wonders, deep and pristine. Its 183 square miles (494 sq km) of water is 99 per cent pure, plunging to a depth of 1,660 feet (506 m).

Tahoe's magic lies in its moods as much as in its size. In summer, the wind over the surrounding peaks becomes calm, and the surface of that deep water goes smooth. On a spring morning, mist in the basin might blend Tahoe's glassy surface into mountains and sky, like the wash of a blue Monet painting. Winter gives the lake its most dramatic look: February storms drop over the high mountains and rip the surface of the lake into ocean waves. The wind and clouds

Above: Scandinavian architecture in California: Vikingsholm on Emerald Bay.

paint Lake Tahoe differently every day, every season.

A Brief History

Washoe and Paiute Indians were the earliest humans to inhabit the area, fighting for control of "Big Water's" summer fishing and hunting grounds. During the harsh winters, however, the Indians retreated to lower ground in the nearby Nevada deserts.

The first white men to set eyes on Tahoe were Captain John Fremont and his guide, Kit Carson. Near-starvation of his troops had forced Fremont into a winter crossing of the Sierra. Reaching the summit of a peak near modern Carson Pass on February 14, 1844, he saw "a beautiful view of a mountain lake ... so entirely surrounded by mountains that we could not discover an outlet."

Only two years later, settlers en route to the fertile Central Valley tried new routes across the Sierra. The most infamous attempt took place in 1846. The Donner party, delayed by a troublesome crossing of Nevada, arrived in the Sierra late in the fall. North of Tahoe, they became trapped by a tremendous snowstorm. Of the 82 travelers, 32 survived until spring by cannibalizing their dead.

Despite such gruesome stories, the westward flow of pioneers continued. With the 1848 discovery of gold in the Sierra foothills at Sutter's Mill, the flow became a flood, and the population of California grew 26-fold in only two years.

At first, the fortune seekers were ill-prepared for the harsh winter climate near Tahoe. In 1856, that changed with the discovery of one of the largest silver deposits in history – the Comstock Lode – just down the mountains from Tahoe at Nevada's Virginia City. The thousands of miners who raced to Nevada needed lumber and water, and Tahoe became the center of those industries. Settlements sprang

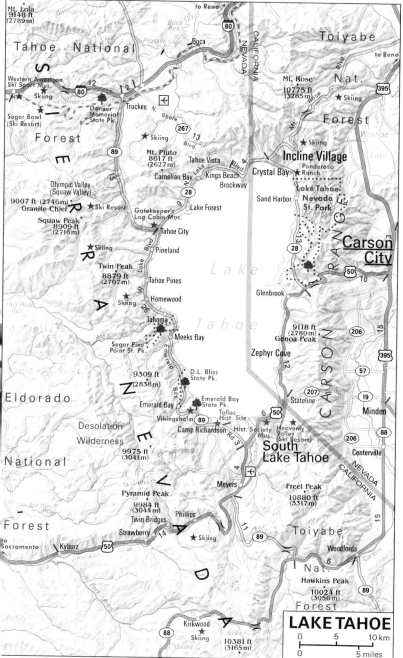

to Reno

80

Boca
Boca
Res.

Prosser Creek Res.

Prosser
Independence L.

Mt. Lola
9148 ft
(2789m)

Tahoe National

NEVADA
CALIFORNIA

Toiyabe

to Reno

Nat.

395

Western American
Ski Sport Mus.
★ Skiing

80

12

12

Donner L.

Donner
Memorial
State Pk.

N. Shore

Truckee

Mt. Rose
10775 ft
(3285m)
★ Skiing

Forest

Sugar Bowl
(Ski Resort)

Forest

267   13

★ Skiing

Mt. Rose Blvd.

Washoe

Skiing

89

★ Skiing

Mt. Pluto
8617 ft
(2627m)

Tahoe Vista

Carnelian Bay

Kings Beach
Brockway

Incline Village

Lake Tahoe Blvd.

Crystal Bay ★
Ponderosa
Ranch

Lake Tahoe
Nevada
St. Park

Lake

9007 ft (2746m)
Granite Chief

★ Ski Resort

Olympic Valley
(Squaw Valley)

Gatekeeper's
Log Cabin Mus.

28

Lake Forest

Sand Harbor

Squaw Peak
8909 ft
(2716m)

Tahoe City

S I E R R A

★ Skiing

Pineland

Lake Tahoe Blvd.

Lake

Carson
City

28

Twin Peak
8879 ft
(2707m)

Tahoe Pines

Tahoe

50

10

Homewood

Glenbrook

RANGE

★ Skiing

Hell Hole

Tahoma

Rte 26

Meeks Bay

9118 ft
(2780m)
Genoa Peak

206

15

Sugar Pine
Point St. Pk.

Emerald Bay

McKinney

Zephyr Cove

Carson

395

Coon L.

9309 ft
(2838m)

D.L. Bliss
State Pk.

57

Eldorado

Emerald Bay
State Pk.

Emerald Bay

Vikingsholm

89

Tallac
Hist. Site

207

Stateline

19

Minden

N E V A D A

Desolation
Wilderness

Camp Richardson

Rd 3

Hist. Society
Mus.

6

50

Heavenly
Valley
(Ski Resort)

206

88

9975 ft
(3041m)

Fallen
Leaf L.

South
Lake Tahoe

Centerville

National

4

Aloha L.

Meyers

NEVADA
CALIFORNIA

Stony Valley

Pyramid Peak
9984 ft
(3044m)

Freel Peak
10880 ft
(3317m)

15

Forest

Ice House Res.

Twin Bridges

Phillips

to
Sacramento

Kyburz

50

American River

Strawberry

★ Skiing

11

89

Toiyabe

Woodfords

6

Carson

Silver Fork

South Fork

Hawkins Peak
10024 ft
(3056m)

89

Nat.

Forest

Kirkwood

88

★ Skiing

10381 ft
(3165m)

Silver L.

Maples

LAKE TAHOE

0   5   10 km

0   5 miles

up around the lake, and large boats began to ply its surface. These small outposts were built solely to support the mines, but they soon developed into resorts catering to the new wealth. Thus began what would become Tahoe's primary industry: tourism.

With the help of 10,000 Chinese laborers, the first transcontinental railroad was completed in 1868, opening a new era for the Tahoe region. Travel from the rail line to Tahoe was conducted by horse-drawn stage coach, until a new line was built in 1900, connecting the town of Truckee with Tahoe City. From there, a growing fleet of steam boats brought passengers to the various resorts along the shore. Tahoe became the fashionable place for rich San Franciscans to have a "summer home". Many of these homes looked more like castles – as one can readily see today, by visiting the well-

Above: Lake Tahoe, the home away from home for many San Franciscans. Right: Lake Tahoe seen from Heavenly Valley.

preserved **Ehrman Mansion,** or **Vikingsholm** on Tahoe's west shore. When gambling came to Tahoe in the 1930s at the north shore's Brockway, a whole new type of visitor was attracted to the area. **Stateline**, Nevada, on the south shore, is now the main gaming center.

Recreational Playground

Winter sports had long been a part of the Tahoe scene. The first ski races in the United States were held on mountains near here in the 1860s. **Sugar Bowl** ski resort opened in 1939 and initiated a race contested by the best skiers of the time. But Tahoe's reputation for world-class winter sports truly began in 1960 with the opening of the Winter Olympic Games at **Squaw Valley,** 5 miles (8 km) from Tahoe City. Squaw's Olympics not only sparked the growth of skiing locally, but helped to boost the sport's popularity throughout the United States.

There are now 20 ski resorts surrounding Lake Tahoe, with 160 lifts – the

largest concentration of skiing in America. They include **Heavenly Valley,** on the south shore, whose international fame approaches that of Squaw. Cross-country skiing, snowmobiling, and sleigh rides are all popular at Tahoe from early November until late in May.

Tahoe lives up to its billing as a "year-round playground". Despite its fame for winter sports, the summer season is Tahoe's busiest. The ski season begins to fade after April; **Alpine Meadows** is the last resort to close, usually at the end of May.

By that time, the snow has long since left the lake shore, and the summertime pursuits of water skiing, sailing, fishing, hiking, climbing, mountain biking, and just-plain sunbathing are in full swing. The lake is extremely cold, however: It requires a wetsuit until late August! A few feet beneath the surface Tahoe's temperature never varies, its tremendous volume keeping it cool in summer and preventing it from freezing in winter. Summer is in full glory by June, and continues through September. Temperatures average around 75 °F (24 °C) with very little rain. By mid October, autumn turns the area's aspen trees to a brilliant yellow. Snow arrives soon after; the ski resorts usually open by mid November.

Like many recreation areas, Tahoe is largely populated by young outdoor enthusiasts. The expensive homes around the lake are the property of old money, but the spirit of the place is in the firm possession of their sons and daughters. Many work during the busy summer season, saving for their ski pass; then they work only part-time, or not at all, during the winter.

Tahoe's Towns

Not everyone is a member of the young leisure class, however. The sizable communities of South Lake Tahoe, Incline Village, King's Beach, Tahoe City, and Truckee support a significant number of middle-aged families and older retirees. The diversity among these moun-

and seafood restaurants, which continues today along the north shore.

On the opposite side of the lake is **South Lake Tahoe,** the real "city" of the region. Taxis cruise from the high-rise casinos of Harrah's, Harvey's, Caesar's, the High Sierra and others in adjoining **Stateline** down the lakeside strip to myriad hotels and restaurants. Most visitors seem more interested in the nightlife than in the day life of Tahoe's outdoors. Bill Cosby and Frank Sinatra are just a couple of the big-name performers who appear at the casinos throughout the year.

Around and near the Lake

There are many worthwhile places to explore within a few hours' drive of Lake Tahoe. **Truckee,** once a thriving railroad and lumber town, is only 13 miles (21 km) north of Tahoe City. Here also is **Donner Lake,** with a monument to those ill-fated pioneers. Further north are a number of tiny wilderness towns along Routes 49 and 70, relatively unchanged since the '49er miners left. South of Tahoe, the mountains become larger and more dramatic, with few settlements except "Old West" **Markleeville** along Route 4.

The one drive that should not be missed by any visitor is the 71-mile (114-km) circuit around Lake Tahoe. The wilderness land along the lake's east and west shores is particularly spectacular, especially the white beaches near **Sand Harbor** on the east and the precipitous cliffs dropped to the picturesque inlet of **Emerald Bay** on the west. This isolated beauty can also be watched from large vessels, departing from **Zephyr Cove**, Nevada, for cruises on the lake. Although development has caused some deterioration of the water quality, growth in the Tahoe basin is now strictly limited by a government agency. Tahoe is one inhabited area of earth that is destined to change very little in the future.

tain communities is one of Tahoe's major attractions.

Incline Village, in Nevada at the lake's north end, received its name from the steeply "inclined" flume that carried logs nearly 1,400 feet (425 m) down into the lake in the 1850s. Boise Cascade Corporation, a lumber company, developed the present town in 1968 with a small ski resort and a couple of golf courses.

Across the border in California is **King's Beach,** a community that houses workers from the three small casinos located on the Nevada border. King's Beach is the center of inexpensive housing, hotels, and tourist shops on the north shore.

Tahoe City, 5 miles (8 km) west along the lake shore, is the focal point of most of the shopping, nightlife, and sporting activity in north Tahoe. Europeans originally attracted to Tahoe by the Olympics began a tradition of fine German, French,

Above: Les jeux sont faits for the blackjack players at Harrah's Casino in Stateline.

LAKE TAHOE

(Telephone area code 916 unless otherwise noted.)

NORTH LAKE TAHOE
Accommodation

LUXURY: **Club Tahoe,** P.O. Box 4650, Incline Village, NV 89450 (Tel. 702-831-5750, 800-527-5154). *MODERATE:* **Squaw Valley Inn,** 1920 Squaw Valley Rd., Tahoe City 95730 (Tel. 583-1576, 800-323-7666); **Tahoe Sands Resort,** 6610 N. Lake Blvd., Tahoe Vista 95732 (Tel. 546-2592). *BUDGET:* **Cedar Glen Lodge,** 6589 N. Lake Blvd., Tahoe Vista 95732 (Tel. 456-4281); **Truckee Tahoe Inn,** 11331 Hwy. 267, Truckee 95730 (Tel. 800-528-1234). *CASINO HOTELS:* **Cal-Neva Lodge,** 5 Stateline Dr., Crystal Bay, NV 89402 (Tel. 702-832-4000); **Hyatt Lake Tahoe Resort,** Country Club Dr. and Lakeshore Blvd., Incline Village, NV 89450 (Tel. 702-831-1111, 800-228-9000).

Restaurants
AMERICAN: **Rosie's Cafe,** 571 N. Lake Blvd., Tahoe City. *CONTINENTAL:* **The Bohn House,** 8160 N. Lake Blvd., Kings Beach. *FRENCH:* **Le Petit Pier,** 7252 N. Lake Blvd., Tahoe Vista. *MEXICAN:* **Pepper's Taqueria,** 565 N. Lake Blvd., Tahoe City. *SEAFOOD:* **River Ranch,** Hwy. 89 at Alpine Meadows Rd., Truckee.

Attractions
Gatekeeper's Log Cabin Museum, 130 W. Lake Blvd., Tahoe City (Tel. 583-1762), 11am-5pm May 15-Oct 15, free; **North Tahoe Cruises,** Roundhouse Mall, Tahoe City (Tel. 583-0141), mid May-Oct; **Ponderosa Ranch,** Hwy. 28, Incline Village (Tel. 702-832-1606), 9:30am-5pm mid Apr-Oct; **Western American Ski Sport Museum,** Soda Springs (Tel. 426-3313), 11am-5pm Tue-Sun winter, 11am-5pm Wed-Sun summer.

Major Ski Areas
Alpine Meadows, 11 miles north of Tahoe City (Tel. 583-4232); **Northstar-at-Tahoe,** 6 miles north of Tahoe Vista (Tel. 562-1010); **Squaw Valley,** 11 miles north of Tahoe City (Tel. 583-6985); **Sugar Bowl,** Norden, 9 miles west of Truckee (Tel. 426-3651).

Tourist Information
Tahoe North Visitors and Convention Bureau, 950 N. Lake Blvd. (P.O. Box 5578), Tahoe City 95730 (Tel. 583-3494, 800-824-6348); **Incline Village/Crystal Bay Visitor & Convention Bureau,** 969 Tahoe Blvd., Incline Village, NV 89451 (Tel. 702-832-1606, 800-468-2463); **Truckee-Donner Visitors Center,** 10065 Donner Pass Road (P.O. Box 2757), Truckee 95734 (Tel. 587-2757, 800-548-8388).

SOUTH LAKE TAHOE
Accommodation

LUXURY: **Tahoe Seasons Resort,** Heavenly Valley (P.O. Box 5656), S. Lake Tahoe 95729 (Tel. 541-6010). *MODERATE:* **Sorensen's Resort,** Hope Valley 96120 (Tel. 694-2203); **Station House Inn,** 901 Park Ave., S. Lake Tahoe 95729 (Tel. 542-1101, 800-822-5953). *BUDGET:* **Tahoe Sands Inn,** 3600 Hwy. 50, S. Lake Tahoe 95705 (Tel. 544-3476, 800-237-8882); **Zephyr Cove Resort,** 760 Hwy. 50, Zephyr Cove, NV 89448 (Tel. 702-588-6644). *CASINO HOTELS:* **Caesars Tahoe,** P.O. Box 5800, Stateline, NV 89449 (Tel. 702-588-3515, 800-648-3353); **Harrah's Lake Tahoe Resort,** P.O. Box 8, Stateline, NV 89449 (Tel. 702-588-6611, 800-648-3773); **Harvey's Resort,** P.O. Box 128, Stateline, NV 89449 (Tel. 702-588-2411, 800-648-3361); **High Sierra,** P.O. Box C, Stateline, NV 89449 (Tel. 702-588-6211, 800-648-3322).

Restaurants
AMERICAN: **Heidi's,** 3485 Hwy. 50, S. Lake Tahoe (Tel. 544-8113), dinner cruise. *CALIFORNIA:* **The Beacon,** Hwy. 89 at Camp Richardson, S. Lake Tahoe (Tel. 541-0630). *CONTINENTAL:* **Christiania Inn,** 3819 Saddle Rd., S. Lake Tahoe (Tel. 544-7337). *MEXICAN:* **Carlos Murphy's,** 3678 Hwy. 50, S. Lake Tahoe (Tel. 542-1741). *SEAFOOD:* **Dory's Oar,** 1041 Fremont St., S. Lake Tahoe (Tel. 541-6603).

Attractions
Emerald Bay State Park, Hwy. 89, S. Lake Tahoe (Tel. 525-7277), includes Vikingsholm castle. **Grover Hot Springs State Park,** Hot Springs Rd., Markleeville (Tel. 694-2248); **Lake Tahoe Cruises,** S. Lake Tahoe (Tel. 541-3364, 800-238-2463); **Lake Tahoe Historical Society Museum,** S. Lake Tahoe (Tel. 544-5050), 10am-5pm Memorial Day-Labor Day; **Tallac Historical Site,** Hwy. 89 near Camp Richardson (Tel. 542-2787).

Major Ski Areas
Heavenly Valley, South Lake Tahoe (Tel. 541-1330); **Kirkwood,** 36 miles south of S. Lake Tahoe (Tel. 258-6000); **Sierra Ski Ranch,** Twin Bridges, 19 miles southwest of S. Lake Tahoe (Tel. 659-7453).

Tourist Information
Lake Tahoe Visitors Authority, 1156 Ski Run Blvd. (P.O. Box 16299), S. Lake Tahoe 95706 (Tel. 544-5050, 800-822-5922); **Lake Tahoe Visitor Center,** Hwy. 89 just north of S. Lake Tahoe (Tel. 573-2600 or 573-2674), June-Oct; **Alpine County Chamber of Commerce,** P.O. Box 265, Markleeville 96120 (Tel. 694-2475).

THE GOLD COUNTRY

Gold is a powerful word. Its power changed California. After the yellow metal had been found in January, 1848, 546 mining towns sprang up within a few months. Today, about 250 of the camps remain. Many look much as they did when the Mother Lode was blooming. State Route 49 connects the main towns as it winds through the Gold Country from Oakhurst, near Yosemite, north to Sierra City.

Oakhurst, at the southern end of "The Golden Chain" of Gold Country towns, began as a small camp in the 1850s. Little of the town's original character remains, though **Fresno Flats Historical Park** south of town recreates life of a century ago. Not far north is **Mariposa,** site of the **California State Mineral and Mining Museum** at the Mariposa County Fairgrounds. The museum contains a rich

Above: The ghost town of Bodie, a left-over from the gold rush of 1849.

collection of minerals, gems, mining equipment, a mine shaft, a working replica of a stamp mill, and rotating exhibits of gold and other impressive finds.

Merchants in supply towns like **Coulterville,** north of Mariposa, usually became richer than the miners. That was no wonder. A slice of bread could cost $1, or $2 if it was buttered; and a shovel would draw $50 from a miner's thin wages. Coulterville's Magnolia Saloon, at the Jeffery Hotel, remains much as it was in the 1850s. **Chinese Camp** was settled by Chinese miners banished by intolerant Americans. In 1856, it boasted 5,000 residents, most of them Chinese, all of them attracted by rich gold deposits. A Wells Fargo stage coach station and other original buildings remain.

When Hollywood went to film Gary Cooper's *High Noon,* it found the ideal Western setting in **Jamestown.** Two-storied balconied buildings and a park with a gazebo are part of the town's rustic charm. **Railtown 1897 State Historic Park,** a collection of railroad buildings, roundhouse and turntable, cars and steam locomotives from the old Sierra Railway, is often used by movie companies.

Early in the gold rush, **Sonora** was the wealthiest and rowdiest town in the southern Mother Lode. Numerous attractive Victorian homes and classic Gold Country architecture are seen along Main Street. Two miles north, **Columbia State Historic Park** is a living history center where life in the 1850s is reenacted every day. Columbia was once California's second-largest city with 5,000 residents, four banks, eight hotels, two fire companies, three churches, a school, three theaters, 53 stores, 40 saloons, and 159 gambling dens!

Angels Camp was one of the towns that authors Mark Twain and Bret Harte made famous. Twain's *Celebrated Jumping Frog of Calaveras County* helped launch his career and led to the annual **Jumping Frog Jubilee** every May at the Calaveras County Fairgrounds.

San Andreas gained a reputation not only as a rich mining town. It was the locale of racial confrontations between American miners and "foreigners". Tension turned into war at nearby Chili Gulch when American miners battled Chileans in 1849, and again at French Hill near **Mokelumne Hill,** when the Frenchmen raised the tricolor in celebration of a rich gold find.

Jackson became richer from its location near water, and as a supply center, than it did from mining. Still, the impressive Kennedy Mine overlooks the town. The National Hotel is one of several gold rush-era landmarks along Main Street.

Indian Grinding Rock State Park, between Pine Grove and Volcano, was a seasonal meeting place for Miwok Indians. Some 1,200 mortar holes are located in the surrounding rocks, used to grind flour from acorns. Lodges and an Indian Cultural Center are worth exploring.

Sutter Creek, 4 miles (6.5 km) north of Jackson, has one of the most pic-

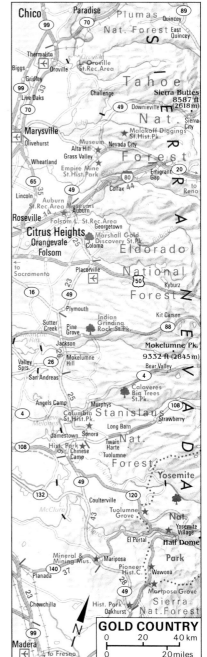

169

turesque main streets in the Gold Country. Wooden storefronts with overhanging balconies and lovely wood-frame homes are meticulously kept. Sutter Creek's many antique and craft shops and festivals attract visitors year-round.

Placerville was an important crossroads during gold rush days. Mail routes, wagon trains and the Pony Express passed through the town. Today, travelers on U.S. Highway 50 enjoy a refreshing stop at this community. Placerville's role in western history is remembered in several annual street festivals.

Almost all of **Coloma,** 9 miles (14 km) north of Placerville, is within the boundaries of **Marshall Gold Discovery State Park.** The park includes the discovery site, Sutter's Mill, a visitor center, excellent exhibits, and various other interpretive sites. Shaded picnic areas are located throughout the park and near the American River.

Above: Nevada City still keeps its 19th century face, the National Hotel.

Auburn, like Placerville, sits on a major route to Lake Tahoe and Reno (Interstate 80). The town has a split personality: a newer Upper Town and an older Lower Town. The latter features a striking red-and-white 1891 firehouse, said to be the most photographed firehouse in California, and the state's oldest continuously used post office, built in 1849. The county museum is one of the best in the Gold Country.

Empire Mine State Historic Park near Grass Valley is the site of the richest hard-rock mine ($960 million) in California history. The park contains offices and shops of the mine, along with **Bourn Mansion,** a baronial brick estate that was the summer home of the mine's owner.

Lola Montez was a famous courtesan of kings and celebrities. Her **Grass Valley** house now contains a fascinating museum. Nearby, the **North Star Powerhouse Mining Museum** displays a massive Pelton waterwheel, once the largest in the world. Built on hilly terrain like many other Gold County towns, **Nevada City**, 4 miles (6.5 km) beyond Grass Valley, has many iron-shuttered brick buildings dating to the 1850s. The National Hotel (1854) is the oldest continuously operated hotel in the state, with rooms furnished with period antiques.

Sixteen miles (26 km) further north is **Malakoff Diggings State Historic Park,** where the world's largest hydraulic mine once operated. From 1853 until the 1880s, gigantic nozzles (called monitors) redirected a river of water against hillsides, cutting open a huge pit.

Beyond **Nevada City,** another 43 miles (69 km), the rustic beauty of **Downieville** – set beside the North Yuba River in a lovely forested canyon – disguises the town's rough past.

Sierra City, northernmost town in the golden chain, combined gold-rush architecture with mountain scenery. Among the millions found was one nugget which weighed 141 pounds (64 kg)!

NORTHERN GOLD COUNTRY
(Telephone area codes 916)
Accommodation
MODERATE: **Placerville Inn,** 6850 Greenleaf Dr., Placerville 95667 (Tel. 622-9100, 800-528-1234). *BUDGET:* **Auburn Inn,** 1875 Auburn Ravine Rd., Auburn 95603 (Tel. 885-1800, 800-272-1444); **National,** 211 Broad St., Nevada City 95959 (Tel. 265-4551).
Restaurants
AMERICAN: **Dingus McGees,** 2121 S. Auburn St., Colfax. *CALIFORNIA:* **Selaya's,** 320 Broad St., Nevada City. *CONTINENTAL:* **Butterworth's,** 1522 Lincoln Way, Auburn.
Attractions
Bernhard Museum, 291 Auburn-Folsom Rd., Auburn (Tel. 889-4156), 11am-3pm Tue-Fri, 12-4pm Sat-Sun; **El Dorado County Historical Museum,** 100 Placerville Dr., Placerville (Tel. 621-5865), 10am-4pm Wed-Sat; **Empire Mine State Historic Park,** 10791 E. Empire St., Grass Valley (Tel. 273-8522); **Gold Country Museum,** 1273 High St., Auburn (Tel. 889-4155), 10am-4pm Tue-Sun; **Hangtown's Gold Bug Park,** 549 Main St., Placerville (Tel. 622-0832), 10am-4pm daily May-Sept, weekends spring and fall, 50c; **Malakoff Diggins State Historic Park,** 23579 N. Bloomfield Rd., North Bloomfield (Tel. 265-2740); **Marshall Gold Discovery State Historic Park,** 310 Back St., Coloma (Tel. 622-3470). 10am-5pm daily, $3; **Sierra County Historical Park,** Hwy. 49, Sierra City (Tel. 862-1310), 10am-5pm Wed-Sun May-Sept, $1.50; **Sierra Valley Museum,** Loyalton City Park, Loyalton (Tel. 993-4454). 12-4:30pm Wed-Sun, June-mid Oct, free.
Tourist Information
Gold Chain Council of the Mother Lodge, 685 Placerville Dr., Placerville 95667 (Tel. 621-5885); **Auburn Area Visitor and Convention Bureau,** 521 Auburn Ravine Rd., Auburn 95603 (Tel. 916-885-5616, 800-433-7575); **El Dorado County Chamber of Commerce,** 542 Main St., Placerville 95667 (Tel. 916-621-5885); **Grass Valley and Nevada County Chamber of Commerce,** 248 Mill St., Grass Valley 95945 (Tel. 916-273-4667, 800-752-6222); **Sierra County Commission on Tourism,** P.O. Box 473, Downieville 95936.

SOUTHERN GOLD COUNTRY
(Telephone area codes 209)
Accommodation
MODERATE: **Shilo Inn,** 40644 Hwy. 41, Oakhurst 93644 (Tel. 683-3555, 800-222-2244); **Sonora Inn,** 160 S. Washington St., Sonora 95370 (Tel. 532-7468, 800-321-5261); **Yosemite Gold Rush Inn,** 4994 Bullion St., Mariposa 95338 (Tel. 966-4344, 800-321-5261). *BUDGET:* **Amador Inn,** 200 Hwy. 49 S., Jackson 95642 (Tel. 223-0211, 800-528-1234); **Sonora Country Inn,** 18755 Charbroullian Lane, Sonora 95327 (Tel. 984-0315, 800-847-2211).
Restaurants
AMERICAN: **Kelly's Kitchen,** Hwy. 108, Sugar Pine. *CONTINENTAL:* **The Balcony,** 164 Main St., Jackson. *FRENCH:* **City Hotel,** Main Street, Columbia; **Erna's Elderberry House,** Hwy. 41 at Victoria Lane.
Attractions
Amador County Museum, 225 Church St., Jackson (Tel. 223-6386), 10am-4pm Wed-Sun, free; **Calaveras Big Trees State Park,** 1170 E. Hwy. 4, Arnold (Tel. 795-2334); **California State Mining and Mineral Museum,** Mariposa County Fairgrounds, Mariposa (Tel. 742-7625). 9am-8pm Mon-Sat, 9am-5pm Sun summer; 10am-6pm Wed-Sun winter; **Columbia State Historic Park,** P.O. Box 151, Columbia (Tel. 532-4301); **Coulterville History Center and Museum,** Hwys. 49 and 132, Coulterville (Tel. 878-3015), 10am-4pm daily, summer; weekends winter; free; **Indian Grinding Rock State Historic Park,** 14881 Pine Grove-Volcano Rd., Volcano (Tel. 296-7488); **Mariposa Museum and History Center,** 12th and Jessie streets, Mariposa (Tel. 966-2924), 10am-4:30pm daily Apr-Oct, 10am-4pm weekends winter, free; **Mercer Caverns,** Sheepranch Rd., Murphys (Tel. 728-2101), 9am-5pm daily June-Sept, 11am-4pm Sat-Sun Oct-May; **Moaning Cave,** Parrotts Ferry Rd., Vallecito (Tel. 736-2708), daily; **Railtown 1897 State Historic Park,** Jamestown (Tel. 984-3953), Apr-Oct; Roaring Camp Mining Company, Pine Grove (Tel. 296-4100), May-Sept; **Tuolumne County Museum and History Center,** 158 W. Bradford Ave., Sonora (Tel. 532-1317), 10am-3:30pm Mon-Sat, free.
Tourist Information
Amador County Chamber of Commerce, P.O. Box 596, Jackson 95642 (Tel. 223-0350); **Calaveras County Chamber of Commerce,** Box 111, Angels Camp 95222 (Tel. 736-4444, 800-999-9039); **Mariposa County Chamber of Commerce,** P.O. Box 425, Mariposa 95338 (Tel. 966-2456); **Southern Yosemite Visitors Bureau,** P.O. Box 1404, Oakhurst 93644 (Tel. 683-4636); **Tuolumne County Visitors Bureau,** P.O. Box 4020, Sonora 95370 (Tel. 533-4420, 800-446-1333).

THE CENTRAL VALLEY

SACRAMENTO

SAN JOAQUIN VALLEY

SACRAMENTO

Sacramento is the Rodney Dangerfield of California cities. It simply does not get any respect.

Despite its status as state capital, booming metropolis, agricultural center, and cradle of California history, Sacramento is the butt of more bad jokes than any other Golden State city. Cabbies call it "Sack-a-tomatoes". San Francisco snobs say it is merely a "cow town".

But look again. This metropolis of nearly 400,000 is rapidly emerging from San Francisco's shadow to stake its own claim on the future of California. As a center of government in the United States, Sacramento is second only to Washington, D.C. It is the training ground of U.S. presidents and Supreme Court justices, and the home of innovative government policy.

But government is not its only face, though. Sacramento is a gentle city of Victorian splendor, ancient cedar trees and blooming camellias. It is a riverboat town, and a fertile valley that supplies the world with fresh produce. A visit to Sacramento is a trip back to the 1849 California gold rush, and a glimpse into the

Previous pages: Sacramento's gold also includes also this pumpkin field.

future of the state as it approaches the 21st century.

The city of Sacramento is located at the confluence of the Sacramento and American rivers. To the east loom the Sierra Nevada mountains. To the west, the Sacramento River delta spreads to the San Francisco Bay. Between mountain and ocean lies the Central Valley, with some of the richest farmland in the world.

History and People

John Augustus Sutter, a Swiss adventurer fleeing a wife and a bankrupt business, created Sacramento in 1839 when he built a fort to protect the 48,000-acre (19,400-hectare) land grant he received from the Spanish government. Called "New Helvetia", the settlement flourished as a safe haven for pioneers and mountain men. But it became a tent city when gold was discovered at Sutter's mill in 1847.

By 1849, 40,000 hungry prospectors descended on the area. Though the discovery was made on his land, a series of land claims and swindles left Sutter broke. In 1880, the founding father of Sacramento died penniless.

Though Sutter did not prosper, his town did. By 1850, tents gave way to bricks and mortar, and in 1854, Sacramento was selected as capital of the nation's 31st state. But more history was to shape Sacramento. In 1860, it became western headquarters for the famed Pony Express. In 1863, the first tracks were laid in Sacramento for the transcontinental railroad – a line conceived and financed by Sacramento businessmen Collis P. Huntington, Mark Hopkins, Leland Stanford and Charles Crocker, better known as "The Big Four".

Today, with a reasonable cost of living, a hometown atmosphere and quiet downtown streets, Sacramento is a comfortable city. It is the nation's grocer, and home to a number of intriguing and historic sites.

Old Town

With its restored buildings, western facades and wooden boardwalk, the historic landmark of **Old Sacramento** provides a nice introduction to the Gold Country. It is a 28-acre (11.3-hectare) historic park with more than 100 buildings in what used to be Sacramento's "skid row" section.

The **B.F. Hastings Building,** 2nd and J streets, was built in 1852. It houses a post office, tourist information center, and Pony Express museum, and is an excellent place to start an Old Town tour. The nearby **Old Sacramento Schoolhouse,** Front and L streets, reproduces the atmosphere of a Wild West school with its 19th century antiques. The **Sacramento History Center,** 101 I St., presents a fine display of state history.

The **Big Four Building,** I Street between 2nd and Front, was once the headquarters of the Central Pacific Railroad. Around the corner, **The California State Railroad Museum,** Front Street between I and J, is the highlight of Old Town. It faithfully recreates the 1876 Central Pacific station, from the "All aboard!" shout of a conductor to the piercing whistle of a steam locomotive. On display are steam engines, passenger trains,

and a model showing construction of the transcontinental railroad.

Sacramento's steamboat history is docked along Old Sacramento's waterfront. Two paddleboats, the *Matthew McKinley* and the *River City Queen,* offer cruises of the Sacramento River. The *Delta King,* a steamboat-turned-hotel, is also docked near the port.

Capitol Area

Look up the tree-lined Capitol Mall boulevard from Old Sacramento. Looming ahead is the **State Capitol** building, on 9th Street between L and N. This magnificent 220-foot-tall (67 m) structure dominates the Sacramento skyline. Built in 1860 and modeled after the nation's capitol, the Roman Corinthian building reflects the grandiose vision Californians have of themselves.

The inside of the Capitol is equally impressive, with rooms restored to their 19th century elegance and open for public tours. On the third floor, a visitor's gallery offers a bird's-eye view of politics, California style.

Surrounding the Capitol is 40-acre (16-hectare) **Capitol Park,** a collection of more than 40,000 trees, shrubs and flowers from every climate and continent in the world. The famous deodar cedar trees along the west side of the Capitol are over 100 years old and were transported from the Himalaya Mountains to Sacramento in 1870. The park also contains trout ponds and a monument to Civil War veterans.

With 15 rooms, five baths, 14-foot (4.3 m) ceilings, Italian marble fireplaces, turrets, and elaborate wooden fretwork, you would think the **Governor's Mansion,** 16th and H streets, was fit for a king. But no governor has lived there since 1967, when Ronald Reagan refused to move in. Today, it is a museum, with rooms restored to reflect the life and times of California executives.

California governors have been homeless since 1967. Reagan commissioned a sprawling suburban ranch house, but he never lived in it as governor because it was completed after his term. The next governor, Jerry Brown, refused to move into the Reagan ranch. Governor George Deukmejian wanted to move in, but state legislators told him "no".

The **Crocker Art Museum,** 2nd and O streets, exhibits art and architecture in the oldest museum in the West. The collection of more than 1,700 drawings and paintings includes works by Rembrandt and Durer, but its strength lies in the richness of its California landscapes. The museum building, a former private home, is a work of art itself, with handcrafted mahogany cabinets, a wonderful ballroom, parquet floors and frescoed walls.

The Edge of Town

In outer Sacramento, **Sutter's Fort,** 2701 L St., is the reconstructed site of the settlement founded by John Sutter in 1839. The two-story adobe building is a recreation of a fortress that once served as civilization in northern California. Survivors of the infamous Donner Party recovered at Sutter's Fort, and famous frontiersmen such as Captain John Fremont and Kit Carson stayed here.

Today, visitors are supplied with hand-held radio wands which give self-guided tours in English, German, Spanish, and Japanese. Exhibits depicting daily life in 1848 include a carpenter's shop and a blacksmith shop.

Adjacent to the fort is the **California State Indian Museum,** which contains an extensive collection chronicling native American life. The museum depicts the lifestyles of the Miwok, Hupa, Pomo, and several other tribes, and contains one of the finest basket collections in existence.

Though the city offers visitors a myriad of options, it is nice to get a taste of country life and a breath of fresh air. The **American River Parkway** is Sacramento's massive answer to Golden Gate Park. This 12-mile (19-km) greenbelt in the heart of metropolitan Sacramento attracts over three million visitors annually and encompasses more than 20 recreation areas along the Sacramento River. It is a nice place to picnic or exercise.

Outside of the city area are many more Central Valley attractions. **Sacramento National Wildlife Refuge** was established in 1937 as a sanctuary for wintering waterfowl on the Pacific Flyway. **Lake Oroville State Recreation Area** encloses a 165-mile (265-km) shoreline popular among campers, boaters, and fishermen. The **Oroville Chinese Temple** dates to 1856, and gives visitors a peek at one facet of immigrant life in the gold rush.

Many of Sacramento's farmers let visitors wander through fields of fresh produce and groves of fruit trees. The State Department of Food and Agriculture (Tel. toll-free 800-952-5272) can provide a list of farms that welcome visitors.

SACRAMENTO CITY
(Telephone area codes 916)
Accommodation
LUXURY: **Hyatt Regency,** 1209 L St., 95814 (Tel. 443-1234, 800-228-9000); **Riverboat Delta Queen,** 1000 Front St., 95814 (Tel. 444-5464); **Sterling,** 1300 H St., 95814 (Tel. 448-1300, 800-365-7660). *MODERATE:* **Fountain Suites,** 321 Bercut Dr., 95814 (Tel. 441-1444, 800-321-1777); **Hilton,** 2200 Harvard St., 95815 (Tel. 922-4700, 800-344-4321); **Red Lion Inn,** 2001 Point West Way, 95815 (Tel. 929-8855, 800-547-8010); **Sheraton Sunrise,** 11211 Point East Dr., Rancho Cordova 95742 (Tel. 638-1100, 800-325-3535). *BUDGET:* **Central Motel,** 818 16th St., 95814 (Tel. 446-6006); **Desert Sand Inn,** 623 16th St., 95814 (Tel. 444-7530); **Downtown TraveLodge,** 1111 H St. 95814 (Tel. 444-8880); **El Rancho,** 1029 W. Capitol Ave. 95691 (Tel. 371-6731, 800-952-5566).
Restaurants
AMERICAN: **Fat City Bar & Cafe,** 1001 Front St.; **Harry's Bar & Grill,** 400 L St.; **California Fat's,** 1015 Front St. *CHINESE:* **King's,** 5800 Madison Ave. *CONTINENTAL:* **Aldo's,** 2914 Pasatiempo Lane, Stanford & Country Village; **The Firehouse,** 1112 2nd St.
ITALIAN: **Old Spaghetti Factory,** 1910 J St. *MEXICAN:* **Mexico 70,** 1114 8th St.
SEAFOOD: **Stroh's Neptune Table,** 5990 S. Land Park Dr.
Attractions
Blue Diamond Growers, 17th and C streets (Tel. 446-8409), free tours 9 and 10 am, 1 and 2 pm daily, almonds; **California State Archives,** 1020 O St. (Tel. 445-4293), 8am-5pm Mon-Fri; **California State Capitol,** 9th and L streets (Tel. 324-0333), free tours 9am-4pm Mon-Fri, 10am-4pm Sat-Sun; **California State Indian Museum,** 2618 K St. (Tel. 324-0971), 10am-5pm daily; **California State Railroad Museum,** 111 I St. (Tel. 448-4466), 10am-5pm daily, steam train rides Sat-Sun, May-Labor Day; **California Vietnam Veterans Memorial,** 15th and L streets; **Crocker Art Museum,** 216 O St. (Tel. 449-5423), 1-9pm Tue, 10am-5pm Wed-Sun. **Folsom Lake State Recreation Area,** 7806 Folsom-Auburn Rd., Folsom (Tel. 988-0205); **Gibson Ranch County Park,** Watt Ave. at Elverta Rd. (Tel. 366-2061), 7am-dusk daily; **Old Governor's Mansion,** 1526 H St. (Tel. 323-3047), tours 10am-4pm daily.; Old Sacramento Visitor Center, 917 Front St. (Tel. 443-7815); **River City Queen,** 1401 Garden Hwy. (Tel. 921-1111), four cruises daily; **Sacramento History Center,** 101 I St. (Tel. 449-2057), 10am-5pm daily; **Sacramento Science Center,** 3615 Auburn Blvd. (Tel. 449-8255), 9:30am-5pm Mon-Fri, 12-5pm Sat-Sun; **Sacramento Zoo,** 3930 W. Land Park Dr. (Tel. 449-5885), 9am-4pm daily; **Silver Wings Aviation Museum and Planetarium,** Mather Air Force Base, Rancho Cordova (Tel. 364-2908), 10am-4pm Mon-Fri, 12-4pm Sat-Sun, free; **Stanford House,** 800 N St. (Tel. 324-0575); **Sutter's Fort State Historic Park,** 2701 L St. (Tel. 445-4422), 10am-5pm daily.; Towe Ford Museum, 2200 Front St. (Tel. 442-6802), 10am-6pm daily; **Waterworld USA,** 1600 Exposition Blvd. (Tel. 924-0555), daily May-Sept.
Tourist Information
Sacramento Convention and Visitors Bureau, 1421 K St., Sacramento 95815 (Tel. 445-4209).

NORTHERN CENTRAL VALLEY
(Telephone area codes 916)
Accommodation
BUDGET: **Bonanza Inn,** 1001 Clark Ave., Yuba City 95991 (Tel. 674-8824); **Golden Pheasant Inn,** 249 N. Humboldt Ave., Willows 95988 (Tel. 934-4603, 800-528-1234); **Heritage Inn,** 25 Heritage Lane, Chico 95926 (Tel. 894-8600, 800-446-4291); **Oxbow Motel,** 1078 N. Beale Rd., Marysville 95901 (Tel. 742-8238).
Restaurants
AMERICAN: **The Depot,** 2191 High St., Oroville. **The Levee House,** 610 J St., Marysville. *ITALIAN:* **Franco's,** 610 S. Tehama St., Willows.
Attractions
Bidwell Mansion State Historic Park, 525 Esplanade, Chico (Tel. 895-6144), tours 10am-5pm daily; **Gold Nugget Museum,** 502 Pearson Rd., Paradise (Tel. 872-8722), 12-4pm Wed-Sun, free; **Gray Lodge Wildlife Area,** west of Live Oak (Tel. 846-3315); **Lake Oroville State Recreation Area,** 400 Glen Dr., Oroville (Tel. 538-2200); **Oroville Chinese Temple,** 1500 Broderick St., Oroville (Tel. 538-2496), 1-4pm Tue-Wed, 11am-4:30pm Thu-Mon; **Sacramento National Wildlife Refuge,** 7 miles south of Willows on County Road 99; **Sacramento Valley Museum,** 1491 E St., Willows (Tel. 473-2978), daily, hours vary.
Tourist Information
Davis Area Chamber of Commerce, 226 B St., Davis 95616 (Tel. 756-5160); **Greater Chico Chamber of Commerce,** P.O. Box 3038, Chico 95927 (Tel. 891-5556); **Oroville Area Chamber of Commerce,** 1789 Montgomery St., Oroville 95965 (Tel. 533-2542); **Yuba-Sutter Chamber of Commerce,** P.O. Box 1429, Marysville (Tel. 743-6501).

SAN JOAQUIN VALLEY

From the window of an airplane, the San Joaquin (pronounced "wah-keen") Valley reveals its true colors. Spread beneath coastal foothills and the western slopes of the Sierra Nevada is a vast patchwork quilt of pastures, fields, orchards and vineyards, laced together by silver waterways and deep-blue lakes.

Over the last two centuries, generations of farmers have transformed the valley's marshland and desert into some of the world's most productive farmland. This is the green belly of California, and the agricultural heartland of the United States. From Fresno to Bakersfield, the San Joaquin opens its bounty to a hungry world. Three of the top ten agricultural counties in the USA are located there. More than 250 crops are grown.

The valley's vastness and incredible productivity inspired author John Stein-

beck to write his epic Depression-era novel, *The Grapes of Wrath.* Its rich soil and warm climate have inspired an agricultural revolution.

The San Joaquin is the fastest growing region in California. Spilling into the valley are coastal residents fleeing high housing costs and Asian and Latin American immigrants seeking a new life. The valley has become a vast melting pot of Western cowboys and Eastern religion, of Mexican machismo and homecoming queens.

U.S. Highway 99 cuts a swath through the valley from Sacramento to Los Angeles. The string of communities along this route includes Fresno, Visalia, Hanford and Bakersfield.

Fresno

Fresno, California's eighth largest city, is the financial headquarters for San Joaquin Valley agribusiness. Its roots are firmly planted in the rich soil of history, which makes for an interesting visit.

Above: The Central Valley offers the space for herds as far as the eye can see.

The first settlers came to the Fresno area in the mid 1850s. Although little gold was discovered here, settlers found a bounty of another sort. Rich soil and ample water supplies meant they could live off the fat of the land.

The **Fort Miller Block House** is part of that era. Built to protect settlers and gold prospectors during the 1851 Mariposa Indian War, the block house takes visitors back to the time of valley pioneers. Its exhibits demonstrate how the forests and swamps of the 19th century became the gilded fields of the 20th.

In west Fresno, the turn-of-the-century **Kearney Mansion Museum** chronicles the life and times of raisin baron Martin Kearny, one of the county's agricultural pioneers. Kearny made his fortune on the vine of the sweet grape, and his French Renaissance-style house contains the opulent furnishings and European decorate that dried fruit bought.

The historic **Tower District,** a restored neighborhood that reflects Fresno in the Roaring Twenties, is the city's shopping and dining quarter. A pleasant ambience characteristic of its Art Deco architectural style fills the Tower District, which boasts some of the city's finest restaurants and art galleries.

Fresno features its own Philharmonic Orchestra, a **Community Theater** and the **Metropolitan Museum of Art, Science and History**. In **Woodward Park** visitors can experience the culture of a country on the other side of the Pacific Ocean in the Japanese Garden. Even more bizarre is the work of Baldasare Forestiere, who created a maze of a hundred rooms and courtyards in his **Underground Gardens** at 5021 Shaw Avenue.

Fresno's newest immigrants exhibit their work at **Hmong Art,** a unique collection of art and artifacts of the Hmong tribal people of Laos. These highland refugees, fleeing persecution in their native country, have secured a new community

in Fresno. The work of some 300 craftswomen is on display and for sale.

Nestled in the foothills of the Sierra Nevada are two of Fresno County's favorite getaways. The **Wonder Valley Ranch Resort** 15 miles (24 km) southeast of Fresno is California's original dude ranch. According to legend, the train-robbing Dalton Brothers used it as a hideout. The picturesque **Shaver Lake,** nestled in Sierra National Forest, is a warm and hospitable mountain community. **Visalia**, about 43 miles (69 km) south of Fresno, serves as self-proclaimed "Gateway to the Sequoias". With more than 70 restaurants and 800 hotel rooms, it is the hub of tourist activity in the San Joaquin Valley. Numerous tours of local dairies, nurseries, vineyards and cotton fields are available from Visalia.

In nearby **Hanford,** peek into the past of one of California's largest turn-of-the-century Chinese communities. The numerous restored buildings in town include the **Hanford Taoist Temple,** in the historic China Alley District.

Bakersfield

Further south, at the base of the San Joaquin Valley, is the bustling city of **Bakersfield.** This is the hub of Kern County, the leading oil-producing county in the United States. It is also rich in agriculture and just plain-old culture.

The **Kern County Museum and Pioneer Village** comprises the heart of Bakersfield's historic downtown. A 60-building display stretching across 15 acres (6 hectares), Pioneer Village has won national recognition for its representations of architectural styles of 1860-1930. Many of Bakersfield's musicians like to think their city put the "western" in country-and-western music. They may be right. With its proliferation of C&W honky-tonks, the city enjoys a reputation as the second home of country music behind Nashville, Tennessee. Organizers

plan a **Bakersfield Country Music Museum** next to Kern County Museum.

Bakersfield's culture runs deeper than its music. The city is home to one of the largest Basque populations outside of Spain's Pyrenees. The Kern Basque community preserves its much-beloved cultural heritage through annual festivals and events.

On the doorstep of the Mojave Desert and the Sequoia National Forest, Bakersfield also offers several nearby outdoor activities. The **California Living Museum** displays desert animals in their natural habitat. It is located 6 miles (10 km) northeast of Bakersfield on the Alfred Harrell Highway. About 15 miles (24 km) west of Bakersfield is the **Tule Elk State Reserve,** home to the smallest and rarest of all elk. Nearly decimated by the arrival of prospectors and settlers, the elk are protected on this 950-acre (384-hectare) preserve. The herd of 70 can be

Above: The skyline of Bakersfield includes the lumbering oil wells.

seen from a viewing area, where picnic tables and exhibits are maintained.

Western Kern County will soon be the canvas the the Bulgarian-born avant-garde artist Christo. The man who covered the oldest bridge in Paris with champagne-colored cloth, and who draped cloth along the north coast of California, has another work up his sleeve: In October 1991 Christo will exhibit 1,700 bright yellow umbrellas, each about 30 feet (10 m) across, along Interstate 5 near **Gorman.** The exhibit will coincide with a similar umbrella display in Japan.

Eastern Kern County opens into the vastness of the Mojave Desert. It is home to several ghost towns, including **Randsburg, Garlock** and **Goler.**

The community of **Boron,** home of the world's largest borax mine, is also worth a visit. Its claim to fame is a household item: Borax is used to make household cleansers. Boron is also home to the famous Twenty Mule Teams that once hauled borax from the mines.

BAKERSFIELD AREA
(Telephone area codes 805)
Accommodation
MODERATE: **Red Lion Inn,** 3100 Camino Del Rio Ct., 93308 (Tel. 323-7111, 800-547-8010); **Sheraton Valley Inn,** 5101 California Ave., 93309 (Tel. 325-9700, 800-325-3535).
Attractions
Al Bussell Ranch, 12 miles west, 26500 Stockdale Hwy. (Tel. 589-2677), 7am-7pm Apr-Oct; **California Living Museum,** 13 miles east, 14000 Old Alfred Harrell Hwy. 178 (Tel. 872-2256), 10am-sunset Tue-Sun; **Colonel Allensworth State Historic Park,** 20 miles north of Wasco on Hwy. 43 (Tel. 849-3433); **Fort Tejon State Historic Park,** 40 miles south on I-5, Lebec; **Kern County Museum,** 3801 Chester Ave. (Tel. 861-2132), 8am-5pm Mon-Fri, 10am-5pm Sat-Sun; **Kern National Wildlife Ref.** 19 miles west of Delano, Garces Hwy. and Corcoran Rd., dawn-dusk daily mid Jan-mid Oct, restricted times mid Oct-mid Jan; **Kern Valley Museum,** Sierra Way and Kernville Rd., Kernville (Tel. 714-379-2087), 1-4pm Sat-Sun, free.
Tourist Information
Gr. Bakersfield Conv. and Visitors Bureau, 1033 Truxtun Ave. (P.O. Box 192), 93302 (Tel. 325-5051).
Kern County Board of Trade Visitors Ctr., 2101 Oak St., 93302 (Tel. 861-2367).

FRESNO-VISALIA AREA
(Telephone area codes 209)
Accommodation
MODERATE: **Fresno Hilton,** 1055 Van Ness Ave., Fresno 93721 (Tel. 485-9000, 800-652-1094); **Holiday Inn Plaza Park,** 9000 W. Airport Dr., Visalia 93277 (Tel. 651-5000, 800-465-4329).
BUDGET: **Econo Lodge,** 1804 W. Olive Ave., Fresno 93728 (Tel. 442-1082, 800-321-5261).
Attractions
Duncan Water Gardens, 691 Temperance Ave., Fresno (Tel. 255-7233), 9am-5pm Wed-Sat, 10am-4pm Sun; **Fort Miller Block House,** Olive Ave. and Hwy. 99, Fresno (Tel. 441-0862), 1-4pm Sat-Sun, May-Sept, free; **Fresno Art Museum,** 2233 N. First St., Fresno (Tel. 485-4810), 10am-5pm Tue-Sun; **Fresno Metropolitan Museum of Art, History and Science,** 1555 Van Ness Ave., Fresno (Tel. 441-1444), 11am-5pm Wed-Sun; **Fresno Zoo,** 894 W. Belmont Ave., Roeding Park, Fresno (Tel. 488-1111), 10am-5pm daily; **Hanford Courthouse Square,** 113 Court St. Hanford, 10am-5pm daily; **Hanford Taoist Temple,** 12 China Alley, Hanford

(Tel. 584-3236), free tours by appointment; **Hmong Art,** 842 N. Fulton St., Fresno (Tel. 237-7106); **Kearney Mansion,** 7160 W. Kearney Blvd., Kearney Park, Fresno (Tel. 441-0862), 1-4pm Fri-Sun; **Kingsburg Swedish Village,** California St., Kingsburg (Tel. 897-2925); **Madera County Museum,** 210 W. Yosemite St., Madera, 1-4:30pm Sat-Sun; **Mennonite Quilting Center,** 1010 G St., Reedley (Tel. 638-6911), 9:30am-5pm Mon-Sat; **Zalud House,** Morton and Hockett streets, Porterville (Tel. 782-7548), 10am-4pm Wed-Sat, 2-4pm Sun.
Tourist Information
Central Valley Tourism Association/Fresno Conv. and Visitors Bureau, 808 M St. (P.O. Box 1792), Fresno 93717 (Tel. 233-0836, 800-543-8488); **Hanford Chamber of Commerce and Visitor Agency,** 213 W. Seventh St., Hanford 93230 (Tel. 582-0483, 800-722-1114); **Visalia Conv. and Visitors Bureau,** 720 W. Mineral King Ave., Visalia 93291 (Tel. 734-5876).

STOCKTON-MODESTO AREA
(Telephone area codes 209
Attractions
Bright's Pioneer Exhibit, 5246 S. Plainsburg Rd., LeGrand (Tel. 389-4511, 8am-4pm Mon-Fri; **Castle Air Museum,** Castle Air Force Base, Atwater (Tel. 723-2178 or 723-2177), 10am-4pm daily; **Great Valley Museum of Natural History,** 1100 Stoddard Ave., Modesto (Tel. 575-6196), 12-4:30pm Tue-Fri, 10am-4pm Sat; **Haggin Museum,** 1201 N. Pershing Ave., Stockton (Tel. 462-4116), 1:30-5pm Tue-Sun.; **Los Banos Wildlife Area,** north of Los Banos (Tel. 826-0463); **McHenry Museum and Mansion,** 15th and I streets, Modesto (Tel. 577-5366 or 577-5344), 12-4pm Tue-Sun; **Micke Grove Park and Zoo,** 11793 N. Micke Grove Rd., Lodi (Tel. 953-8800), 10am-5pm daily; **Pollardville Showboat & Ghost Town,** 10464 N. Hwy. 99, Stockton (Tel. 931-0274); **San Joaquin County Historical Museum,** 11793 N. Micke Grove Rd., Lodi (Tel. 368-9154); **Yosemite Wildlife Museum,** 2040 Yosemite Pkwy., Merced (Tel. 383-1052), 10am-5pm Mon-Sat.
Tourist Information
Merced Convention and Visitors Bureau, 1880 N St. (P.O. Box 3107), Merced 95344 (Tel. 384-3333, 800-446-5353).
Modesto Convention and Visitors Bureau, 1114 J St. (P.O. Box 844), Modesto 95353 (Tel. 577-5757).
Stockton-San Joaquin C. Convention and Visitors Bureau, 46 W. Fremont St., Stockton 95202 (Tel. 943-1987, 800-888-8016).

THE FAR NORTH

SHASTA-CASCADE
THE NORTH COAST

SHASTA-CASCADE

The Shasta-Cascade county is California's Eden, a sprawling and sparsely populated evergreen paradise stretching from Redding to the Oregon border and from Nevada to the coastal range. Parts of it have so far been left virtually untouched.

Six mountain ranges – the Cascade, Klamath, Marble, Salmon, Trinity and Warner – form a series of peaks and valleys that harbor crystal lakes and rivers. Lush forests and wilderness areas provide miles and miles of backpacking terrain. Shasta-Cascade is the size of Ohio, yet it is 65 per cent federally owned, with six national forests and eight national and state parks.

Mount Shasta lords over the land. Rising from the northern edge of the Central Valley, this 14,162-foot (4,316-m) giant commands attention with its brilliant snow-covered peak and its gray granite face. Within its sight are 30,000-acre (12,140-hectare) the Shasta Lake, the state's largest lake; and the 10,457-foot (3,187-m) Lassen Peak, the world's largest plug-dome volcano.

Preceding pages: Mount Shasta keeps a vigilant eye over the Central Valley. Steam and boiling mud at Bumpass Hell.

Redding and the Trinity Alps

Few California cities are located as strategically as **Redding**. This city of 45,000 is the perfect base from which to explore the region. North of Redding, Highway 299 follows the Trinity River through historic towns like **Shasta** and **French Gulch.** During the halcyon days of the 1850s, more than $100,000 in gold dust was processed every week. The 13-acre (5.3-hectare) **Shasta State Historical Park** relives those days with exhibits that include a general store and a courthouse.

In **Weaverville,** a charming Western city with swinging bar-room doors and ornate building facades, the **Joss House State Historic Park** tells of gold fever through the eyes of Chinese miners. The park features the "Temple Amongst the Forest Beneath the Trees", a 19th century Taoist temple complete with carved altars and other works of Chinese art.

Nestled at the base of jagged peaks that soar to 8,000 feet (2,500 m), Weaverville is the gateway to the **Trinity Alps Wilderness Area.** This 500,000-acre (200,000-hectare) preserve of alpine meadows and glacial lakes protects four distinct ecological zones from development. Route 3 cuts through striking mountain valleys and isolated villages to

Yreka, christened with the Indian name for Mount Shasta. Besides excellent fishing in the **Klamath River,** the Shasta country's northern outpost of civilization boasts the time-worn buildings of **Miner Street,** a county courthouse with a gold-nugget display, and the **Siskiyou County Museum,** which exhibits artifacts of native Indians and immigrant miners.

Shasta and Lassen

North of Redding on Interstate 5 is manmade **Shasta Lake,** a recreational plum and an engineering feat. The 465-foot (141-m) dam traps water from three rivers and creates a lake with 370 miles (595 km) of shoreline and a depth of 517 feet (157m). The dam's spillway is three times the height of Niagara Falls.

Shasta Caverns, a series of chambers with thousands of stalactites and stalagmites up to 20 feet (6 m) long, are hidden

Above: The northern country lives in part from logging.

along Shasta Lake's shoreline. So isolated are they that the only access is by Forest Service ferry. The service operates year-round from the town of **O'Brien.**

About 25 miles (40 km) north of Shasta Lake is **Castle Crags State Park,** glacier-polished outcroppings that tower over the Sacramento River.

All descriptions of the Shasta-Cascade region begin and end with **Mount Shasta** and its twin volcanic cones. Five glaciers hug its slopes and hot springs bubble up from its depths. Shasta's beauty has inspired writers and philosophers, and spawned a crop of legends. Poet Joaquin Miller wrote that Shasta is "lonely as God and white as a winter moon". New Age spiritualists gathered here for the 1987 Harmonic Convergence.

Locals in **Mount Shasta City** swear the mountain purposely shoved an irritating ski lift off its back in the winter of 1989. The ski area has not reopened. An access road winds up Shasta to 6,800 feet (2,072 m). From here, there are several enjoyable hikes.

Southeast along Route 89 **McArthur-Burney Falls Memorial State Park** is situated. With its mist painting rainbows in the sky, the 129-foot (39-m) Burney Falls was once described by U.S. President Theodore Roosevelt as the eighth wonder of the world.

Lassen Volcanic National Park puts the region's awesome origins on display. **Lassen Peak** erupted 300 times between 1914 and 1917, covering the area with ash and lava flows and leaving a legacy of boiling lakes, bubbling mud and fumaroles which can still be viewed. The still-active volcano marks the southern edge of the Cascade Range.

A 34-mile (55-km) road loops through the park and climbs to 8,500 feet (2,590 m). Hiking trails through the 106,000-acre (42,900-hectare) park show many spectacular volcanic features, including **Bumpass Hell,** its hot waters and gases bubbling up from the earth's surface.

SHASTA COUNTY

(Telephone area codes 916)

Accommodation

LUXURY: **Drakesbad Guest Ranch,** Chester 96020 (Tel. Susanville operator, Drakesbad No. 2), 47 miles southeast of park HDQ off Chester-Warner Valley road.
MODERATE: **Hilltop Inn,** 2300 Hilltop Dr., Redding 96002 (Tel. 221-6100, 800-528-1234); **Red Lion Motor Inn,** 1830 Hilltop Dr., Redding 96001 (Tel. 221-8700, 800-547-8010).
BUDGET: **Bridge Bay Resort,** 10300 Bridge Bay Rd., Redding 96003 (Tel. 275-3021, 800-752-9669), on Lake Shasta; **Shasta Inn,** 2180 Hilltop Dr., Redding 96002 (Tel. 221-8200).

Restaurants

AMERICAN: **Andy's Cow Patty Palace,** 2105 Hilltop Dr., Redding; **Hatch Cover,** 202 Hemsted Dr., Redding.
CONTINENTAL: **T.R.'s,** 2180 Hilltop Drive, Redding.

Attractions

Ahjumawi Lava Springs State Park, 3.5 miles northeast of McArthur on Hwy. 299 (Tel. 335-2777); **Carter House Natural Science Museum,** Caldwell Park, Redding (Tel. 225-4125), 10am-5pm Tue-Sun; **Castle Crags State Park,** Castella, 6 miles south of Dunsmuir off I-5 (Tel. 235-2684); **Fort Crook Museum,** Fall River Mills, 4 miles southwest of McArthur on Hwy. 299 (Tel. 336-5100), 12-4pm May-Oct, free; **Lake Shasta Caverns,** O'Brien (Tel. 238-2341 or 238-2386), hourly tours from 9am Apr-Sept, tours three times daily from 10am Oct-Apr; **Lassen Volcanic National Park,** P.O. Box 100, Mineral (Tel. 595-4444); **McArthur-Burney Falls Memorial State Park,** 11 miles northeast of Burney off Hwy. 89 (Tel. 335-2777); **Old City Hall Gallery and Performing Arts Center,** 1313 Market St., Redding (Tel. 241-7320), 9am-4pm Mon-Fri, free; **Redding Museum and Art Center,** Caldwell Park, 56 Quartz Hill Rd. and Rio Dr., Redding (Tel. 225-4155), 12-5pm Tue-Sun; **Shasta Dam,** Visitors Information, Redding (Tel. 275-1554); **Shasta State Historic Park,** Shasta, 6 miles west of Redding on Hwy. 299 (Tel. 225-2065), 10am-5pm daily Mar-Oct, Thu-Mon Nov-Feb; **Whiskeytown Lake,** Whiskeytown (Tel. 241-6584).

Tourist Information

Redding Convention and Visitors Bureau, 777 Auditorium Drive, Redding 96001 (Tel. 225-4100); **Shasta Cascade Wonderland Association,** 1250 Parkview Avenue, Redding 96001 (Tel. 243-2643).

SISKIYOU COUNTY

Accommodation

MODERATE: **Tree House Motor Inn,** I-5 at Central Mt. Shasta exit (P.O. Box 236), Mount Shasta 96067 (Tel. 926-3101, 800-528-1234).
BUDGET: **Cedar Lodge Motel,** 4201 Dunsmuir Ave., Dunsmuir 96025 (Tel. 235-4331); **Miner's Inn,** 122 E. Miner St., Yreka 96097 (Tel. 842-3392, 800-528-1234).

Attractions

Fort Jones Museum, 11913 Main St., Fort Jones (Tel. 486-2631), 10am-4pm Mon-Sat late May-Oct 1, free; **Klamath Basin National Wildlife Refuge,** Tulelake (Tel. 667-2231); **Klamath National Forest Interpretive Museum,** 1312 Fairlane Rd., Yreka (Tel. 842-6131), 8am-4:30pm Mon-Fri, free; **Lava Beds National Monument,** Tulelake (Tel. 667-2282); **Mount Shasta,** Information Center, 104 Siskiyou Ave., Mount Shasta (Tel. 926-5254); **Siskiyou County Museum,** 910 S. Main St., Yreka (Tel. 842-3836), 9am-5pm Mon-Sat, 1-5pm Sun, June-Aug; 9am-5pm Tue-Sat, Sept-May; free; **Sisson Hatchery Museum,** 1 Old Stage Rd., Mount Shasta (Tel. 926-5508 or 926-4738), 10am-5pm daily summer, 12-4pm daily winter, free.

Tourist Information

Mount Shasta Chamber of Commerce, 300 Pine St., Mount Shasta 96067 (Tel. 926-4865); **Weed Chamber of Commerce,** P.O. Box 366, Weed 96094 (Tel. 938-4624); **Yreka Chamber of Commerce,** 1000 S. Main St., Yreka 96097 (Tel. 842-1649).

TRINITY COUNTY

Accommodation

BUDGET: **Motel Trinity,** Hwy. 299 (P.O. Box 1179), Weaverville 96093 (Tel. 623-2129); **Weaverville Hotel,** 201 Main St., Weaverville 96093 (Tel. 623-3121).

Attractions

Jake Jackson Memorial Museum-Trinity County Historical Park, Weaverville (Tel. 623-5211), 10am-5pm May-Oct, 12-4pm Apr and Nov, free; **Scotts Museum,** Weaverville (Tel. 623-5211), 10am-5pm May-Nov; **Trinity Alps Wilderness,** Weaverville (Tel. 623-2121); **Weaverville Joss House State Historical Park,** Hwy. 299, Weaverville (Tel. 623-5284), 10am-5pm daily Mar-Oct, Thu-Mon Nov-Feb; **Whiskeytown-Shasta-Trinity National Recreation Area,** Hwy. 3, north of Weaverville.

Tourist Information

Trinity County Chamber of Commerce, 317 Main St. (P.O. Box 517), Weaverville 96093 (Tel. 623-6101).

THE NORTH COAST

With its sheer cliffs and pounding waves, California's North Coast marks a dramatic division between land and sea. The unspoiled coastline, which stretches some 200 miles (320 km) south from the Oregon border, is dominated by the Pacific Ocean, red wood forests and coastal mountains.

This is a land where morning fog shrouds towns in splendid isolation, and sunsets explode with salmon-colored light. Its rugged natural beauty provides a breathtaking backdrop and a breath of fresh air for travelers seeking respite from city sights.

The region's beauty and low cost of living are a lure. Humboldt County is home to more artists per capita than any other part of California. The coast's rural ambience lures many who seek an alternative to the hectic cities.

Above: Highway 1 hugs the scenic Pacific coast. Right: The cliffs near Fort Bragg.

North Coasters use ingenuity to scratch out a living in this region, which has higher unemployment and less economic opportunity than other parts of California. In Eureka, for example, they have restored dilapidated Victorian homes to create a cottage industry of bed-and-breakfast inns. Deep in the backwoods of southern Humboldt County thrives an illegal marijuana industry: entrepreneurial farmers harvest potent plants that grow 12 feet (3.6 m) tall and sell easily.

The lumber industry, still the major employer, has been less inventive. In its 130-year history, the industry cut over 90 per cent of the redwood forest without providing adequate reforestation. Now it faces a timber shortage and court battles with environmentalists, bent on rescuing remaining virgin forests. Logging trucks, a common sight on coast roads, soon may be an endangered species.

The main coastal road is scenic Route 1, a winding byway that follows the crashing surf. Inland, Highway 101 pursues a similar course, but at faster and less charming speeds. The roads meet at the town of **Leggett**.

The Sights of Highway 1

Perched on a promontory, surrounded on three sides by ocean and wearing the soft, faded colors of yesterday, the town of **Mendocino**, with a population of 1,200, has a character of its own. Its New England-style houses, moss-covered fences and wooden water towers are carefully preserved with strict zoning. The setting is a favorite among Hollywood directors.

The town's reputation as an artists' colony is well deserved, as a visit to the **Mendocino Art Center and Gallery** on Little Lake Street will attest. The center features exhibits, classes in painting, pottery and textiles, and Sunday concerts.

Neighboring **Fort Bragg** (population 5,000) is home to the **California Western Railroad's** "Skunk Line", which runs east through mountains to the town of **Willits.** Next to the station is the **Guest House Museum,** with local history and railroad displays.

North of Fort Bragg is the rugged **Lost Coast,** dominated by scrub chaparral and the dramatic King Range. One of the wettest areas on the Pacific shoreline, the Lost Coast is also one of the wildest. Hikers enjoy the isolated trails that follow the coastal ridges and dunes.

Highway 101 to Eureka

Heading inland at Humboldt County, the North Coast takes on a new feeling. Ocean yields to towering redwoods, crashing tides give way to forest stillness, and boundless horizon becomes a sliver of misty sunlight through a canopy of conifers. This is **Redwood Country**, home to *Sequoia sempervirens*, a tree that dates to the age of dinosaurs.

At **Avenue of the Giants,** a 33-mile (53-km), two-lane section of old High-

way 101, visitors find themselves in the middle of an ancient redwood forest. The road starts at **Garberville** and snakes through the 51,000-acre (20,600-hectare) **Humboldt Redwoods State Park.**

In addition to magnificent trees, the avenue is a showcase of kitsch, the popular Americana that flourished in the years following World War II. It winds through small towns and past homespun places like Chimney Tree and Mystery Mountain, north to **Klamath,** home of a drive-through tree and the **Trees of Mystery.** This theme park features a grove of strangely formed trees, huge wood carvings, and a 50-foot (15-m) concrete-and-plaster model of legendary American woodsman Paul Bunyan.

Eureka, with 25,000 people, is the region's largest city and its hub of commerce. Chartered in 1856, and built by timber and fishing, the city is filled with sights reflecting its Victorian heritage.

Old Town along the Humboldt Bay waterfront is a restored district of gourmet restaurants, stylish bars, antique

189

shops, and inns. The **Carson Mansion,** built around 1880 by a lumber merchant and today the most photographed Victorian home in the U.S., is queen of late 19th century American architecture. Unfortunately it is not open to the public as the most distinguished members of the club that owns it prefer to remain private.

Eureka also is home to much of the North Coast's creative genius. **Humboldt State University** is the only institution of higher learning on the North Cost. The **Humboldt Cultural Center,** 422 First St., and **Old Town Art Guild,** 233 F St., both feature exhibits by regional artists. But almost any open wall space is a potential gallery. Check banks, bars, restaurants, or hotels for local talent.

The salty air also inspires the strange and exotic. **Romano Gabriel's Wooden Sculpture Garden,** 315 Second St., built from vegetable crates, is a classic work of American folk art.

Above: The Redwood National Park graces the coastal region.

Redwood National Park

With 106,000 acres (42,900 hectares) of old-growth redwood groves and outstanding coastal scenery, **Redwood National Park** is the crowning jewel of a North Coast tour. Founded in 1968, the park combined land from three established state parks – Prairie Creek, Del Norte and Jedediah Smith into one federally managed property.

Hiking trails abound in the park, and lead trekkers deep into the damp primordial home of the ancient redwood trees, whose heritage stretches back before the birth of Christ. **Tall Trees Grove** claims the world's tallest tree at 367.8 feet (112.1 m) and 14 feet (4.3 m) in diameter. **Fern Canyon Grove** provides miles of trails through virgin timber. Park officials are pursuing a program of stabilizing and reforesting logged-over lands in the national park. They are reshaping logging roads to the natural contour of the land, planting thousands of redwood seedlings, and restoring prairies.

(Telephone area codes 707)

DEL NORTE COUNTY
Accommodation
MODERATE: **Northwood Inn,** 655 Hwy. 101 S., Crescent City 95531 (Tel. 464-9771, 800-528-1234). *BUDGET:* **Crescent TraveLodge,** 725 Hwy. 101 N., Crescent City 95531 (Tel. 464-6106, 800-255-3050); **Motel Trees,** Hwy. 101, Klamath 95548 (Tel. 482-3152).

Restaurants
CONTINENTAL: **House of Rowland's,** 400 Hwy. 101 N., Crescent City (Tel. 464-4727). *SEAFOOD:* **Harbor View Grotto,** 155 Citizen's Dock Rd., Crescent City (Tel. 464-3815).

Attractions
Battery Point Lighthouse, Crescent City (Tel. 464-3089); **Del Norte Coast Redwoods State Park,** Hwy. 101, 7 miles south of Crescent City (Tel. 445-6547 or 458-3310); **Del Norte County Historical Society Museum,** 577 H St., Crescent City (Tel. 464-3922), 10am-4pm May-Sept; **Jedediah Smith Redwoods State Park,** Hwy. 199, 9 miles east of Crescent City (Tel. 464-9533 or 458-3310); **Redwood National Park,** office 1111 Second St., Crescent City (Tel. 464-6101); **Trees of Mystery,** Hwy. 101 N., Klamath (Tel. 482-5613), daylight hours.

Tourist Information
Del Norte County Chamber of Commerce, P.O. Box 246, Crescent City 95531 (Tel. 464-3174).

HUMBOLDT COUNTY
Accommodation
MODERATE: **Eureka Inn,** 7th and F streets, Eureka 95501 (Tel. 442-6441, 800-862-4906); **Thunderbird Lodge,** 5th Street and Broadway, Eureka 95501 (Tel. 443-2234, 528-1234). *BUDGET:* **Miranda Gardens Resort,** Avenue of the Giants (P.O. Box 186), Miranda 95553 (Tel. 943-3011).

Attractions
Clarke Memorial Museum, 3rd and E streets, Eurcka (Tel. 443-1947), 12-4pm Tue-Sat, free; **Ferndale State Historic Landmark,** Ferndale (Tel. 786-4477); **Ferndale Museum,** 3rd and Shaw streets, Ferndale (Tel. 786-4466), 11am-4pm Wed-Sat, 1-4pm Sun; **Fort Humboldt State Historic Park,** 3431 Fort Ave., Eureka (Tel. 445-6567), 9am-5pm, free; **Fortuna Depot Museum,** 4 Park St., Fortuna (Tel. 725-2495), 12-5pm daily June-Sept, Sat-Wed Sept-May, free; **Humboldt Bay Maritime Museum,** 1410 Second St., Eureka (Tel. 444-9440), 11am-4pm daily; **Humboldt Cultural Center,** 422 First St., Eureka (Tel. 442-2611); **Humboldt Redwoods**

State Park, Hwy. 101 and 254, Weott (Tel. 946-2311), visitor center 10am-5pm daily Apr-Sept; Includes Avenue of the Giants; **Old Town Art Guild,** 233 F St., Eureka (Tel. 445-2315); **Prairie Creek Redwoods State Park,** Hwy. 101 north of Orick (Tel. 488-2171); **Redwood Information Center,** Hwy. 101, Orick (Tel. 488-3461), 9am-5pm daily.

Tourist Information
Eureka/Humboldt County Convention and Visitors Bureau, 1034 Second St., Eureka 95501 (Tel. 443-5097, 800-346-3482); **Redwood Empire Association,** 1 Market Plaza, Spear Street Tower, Suite 1001, San Francisco 94105 (Tel. 415-543-8334).

MENDOCINO COUNTY
Accommodation
LUXURY: **Stanford Inn by the Sea,** Comptche-Ukiah Rd. (P.O. Box 487), Mendocino 95460 (Tel. 937-5025). *MODERATE:* **MacCallum House,** 45020 Albion St., Mendocino 95460 (Tel. 937-0289); **Mendocino Hotel,** 45080 Main St., Mendocino 95460 (Tel. 937-0511, 800-548-0513). *BUDGET:* **Discovery Inn,** 1340 N. State St., Ukiah (Tel. 462-8873); **Quality Inn Seabird,** 191 South St., Fort Bragg 95437 (Tel. 964-4731, 800-228-5151).

Restaurants
CONTINENTAL: **Cafe Beaujolais,** 961 Ukiah St., Mendocino (Tel. 937-5614). *FRENCH:* **St. Orres,** Hwy. 1, Gualala (Tel. 884-3303).

Attractions
California Western Railroad's Skunk Trains, Fort Bragg to Willits (Tel. 964-6371), daily runs; **Grace Hudson Museum and Sun House,** 431 S. Main St., Ukiah (Tel. 462-3370), 10am-4:30pm Tue-Sat, 12-4:30pm Sun, July 4-Labor Day; **Kelley House Museum,** 45007 Albion St., Mendocino (Tel. 937-5791); **Mendocino Art Center,** 54200 Little Lake St., Mendocino (Tel. 937-5818); **Mendocino Coast Botanical Gardens,** 18220 N. Hwy. 1, Fort Bragg (Tel. 965-4352), 9am-5pm Mar-Oct, 10am-4pm Nov-Feb, $4; **Mendocino County Museum,** 400 E. Commercial St., Willits (Tel. 459-2736), 10am-4:30pm Wed-Sun, free; **Mendocino National Forest,** office 420 E. Laurel St., Willows (Tel. 934-3316); **Point Arena Lighthouse,** Point Arena (Tel. 882-2777).

Tourist Information
Fort Bragg-Mendocino Coast Chamber of Commerce, P.O. Box 1141, Fort Bragg 95437 (Tel. 964-3153); **Mendocino County Convention and Visitors Bureau,** P.O. Box 244, Ukiah 95482 (Tel. 462-3091).

SIDE TRIPS

LAS VEGAS

RENO

LAS VEGAS AND RENO

Not far from the golden beaches and tourist centers of California lie two Nevada cities, attractions in their own right. Las Vegas and Reno are playgrounds for Californians. Those who get the urge to splurge on gambling, live entertainment and lavish buffets head for Las Vegas, just under 280 miles (450 km) east of Los Angeles, or Reno, just 220 miles (350 km) east of San Francisco. Both cities are less than an hour by plane from their metropolitan California neighbors.

Ever since the state of Nevada legalized gambling in 1931, Las Vegas and Reno have boomed. Not since the mining days of the 19th century has Nevada drawn so many people with dreams of striking it rich. In fact, despite its nickname, "Lost Wages", Las Vegas is known as "the entertainment capital of the world". In 1989, more than 19 million visitors left over $3.7 billion on the gambling tables in Las Vegas and other Clark County towns alone!

There are more than 70,000 slot machines in Las Vegas. The cost of pulling the lever of a "one-armed bandit" ranges

Previous pages: The glitz and glitter of the Las Vegas Strip, also known as "Glitter Gulch".

from 1 cent to $500! Other casino games in Las Vegas and Reno include black jack, poker, baccarat, roulette, keno, and craps.

But gambling is not the only diversion. Las Vegas and Reno are also known for their glitzy shows, featuring dozens of scantily clad show girls, and for performances by top-name stars such as Frank Sinatra, Bill Cosby, and The Pointer Sisters. And there is lots more to see in the hinterlands – museums, parks, and historic mining towns.

Las Vegas

Las Vegas is located near the southernmost tip of Nevada, a straight shot from Los Angeles via Interstate 15.

Spanish explorers first visited the site in 1829. They named it "the meadows", for the arid grasses surrounding the valley's artesian springs. Mormons from Utah settled here in 1855 and cultivated the land for a couple of years, but found it too inhospitable. The U.S. Army's Fort Baker, built in 1864, attracted more permanent settlement. The 1905 completion of a railroad line between Los Angeles and Salt Lake City, Utah, helped the town's growth; it further prospered when nearby Hoover Dam was built on the Colorado River in 1930.

In 1931, the Nevada state legislature voted to legalize gambling, and licensed casinos sprouted like weeds. Another growth spurt came after World War II, when developers created the now-famous Las Vegas Strip, nicknamed "Glitter Gulch". Hotel names like Caesar's Palace, the Golden Nugget, and the MGM Grand (now Bally's) became synonymous with the city.

Las Vegas became a haven for the rich and famous. Among them was the late millionaire Howard Hughes, who settled there in the 1950s and invested heavily in local real estate, buying several hotels – including the Desert Inn, the Silver Slipper and The Sands. After Hughes' death in 1975, his Suma Corporation sold all but 20,000 acres (8,093 hectares) of undeveloped land, which it plans to develop as a residential site.

Today, Las Vegas is more than a tourist draw. Clark County is the fastest growing area in the west, adding some 3,500 residents per month. The area's population is nearly 750,000 (262,000 in Las Vegas alone), and is expected to reach one million by the year 2000.

Visitors who are tired of gambling and nightlife find plenty of well-kept secrets waiting to be discovered. The **Imperial Palace Auto Collection**, in the Imperial Palace Hotel, displays more than 200 vintage automobiles. Included are rarities like Adolf Hitler's 1939 Mercedes-Benz and actor Steve McQueen's favorite motorcycle.

Another unique museum is the **Liberace Museum,** 1775 E. Tropicana Ave. Displaying memorabilia of one of the more flamboyant performers of our time, it houses a jewel collection, custom-built pianos, and other possessions of the late entertainer. Downtown at the Four Queens Hotel is an incredible display. **Ripley's Believe It or Not** features more than 1,000 items from the Robert Ripley collection of the bizarre, from primitive oddities to freaks of nature.

The **Nevada State Museum**, 700 Twin Lakes Dr., reveals a more cultural side of Vegas. Surrounded by a park with spring-fed ponds, the museum chronicles the environment and history of the region.

In the nearby town of **Henderson,** chocolate lovers can sample some of the richest sweets at the **Ethel M Chocolate Factory,** 2 Cactus Garden Drive. Owned by the Mars family of candy-bar fame, the factory offers tours. Adjacent is a botanical garden and cactus display.

Also in Henderson is the **Clark County Heritage Museum,** formerly the Southern Nevada Museum, at 1830 S. Boulder Highway. The museum houses a turn-of-the-century railroad town with depot, ghost town, and working railroad stock.

About 15 miles west of Las Vegas off Highway 159, the **Red Rock Recreation Area** offers picnicking, hiking, and stunning views. Within the park is **Old Nevada,** a mock-up village with a wax museum, opera house, staged shootouts, and other Old West amusements.

Southern Nevada's biggest sightseeing attraction is **Hoover Dam.** Located 30 miles (48 km) southeast of Las Vegas off Highway 93, the dam stands 70 stories high and supplies electrical power to Nevada, California, and Arizona. The dam is the gateway to **Lake Mead National Recreation Area,** with beaches, water skiing, sailing, and scuba diving.

Nevada's oldest state park, the **Valley of Fire,** is at the north end of Lake Mead off Highway 169. Blazing red sandstone formations and Indian petroglyphs decorate the area. Visitors can either spend the day or camp overnight.

Reno

Reno lies in northern Nevada, a half-hour drive from Lake Tahoe on Interstate 80 from San Francisco. Gold and silver first drew settlers to nearby Virginia City

in the late 1850s, more than a decade after explorers John Fremont and Kit Carson traversed the area.

The transcontinental Union Pacific Railroad mapped out the first lots for Reno and used the city as a major depot. The Pony Express ran through on its way to its Carson City depot in 1860 and 1861. During the same era, a young Samuel Clemens wrote articles for Virginia City's *Territorial Enterprise* under the pen name Mark Twain.

In the 20th century, after the legalization of gambling, Bill Harrah and other developers erected Reno's world-class hotels and casinos. Today, Reno boasts more than 127,000 residents, and the adjacent city of Sparks has more than 55,000. Mining is still a major industry, and agriculture – cattle and sheep, wheat, oats, barley and other grains – remain important to the economy. But tourism and gambling are the biggest drawing card.

Above: Gambling has also become Reno's most important source of income.

Beyond Reno's Casinos

A highlight of any visit to Reno is the **William F. Harrah Foundation National Automobile Museum,** downtown at the corner of Lake and Mill streets. More than 200 cars from the late gambling magnate's private collection are displayed here. They include the 1949 Mercury driven by James Dean in *Rebel Without a Cause* and the 1907 Thomas Flyer that won the 1908 around-the-world race. Even the architecture of the museum resembles an automobile of the fifties, with rounded corners and horizontal chrome strips.

Another unique collection is the **Harold's Club Gun Collection,** located on the third floor of one of Reno's oldest casinos, 250 N. Virginia St. North of downtown, the **Wilbur D. May Great Basin Adventure and Museum,** 1502 Washington St., features exotic artifacts collected by the department store magnate. The "adventure" portion features a children's park with a dinosaur pit, a stamp-mill replica, and a petting zoo.

Twenty-five miles (40 km) south of Reno off Highway 341 is **Virginia City,** one of the richest cities in the West in the 19th century, when it was known as "Queen of the Comstock." The town still has all of its original structures. The **V&T Railroad** offers a two-mile ride to Gold Hill from its depot at Washington and F streets, and the **Chollar Mine,** at the east end of town on South Street, provides guided tours of the mine shaft of one of the city's original gold mines.

Another historical city is **Carson City,** the Nevada state capital, 35 miles (56 km) south on Highway 395. Visitors can see the **Nevada State Railroad Museum's** displays of working railroad equipment; the **Nevada State Museum's** Indian artifacts, ghost-town replica, and underground mine tour; and the **State Capitol,** with paintings of every Nevada governor on walls of Alaskan marble.

(Phone numbers have 702 area codes.)

LAS VEGAS
Accommodation
LUXURY: **Alexis Park Resort,** 375 E. Harmon Ave., 89109 (Tel. 796-3300); **Caesar's Palace,** 3570 Las Vegas Blvd. S., 89109 (Tel. 731-7110). *MODERATE:* **Bally's,** 3645 Las Vegas Blvd. S., 89109 (Tel. 739-4111); **Desert Inn,** 3145 Las Vegas Blvd. S., 89114 (Tel. 733-4444); **Golden Nugget,** 129 E. Fremont St., 89125 (Tel. 385-7111); **Las Vegas Hilton,** 3000 Paradise Rd., 89193 (Tel. 732-5111); **Sands,** 3355 Las Vegas Blvd. S., 89109 (Tel. 733-5000). *BUDGET:* **Circus Circus,** 2880 Las Vegas Blvd. S., 89109 (Tel. 734-0410); **Four Queens,** 202 E. Fremont St., 89101 (Tel. 385-4011); **Imperial Palace,** 3535 Las Vegas Blvd. S. (Tel. 731-3311), **Union Palace,** 1 Main St., 89101 (Tel. 386-2110).

Restaurants
AMERICAN: **Tony Roma's,** 620 E. Sahara Ave. *CONTINENTAL:* **Alpine Village Inn,** 3003 Paradise Rd. *ITALIAN:* **Philips Supper House,** 4545 W. Sahara Ave. *JAPANESE:* **Benihana Village,** Las Vegas Hilton, 3000 Paradise Rd.

Attractions
Bonnie Springs Old Nevada, 1 Gun Fighter Lane, Bonnie Springs (Tel. 875-4191), 10:30am-5pm daily; **Clark County Heritage Museum,** 1830 S. Boulder Hwy., Henderson (Tel. 565-0907); **Ethel M Chocolate Factory**, 2 Cactus Garden Dr., Henderson (Tel. 458-8864), 9:30am-5:30pm daily, free; **Hoover Dam,** Hwy. 93, Boulder City (Tel. 293-8321), 9am-5pm daily; **Imperial Palace Auto Collection,** Imperial Palace Hotel, 3535 S. Las Vegas Blvd. (Tel. 733-3311), 9:30am-11pm daily; Lake Mead National Recreation Area, southeast of Las Vegas on Colorado River; **Liberace Museum,** 1775 E. Tropicana Ave. (Tel. 798-5595), 10am-5pm Mon-Sat, 12-5pm Sun; **Nevada State Museum,** 700 Twin Lakes Dr. (Tel. 486-5205), 11:30am-4:30pm Mon-Tue, 8:30am-4:30pm Wed-Sun; **Red Rock Recreation Area,** Spring Mountain Ranch State Park, Hwy. 159, 15 miles west of Las Vegas (Tel. 875-4191); **Ripley's Believe It or Not!,** Four Queens Hotel, 202 E. Fremont St. (Tel. 385-4011), 10am-12am Sun-Thu, 10am-2am Fri-Sat; **Valley of Fire State Park,** Hwy. 169, Overton (Tel. 397-2088).

Tourist Information
Las Vegas Convention and Visitors Authority, 3150 Paradise Rd., Las Vegas, NV 89109 (Tel. 733-2323 or 733-2244).

RENO
Accommodation
MODERATE: **Bally's,** 2500 E. Second St., 89595 (Tel. 789-2000, 800-648-5080); **Fitzgerald's,** 255 N. Virginia St. 89501 (Tel. 786-3663); **Harrah's,** Center and Second streets 89520 (Tel. 786-3232); **Hilton,** 255 N. Sierra St. 89501 (Tel. 322-1111). *BUDGET:* **Airport Plaza,** 1981 Terminal Way, 89502 (Tel. 348-6370); **Circus Circus,** 500 N. Sierra St. 89513 (Tel. 329-0711); **Eldorado,** 4th and Virginia streets 89505 (Tel. 786-5700); **River House,** First and Lake streets, 89505 (Tel. 329-0036).

Restaurants
AMERICAN: **The Christmas Tree,** 20007 Mt. Rose Hwy 431, 9 miles southwest of Reno (Tel. 849-0127). *CONTINENTAL:* **Casanova's,** 1695 S. Virginia St. (Tel. 786-6619). *FRENCH:* **La Table Francaise,** 3065 W. Fourth St. (Tel. 323-3200). *ITALIAN:* **Spaughi's,** 1573 S. Virginia St. (Tel. 323-5339). *MEXICAN:* **Micasa Too,** 2205 W. Fourth St. (Tel. 323-6466).

Attractions
Fleischmann Planetarium, University of Nevada-Reno (Tel. 784-4812), 6 shows daily 11am-9:15pm; **Harold's Club Gun Collection,** Harold's Club, 250 N. Virginia St. (Tel. 329-0881), 24 hours, free; **William F. Harrah Foundation National Automobile Museum,** Mill and Lake streets (Tel. 333-9300), 9:30am-5:30pm daily; **Wilbur D. May Great Basin Adventure,** 1502 Washington St. (Tel. 785-4319), 10am-6pm Tue-Sun, summer only; **Wilbur D. May Museum and Arboretum,** 1502 Washington St. (Tel. 785-5961), 10am-5pm Tue-Sun May-Sept, 10am- Wed-Sun Oct-May; **Nevada Museum of Art,** 160 W. Liberty St. and 549 Court St. (Tel. 329-3333), 10am-4pm Tue-Fri, 12-4pm Sat-Sun; **Nevada State Museum,** 600 N. Carson St., Carson City (Tel. 885-4810), 8:30am-4:30pm daily; **Nevada State Railroad Museum,** Hwy. 395 S., Carson City (Tel. 885-5168), 8:30am-4:30pm Fri-Sun, train runs Sat-Sun; **State Capitol,** Carson City (Tel. 885-5000); **Virginia City,** 25 miles south of Reno on Hwy. 341. Includes V&T Railroad (Tel. 847-0380), 10:30am-5:45pm summers; and the Chollar Mine (Tel. 847-0155), 12-5pm daily.

Tourist Information
Nevada Commission on Tourism, Capitol Complex, Carson City, NV 89710 (Tel. 885-4322 or 800-237-0774); **Reno/Sparks Convention and Visitors Authority,** Lake Mansion, 4590 S. Virginia St., Reno, NV 89502 (Tel. 827-7366 or 800-367-7366); **Reno Downtown Visitors Center,** 135 N. Sierra St. (Tel. 329-3558).

BAJA CALIFORNIA

The isolated Mexican peninsula of Baja, or "Lower," California extends for over 1,000 miles (1,600 km) south from California's southern border. This versatile desert country is famous for its fragile flora and fauna, some of it found nowhere else in the world – such as the strange cirio cactus and elephant trees that cast strange silhouettes on the earth. Rugged mountains send peaks over 10,000 feet (3,050 m), and nearly 2,500 miles (4,000 km) of rocky or sandy seashore surround the peninsula.

Geologists say Baja California was once attached to the Mexican mainland. Millions of years of violent upwellings and earth movement along the San Andreas Fault created the peninsula.

The Spanish believed Baja held great deposits of gold and other wealth. Hernan

Above: A prickly issue in the Anza Borrego National Park. Right: Where have all the flowers gone in the Kettleman Hills ?

Cortez, the conquistador of Mexico, took his troops there in 1535 – but the harshness of the weather and low productivity of the land forced them to depart after only two years.

It was a century and a half before a new attempt at settlement was made by Dominican and Jesuit missionaries. In 1697, a mission was established on the Gulf of California coast at **Loreto,** and the settlement became the first capital of Spanish California. But if religion was alive here, it was not so at Land's End, at the peninsula's southern tip. In the area now known as **Los Cabos,** pirates harbored in small bays to attack the treasure-laden Spanish galleons passing by.

In the early 1900s, hearty adventurers explored unmarked roadways by burro. And in the late 1940s, the pearl divers of **La Paz** inspired such writers as John Steinbeck. Virtually untouched by the Mexican Revolution of 1910, Baja California never really developed any industry outside of Tijuana and Mexicali in the north and La Paz in the south.

Baja finally came of age only in 1973, when the Mexican government opened Transpeninsular Highway 1. This serpentine asphalt road runs 1,053 miles (1,695 km) from Tijuana, on the border opposite San Diego, to **Cabo San Lucas**. The two-lane highway not only created economic support for the two underdeveloped Mexican states of Baja California Norte and Baja California Sur; it also brought a flood of tourists, whose money has provided capital for regional growth.

Touring Baja

Visitors to California with a few days to spare can explore a route south along the Pacific Ocean to Ensenada, then across the Sierra San Pedro Martir mountains to the village of San Felipe. The return trip, past the mouth of the Colorado River, crosses the California border at Mexicali.

Several car-rental agencies allow travel across the U.S.-Mexico border into northern Baja California, provided the renter takes out Mexican automobile insurance. Access beyond Ensenada with a rental car is limited.

Tijuana is *the* border town south of San Diego. Its shaggy reputation as a town of brothels, bars and brawls may have been appropriate before World War II, but today, Tijuana is a thriving metropolis of 700,000 people that caters to tourists and high-tech industries.

San Diego visitors can make Tijuana an easy day trip by taking the San Diego Trolley to the border at **San Ysidro**. Taxis await on the Mexican side for those who walk through the world's busiest border crossing. There are shopping delights on the main city streets, horse racing at **Agua Caliente Race Track** on the outskirts of town, and jaialai games at night in the downtown **Fronton** (stadium). In season, natives and tourists alike gather on Sundays at the **Tijuana Bull Ring** to offer "oles" to some of Mexico's and Spain's outstanding bullfighters, displaying their art to the strum of mariachi guitars.

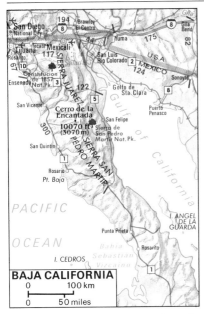

Near the international frontier, the Mexican government in 1982 opened the **Centro Cultural Tijuana** to present all of Mexico to American visitors. The center incorporates a museum, with exhibits on Mexican history and traditional life; an Omnimax theater, performing arts theater, restaurant, and shopping arcade.

South of Tijuana, easily reached by car, is **Rosarito Beach,** a fast-growing city at the edge of the Pacific Ocean. Weekends attract thousands of U.S. citizens, many of whom stay at the landmark Rosarito Beach Hotel, site of a casino in the 1930s. Hundreds more live here permanently in waterfront homes or condominiums, refugees from the crowded urban conditions and highland costs north of the border.

Ensenada and San Felipe

A four-lane toll road leads 65 miles (105 km) south to **Ensenada.** The drive is one of the most picturesque in Baja, reminiscent of the Big Sur coast with cliffs overlooking the changing blues of the Pacific. Ensenada was once known as the "yellowtail capital of the world" for its tuna fishing. But fishing is now secondary to tourism. Almost daily, ships from Los Angeles and San Diego visit the port, allowing passengers several hours for shopping and sightseeing.

About 140 miles (225 km) southeast lies **San Felipe,** a small fishing village where the sun almost always shines. It is unusual for two phenomena: its surging tides and its grunion runs.

Located near the head of the virtually landlocked Golfo de California, the village experiences tides akin to the Bay of Fundy. Coincidental with the tides come the grunion, small fish that mate during daylight hours in the gulf. (They are only seen at night on the Pacific shore.)

The 125 miles (201 km) of highway north to California affords birdwatchers opportunities to sight rare species along the **Rio Hardy** river. The industrial border town of **Mexicali** is the administrative capital of Baja California Norte.

Travelers with more time on their hands find southern Baja especially fascinating. Divers and anglers are enthralled by the hundreds of varieties of fish and underwater life. Moreover, California gray whales migrate to Baja's lagoons to mate and calf, while other species, such as finback and blue whales, dolphins and pinnipeds, have resident populations.

Crossing the border back into the United States can be a long process, depending upon the day and time. Patience is a virtue here.

Every visitor to Mexico is advised to carry a passport or other legal identification, such as a birth certificate. American citizens normally have no problem; visitors from other countries should check ahead into requirements. Travelers who have an indefinite or multiple entry visa for the U.S. in an old or an expired passport might take it along as well as an extra precautionary measure.

(Phone numbers have 706 area codes.)

ENSENADA
Accommodation
MODERATE: **Las Rosas by the Sea,** North Coast Road, Km 105 (P.O. Box 316; Tel. 674-4310); **San Nicolas,** Av. A. Lopez Mateos at Av. Guadalupe (Tel. 676-1901, 800-854-2900).
BUDGET: **Baja Beach & Tennis Club,** Punta Banda Rd., Maneadero (Tel. 678-1101, 800-228-7003); **Ensenada Inn,** Av. San Marcos at Av. Cipres (Tel. 676-2201).
Restaurants
AMERICAN: **Cha-Cha Burgers,** Blvd. L. Cardenas near Av. Sangines. *BAJA:* **Las Cazuelas,** Blvd. L. Cardenas at Av. Sangines.
FRENCH: **El Rey Sol,** 1000 Av. Lopez Mateos at Av. Blancarte.
MEXICAN: **Corralito,** 627 Av. Lopez Mateos near Av. Miramar. *SEAFOOD:* **La Cueva de los Tigres,** Av. Acapulco and Av. Las Palmas.
Attractions
Bodegas de Santo Tomas, winery, 666 Av. Miramar (Tel. 678-2509); **Fish Market,** Av. Gastelum and Blvd. L. Cardenas. **Hussong's Cantina,** 113 Av. Ruiz near Av. Lopez Mateos (Tel. 678-3210); **Riviera del Pacifico,** Blvd. L. Cardenas at Av. Riviera.
Tourist Information
Ensenada Convention Bureau (Tel. 678-2411); **State Tourism Office** (Tel. 676-2222).

MEXICALI
Accommodation
MODERATE: **Rancho la Puerta,** Tecate (P.O. Box 2548, Escondido, CA 92025; Tel. 744-4222, 800-443-7565). *BUDGET:* **Calafia,** 1495 Blvd. Justo Sierra (Tel. 568-3311, 800-262-2656); **Holiday Inn,** 2220 Blvd. N. Benito Juarez (Tel. 566-1300, 800-238-8000).
Attractions
Bosque de la Ciudad, city park, Av. Cardenas at Blvd. Villahermosa (Tel. 555-2833); **Galeria de la Ciudad,** art museum, 1209 Av. Obregon (Tel. 553-5044); **Museum de la Universite,** history museum, Av. de la Reforma (Tel. 562-5715).
Tourist Information
Mexicali Convention Bureau (Tel. 557-2561); **State Tourism Office** (Tel. 552-9795).

ROSARITO BEACH
Accommodation
BUDGET: **Plaza del Mar,** Toll Rd. Km 151, Puerto Nuevo (Tel. 685-9152, 800-262-2656); **Quinta del Mar,** 25500 Blvd. Benito Juarez (Tel. 612-1300, 800-228-7003); **Rosarito Beach,** Blvd. Benito Juarez south (Tel. 612-1106).

Restaurants
CONTINENTAL: **George's,** 75 Av. Costa Azul at Calle Sauce . *MEXICAN:* **Halfway House,** Hwy. 1 Km 53, south of Cantamar; **La Flor de Michoacan,** 146 Av. Benito Juarez. *SEAFOOD:* **El Pescador,** Hwy. 1 Km 44, north of Puerto Nuevo.
Tourist Information
Rosarito Beach Convention Bureau (Tel. 612-0396); **State Tourism Office** (Tel. 612-1005).

SAN FELIPE
Accommodation
MODERATE: **Castel San Felipe,** 148 Av. Mision de Loreto (Tel. 422-6900, 800-262-2656). *BUDGET:* **Riviera,** Frac. Sol y Mar (Tel. 577-1185); **La Trucha Vagabunda,** Av. de los Cedros S. (Tel. 577-1333).
Restaurants
CONTINENTAL: **La Perla,** Av. Mar de Cortez. *MEXICAN:* **Cafe Rosita,** seaside, north end of town.
SEAFOOD: **Corona,** 300 Av. Mar de Cortez (Tel. 577-1121).
Tourist Information
State Tourism Office (Tel. 577-1155).

TIJUANA
Accommodation
MODERATE: **Fiesta Americana,** 4500 Blvd. Agua Caliente (Tel. 681-7000, 800-223-2332). *BUDGET:* **Lucerna,** Paseo de los Heroes at Av. Rodriguez (Tel. 684-0120 or 688-3033); **Radisson-Paraiso,** 1 Blvd. Agua Caliente (Tel. 681-7200, 800-333-3333); **La Sierra,** 3566 Av. 16 de Septiembre (Tel. 686-1601).
Restaurants
BAJA: **Ibirrieria Guanajuato,** 102 Av. Abraham Gonzalez (Tel. 637-7070). *CONTINENTAL:* **Alcazar del Rio,** 564 Paseo de los Heroes (Tel. 684-2672). *ITALIAN:* **Boccaccio's,** 2500 Blvd. Agua Caliente (Tel. 686-2266). *MEXICAN:* **La Fonda Roberto's,** 3566 Ave. 16 de Septiembre (Tel. 686-4687). *SEAFOOD:* **La Marea,** 1935 Calle 5 near Av. Revolucion (Tel. 685-6590).
Attractions
Caliente Racetrack, Blvd. Agua Caliente at Calle Tapachula (Tel. 686-2001), daily; **Centro Cultural Tijuana,** Paseo de los Heroes at Mina Zona Rio (Tel. 684-1111, 684-1132); **Jai Alai Fronton Palacio,** 701 Av. Revolucion (Tel. 619-260-0452), 7pm Fri-Wed; **Plaza de Toros,** downtown (Tel. 686-1510), bullfights May-Sept.
Tourist Information
Tijuana Convention and Visitors Bureau (Tel. 684-0537, 800-522-1516). **State Tourism Office** (Tel. 684-2126).

THE FILM INDUSTRY

The earth rumbles and rattles, then it collapses, pulling a vehicle filled with innocents into a world gone mad. Telephone poles snap and roll, and power cables spark like electronic fireflies. A runaway rig crashes, and its cargo sprays outward. In fright, onlookers read the legend on the truck: "Highly Flammable." And they are sure they smell noxious gases in the air. A roar ... and they see a train wreck. An even more threatening roar ... and a towering, 15-foot (5-m) wall of water rushes furiously in their direction. The onlookers are frozen in horrific fascination. They think: This is a dream, right? No, not a dream, a nightmare. No, not a nightmare, an earthquake. That's it ... it's an earthquake. After all, this *is* Southern California.

Previous Pages: The great surfer's wave. The big Hollywood family on a mural. Above: Place Pigalle in Los Angeles. Right: Making up for Star Wars at Universal Studios.

It is an earthquake, all right – but Mother Nature did not create it. **Universal Studios Hollywood** did.

In fact, *Earthquake: The Big One* is the newest attraction in this movie theme park. It is a carefully staged "natural" phenomenon that utilizes state-of-the-art techniques to baffle and delight visitors caught on a tram in its temblor.

In slightly more than two minutes, 200 times a day, the studio takes trams filled with people through a cataclysm that, if it were really happening, would measure 8.3 on the Richter Scale. But they do it in a gargantuan, 25,000-square-foot (2,322-sq-m) soundstage that has been engineered to withstand the stresses.

Universal Studios Hollywood is an arm of Universal Studios, the world's busiest and biggest motion picture and television studio. Its stock in trade is transporting its guests into the wonderful world of motion-picture magic and illusion through tours behind the scenes in its 420-acre (170-hectare) front and back lots.

Besides the earthquake, the trams – and their passengers – encounter a 6.5-ton (5,900-kg), 30-foot (9-m) King Kong; a collapsing bridge; a flash flood; the shark from the movie *Jaws;* and a parting of the Red Sea. In addition, there are sets from hundreds of classic movies and TV shows. Live filming is often visible from the tram, as well.

When the tram tours are finished, there are live displays of stunts and special effects, with demonstrations from *Star Trek, Conan* and *Miami Vice,* and an animal actors' stage. Everything at Universal Studios Hollywood is geared to putting visitors "in the picture," so to speak, and to help them understand the effects that make movies work.

A Taste of Film History

Because of its theme park, Universal Studios is probably the best-known of Hollywood's dream factories. But it is by no means the only one; nor is it the only one open to the public. And movie studio tours are not the only way visitors can get a sense of film history, or see how movies are made. They can tour a film museum and the forecourt of Mann's Chinese Theater, stroll Hollywood Boulevard and take a bus tour past movie-star homes in Beverly Hills and Bel Air; buy a list of movie and TV shooting-location sites; even visit the graves of famous stars.

The movie industry in the Los Angeles area has come a long way since the early 1900s, when local boarding houses posted signs saying: "No Dogs and No Actors." These days, moviemaking is big business and illusion and so is the business of helping tourists view moviemaking, movie stars, and movie memorabilia.

According to film historians, the industry got its start in 1913, when Cecil B. De Mille began filming at a barn that now houses the **Hollywood Studio Museum.** He chose Hollywood primarily for its weather. De Mille had planned to film in

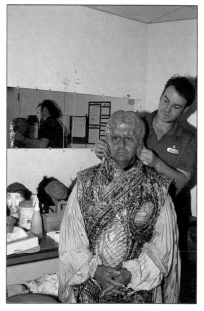

Flagstaff, Arizona, but a downpour greeted him when he stepped off the train there. So he reboarded and rode West until he found sunshine.

The Hollywood Studio Museum, 2300 N. Highland Ave. (Tel. 213-874- 2276), is located across from the Hollywood Bowl. Exhibits include silent movie memorabilia, a recreation of De Mille's office, and a small screening room that presents a short film about Hollywood. The barn itself is an exhibit, too, since it served De Mille as a set at times. In later years, it appeared in the television show *Bonanza.*

The industry is not restricted to Hollywood. Buildings throughout the Los Angeles area have been movie or TV stars. City Hall, for instance, in downtown Los Angeles, was a police station on the television series *Dragnet,* and served as the home of Clark Kent's newspaper, *The Daily Planet,* in *Superman.*

A Glendale warehouse was chosen to be the set for Mack Sennett's *Keystone Kops* comedies.

Universal Studios, 3900 Lankershim Blvd., Universal City (Tel. 818-508-9600), opened in 1915 as the brainchild of another movie pioneer, Carl Laemmle. Although 1989 marked the 25th anniversary of Universal's formal tours, the tour tradition dates back to Laemmle's day: He allowed the public on the lot until the 1920s, when talkies began.

Two other moviemaking establishments, give pleasant, much more intimate looks at studio operations. Bustling **Burbank Studios,** 400 Warner Blvd., Burbank (Tel. 818-954-1744), houses both Warner Brothers (here since 1928) and Columbia Pictures. Guides lead two 10 to 12-person tours daily through sound stages, a $20-million wardrobe inventory, and back lots such as Midwest Street, where Ronald Reagan once starred in *King's Row.* Also on view are prop rooms, including one where a chan-

delier from Errol Flynn's *Captain Blood* and lamps from Humphrey Bogart's *Casablanca* are stored.

Paramount Studios, 5555 Melrose Ave., Hollywood (Tel. 213-468-5575), offers limited two-hour tours that also provide glimpses of movie and TV productions. Among the rooms on view is one in which technicians create and dub sounds that are not recorded with actors' dialogue. That includes everything from footsteps to gunshots.

Other major movie studios include **Metro Goldwyn Mayer (MGM)/United Artists** in Culver City, **20th Century Fox** in Century City, and **Walt Disney Productions** in Burbank. Another tour is offered at **NBC Studios,** 3000 W. Alameda Ave., Burbank (Tel. 818-840-3537). The 75-minute walk not only gives a behind-the-scenes glimpse of TV production; it also puts guests themselves on camera. The two other television giants – **ABC** and **CBS** – are in L.A.

Studio tours vary day-to-day, depending upon daily schedules on their lots.

Above: Only kidding at the western stunt show. Right: You ain't seen nothing yet.

Since most sets stay closed, it is unlikely you will see any actual shooting.

Touring Tinseltown

To find film and TV shooting locations, check with **Hollywood On Location,** 8644 Wilshire Blvd., Beverly Hills (Tel. 213-649-9165). Each morning, this agency issues a list and map detailing street locations where crews are filming that day. Some locations are more active than others, so luck and timing can play a role in what is seen. Lists are available weekdays only, and cover 24 hours.

Serious stargazers will certainly see some in the sidewalks lining **Hollywood Boulevard.** These stars are bronze: Some 2,500 of them with celebrity names are imbedded in concrete.

To see stars' names as signed by the stars themselves – as well as footprints, handprints, and the like – head to **Mann's Chinese Theater,** 6925 Hollywood Blvd. (Tel. 213-464-8111). In 1927, Sid Grauman, who then owned this ornate

theater, began collecting these signatures of moviedom's elite when they attended gala premieres at his pagoda-like movie palace.

Starline Tours, with offices just down the street from Mann's, takes people by van through the Beverly Hills and Bel Air neighborhood, where many of the stars live. Their tours are popular with many movie buffs, who feel there is always the chance to see the celebrities themselves – perhaps at the gate, collecting the mail, or driving by in their Rolls Royces. Note **Pickfair,** 1143 Summit Drive, a colonial-style mansion commissioned by pioneer movie stars Mary Pickford and Douglas Fairbanks in 1919. It is often credited with having started the stars' rush to Beverly Hills.

Diehard movie buffs might prefer the excursions which are offered by **Grave Line Tours** (Tel. 213-876-4286). The company chauffeurs participants on two-and-a-half-hour hearse rides to the death sites and burial places of the movie colony's dearly departed.

THE FINE ARTS

Many California visitors are looking for a place in the sun, an amusing afternoon with Mickey Mouse and the whole Disney gang, or a girding look at the Golden Gate Bridge. Others think that is all well and good, but a vacation is not a vacation unless it includes a visit with a few old masters, or some high-profile avant-garde artists – or both.

California offers that, too. Many cities have fine-arts museums, and certainly the three major cities – Los Angeles, San Francisco and San Diego – have them in abundance. What follows are thumbnail sketches of just some of what is available.

Los Angeles

It was not long ago that "art" and "Los Angeles" seemed mutually exclusive terms. Then the city's **Museum of Con-**

Above: From Botticelli to Braque at the Norton Simon Museum. Right: What's the rush?

temporary Art opened, and even New Yorkers, who rarely credit any place west of the Hudson River as having culture, took notice. With the opening of major exhibition space for modern art, Los Angeles "is on the verge of attaining world-class status," declared the *New York Times Magazine* in 1986.

L.A.'s Museum of Contemporary Art, 250 S. Grand Ave., Los Angeles (Tel. 213-626-6222), is affectionately known to locals as MOCA. It has a permanent collection of international scope, including works by Mark Rothko, Robert Rauschenberg, and Louise Nevelson.

MOCA features art from 1940 to the present in an ultra-modern red sandstone building that looks like a geometry lesson sprung to life. Designed by Japanese architect Arata Isozaki, it is all planes and angles and pyramids – skylights, a sunken courtyard, and seven levels of expansive galleries.

MOCA is by no means the only major institution in the Los Angeles area featuring fine art. Those planning to do some

museum-hopping would do well to spend time, too, in several other galleries.

The **Los Angeles County Museum of Art**, 5905 Wilshire Blvd., Los Angeles (Tel. 213-857-6111), is the largest museum complex in Southern California. It houses paintings, sculptures, and decorative arts from a wide variety of periods and cultures. In the Ahmanson Gallery, for instance, are works by Picasso, Rembrandt, Durer, Hals, and De la Tour, among others.

Also at the museum are the Sinen-Kan collection of more than 300 Japanese scroll paintings and screens; an exhibit of Indian, Tibetan, and Nepalese religious art; 20th century art from the museum's permanent collection; and a tlot of traveling exhibits.

The **Norton Simon Museum**, 411 W. Colorado Blvd., Pasadena (Tel. 818-449-6840), has a fine collection of European paintings, drawings and sculptures from the early Renaissance to the 20th century. There are Rembrandts (*Self Portrait*, for one), Botticellis, Goyas and Rubenses here, as well as works by Van Gogh, Renoir, Matisse, Picasso, Braque and Gris. Not to be missed are the bronzes by Degas and sculptures by Rodin and Henry Moore.

In the same area are **The Huntington Library, Art Gallery and Botanical Gardens,** 1151 Oxford Road, San Marino (Tel. 818-405-2273). This is where Thomas Gainsborough's *Blue Boy* makes its home, amidst a cornucopia of 18th and 19th-century English and French art, including pieces by Van Dyck and Turner, and an exhibit that traces American painting from 1730 through 1930.

But art is only one aspect of this outstanding cultural complex. The library holds some six million rare volumes, including a Gutenberg Bible and the earliest known edition of Chaucer's *Canterbury Tales,* and the beautiful gardens have tropical and temperate blossoms and plants galore.

The **J. Paul Getty Museum**, 17895 W. Pacific Coast Hwy., Malibu (Tel. 213-

454-6541), sits high on a hillside over-looking the ocean. It contains one of America's finest collections of Greek and Roman antiquities in a modern recreation of a first century Roman villa. Also here are rare tapestries, illuminated manu-scripts, Renaissance and Baroque art, and works from other periods. Among the masters represented are Rembrandt, Rubens, De la Tour, Van Dyck, Gains-borough and Boucher.

Also worth viewing are the museum building and environs. The Corinthian columns, reflecting pool, fountains – indeed, the edifice itself – are fashioned after the Villa dei Papyri, which was ex-cavated in 18th-century Herculaneum from the volcanic residue left by the eruption of Mount Vesuvius in 79 A.D.

As with other attractions in the greater Los Angeles area, it takes some traveling to see each of these museums. But every one has collections worth seeing.

San Francisco

Several museums are arrayed in San Francisco's Golden Gate Park. At the **M.H. de Young Memorial Museum** (Tel. 415-750-3600), located on the park's Music Concourse, some 64 galler-ies are gathered around a central court that holds the portal of a 12th century Spanish monastery. This is the oldest museum in the West, but it possesses arti-facts and artworks far older than the United States itself. Some date to ancient Egypt. There are also pieces from early Greece and Rome, from Africa and Oceania, from Asia, Europe and the Americas.

Of special interest is the Nelson Rock-efeller collection of 150 North American paintings by artists such as Copley, Bing-ham, West, Eakins and Sargent. Among artists represented in the museum's per-manent collection are painters like Rem-brandt, Rubens, Titian, Goya, Hals, Fra Angelico, Tintoretto, Pieter de Hooch, and Cranach. In addition, a blockbuster traveling exhibit is often on view.

Sharing a building with the de Young is the **Asian Art Museum** (Tel. 415-668-8921), the only museum in the United States devoted exclusively to Asian art. In its Avery Brundage Collection of more than 10,000 pieces, it has one of the world's major groupings of Asian jades, bronzes, ceramics, and paintings. Fea-tured are works from Japan, Korea, China, Tibet, Nepal, India, Pakistan, Afghanistan, Iran, Syria, Turkey, and Southeast Asia – some of them as many as 6,000 years old. The collection was the legacy of the former head of the Inter-national Olympic Committee.

Not in the park, but conveniently lo-cated in the Veterans Building at the Civic Center, is the **Museum of Modern Art**, Van Ness Avenue at McAllister Street (Tel. 415-863-8800). This is the place to see abstract expressionism, as well as every other major art movement of the 20th century. Its permanent collec-tion includes works by artists like Geor-gia O'Keeffe, Jackson Pollock, Paul Klee, Mark Rothko, Clyfford Still, Alex-ander Calder, Willem de Kooning and Robert Motherwell.

The **California Palace of the Legion of Honor** (Tel. 415-750-3600) graces a hilltop in Lincoln Park, and its facade is equally impressive. Built as a memorial to the state's fallen soldiers of World War I, this shining white neoclassical struc-ture is an exact replica of the Legion of Honor in Paris, with similar arches and columns. The Palace has a noteworthy print collection, with more than 100,000 items; an important collection of French paintings, including works by Monet, Manet, Degas, Corot, and Fragonard; and some fine sculptures, including Rodin's *The Thinker*. There are also displays of furniture, porcelains, tapestries and deco-

Right: The etched face of suffering; the Hulk busting out of a water tank in Sacramento.

rative arts. Outside San Francisco, too, many museums boast fine art collections.

Also of interest architecturally, the **University of Berkeley Museum of Art** (2626 Bancroft Way, Tel. 415-642-1207) contains works of art of the modern era and now incorporates the **Pacific Film Archive**, where rare pieces of international film history can be seen. The **San Jose Museum of Art** (110 S. Market Street, Tel. 408-294-2787) exhibits textiles as well as drawings and prints done by regional artists. Right at the heart of Sacramento's old town stands the **Crocker Art Museum** (216 O Street, Tel. 916-446-4677) with its collection of paintings from the early Renaissance to the present day, sculptures, pottery and textiles.

San Diego

In California's southernmost major city, too, many of the museums are clustered together – in this case, Balboa Park. They include the very interesting **San Diego Museum of Art** and the **Timken Art Gallery.**

The Museum of Art (Tel. 619-232-7931) includes in its collection a number of old masters. There are paintings from other categories as well – Italian Renaissance, Spanish Baroque, French and Dutch impressionist, and contemporary American. On view, too, are a sculpture garden, an Asian art exhibit, and fine touring exhibits.

The Timken Gallery (Tel. 619-239-5548) occupies the only privately owned building in the vast park. Timken is known for its European and early American works. It also has a fine collection of Russian Orthodox icons.

For a look at the avant-garde in this area, the place to visit is the **La Jolla Museum of Contemporary Art**, 700 Prospect St., La Jolla (Tel. 619-454-3541). Housed in a villa overlooking the Pacific Ocean are post-1950s works, including worth viewing sculptures, paintings, photographs, and a design exhibit focusing on objects in everyday use.

213

A LITERARY PILGRIMAGE

In much the same way that it has drawn gold-seekers and sun-worshippers, California has always lured and nurtured writers of all subjects and literary styles.

In the 19th century, it was a magnet for adventurous young writers like Mark Twain, Bret Harte and Robert Louis Stevenson, who found rich material not in the gold streams but in the untamed wilds and lusty atmosphere of a new state, a continent away from the civilized East Coast.

In the 20th century, California produced a native son, John Steinbeck, to immortalize the grasslands of the Salinas Valley, while San Francisco's coffee houses provided sustenance for a generation of "beat" poets and novelists. Like Twain and Harte before them, they found a free-wheeling milieu in which to create.

Above: World famous author Jack London lived here, in Glen Ellen.

Although many of California's prominent literary landmarks have long since fallen victim to earthquake, fire or "progress", many more remain.

Any literary tour of California must begin in San Francisco. Besides the richness of its own literary past, San Francisco makes a central base from which to explore other sites, such as Jack London's estate in Glen Ellen and the Steinbeck house in Salinas.

Much of San Francisco's early literary activity centered in what is now the Financial District. The **Transamerica Pyramid** occupies the former site of the Montgomery Block, an impressive brick structure where Jack London, Ambrose Bierce, George Sterling, and other turn-of-the-century scribes congregated at the **Bank Exchange Saloon.** The lobby of the Pyramid contains memorabilia from the late lamented bar, including photographs of its more famous patrons.

Among other scant traces of 19th century authors is the **Bohemian Club** at Post and Taylor streets. Now an exclusive club with former presidents on its membership rolls, the Bohemian Club was once the domain of scruffier characters like Twain, Harte, Bierce, and poet Joaquin Miller. Embedded in the building's facade is a bronze tablet depicting characters from some of Harte's stories.

Due in part to the great earthquake and fire of 1906, few reminders of Twain's era have survived in downtown San Francisco. The young Samuel Clemens worked as a reporter here in the 1860s and chronicled his impressions of the city in *Roughing It*.

In the 1920s, mystery writer Dashiell Hammett immortalized detective Sam Spade in *The Maltese Falcon*. Hammett had learned the tools of his trade after he signed on at the Pinkerton Detective Agency, Suite 314 of the massive, flatiron **Flood Building** at Powell and Market streets. He turned his experiences into novels and stories while living in various apartments, including one at 620 Eddy St. and another at 891 Post St.

Locations mentioned in *The Maltese Falcon* are scattered throughout the blocks surrounding Union Square. For instance, a bronze plaque on a Bush Street apartment building, bordering a spooky little alley called Burritt Street, proclaims that, "On approximately this spot, Miles Archer, partner of Sam Spade, was done in by Brigid O'Shaughnessy." The grande dame of Union Square, the **Westin St. Francis Hotel,** appeared in the book as the "St. Mark."

After a walking tour of Hammett landmarks, it makes sense to stop for a steak or chop at the author's favorite restaurant – **John's Grill** at 63 Ellis St. Upstairs, in The Maltese Falcon Room, are photographs and memorabilia of the author and of Humphrey Bogart, who played Spade in the movie version.

North of downtown, along Kearny Street, is **Portsmouth Square,** a favorite resting spot for Robert Louis Stevenson. The author of classic adventure stories

lived in the city for a brief period during 1879-1880. Sheltered in a poplar grove, a monument to Stevenson depicts a galleon in full sail: the *Hispaniola* of his best-loved book, *Treasure Island*.

Kearny Street leads to North Beach, the eclectic, Italian-flavored neighborhood where the so-called Beat Generation – among them Jack Kerouac, William Burroughs, Allen Ginsberg, Gary Snyder and Lawrence Ferlinghetti – found a creative haven from the bland Eisenhower years of the 1950s. The era's most prominent landmark, Ferlinghetti's own **City Lights Bookstore** at 261 Columbus Ave., remains a popular place for book browsing and poetry readings. Writers still sip espresso at such former Beat hangouts as **Vesuvio's, Café Trieste** and the **Savoy Tivoli.**

The Haunts of Jack London

Across the bay, in Oakland, the most prominent literary landmark – the waterfront **Jack London Square** – is also an appealing area for restaurants and shopping. Though he was born in San Francisco, London spent his rowdy youth in Oakland, raiding oyster beds and drinking at a saloon called **Heinhold's First and Last Chance.** The wood-frame shack is still open for business at the foot of Webster Street in the Square.

Next door is the **Jack London Cabin,** a tiny log structure moved here from Canada's Yukon. London lived in it in 1897 during the Klondike Gold Rush, and later drew on that material for his novels, *Call of the Wild* and *White Fang*.

Gold rush-era storyteller Bret Harte also spent his early adulthood in Oakland. In the 1860s, he lived in the 500 block of Fifth Street, six blocks from modern London Square. Harte's former street is now the **Bret Harte Boardwalk**, a row of restored Victorian buildings that house restaurants and shops. The **Colonel Starbottle Bar** is named for one of

Harte's characters, and contains a portrait of the author's stepfather – on whom the colonel was based.

There are more literary landmarks north of the Bay Area. In the tiny hamlet of Glen Ellen, an hour's drive from San Francisco in the wine-growing region of Sonoma County, London established a permanent home after his books brought him wealth and success before he was 30. **Jack London State Historic Park** contains the magnificent ruins of Wolf House, his stone-and-redwood estate that burned down in August 1913 shortly before it was completed.

London died three years later at the age of 40. His wife, Charmaine, went on to build the **House of Happy Walls** on a nearby site. Today, that house is a museum of London memorabilia, including his roll-top desk, manuscripts, photographs, and other mementoes from the

Above: Modern poetry on performance in San Francisco. Right: Beat poet Lawrence Ferlinghetti's bookstore in San Francisco.

author's far-flung travels to Alaska and the South Pacific.

Stevenson and Steinbeck

Northeast of Glen Ellen, in the Napa Valley town of St. Helena, the **Silverado Museum** has a sizeable collection of items from Robert Louis Stevenson, who lived in the region during the first year of his marriage in 1876. On display are manuscripts, rare first editions, toys from his childhood, and items from his plantation in Samoa, where he died in 1894.

More Stevenson memories are exhibited 150 miles south in Monterey, where the impoverished Scottish author rented a room in an adobe building now known as the **Robert Louis Stevenson House,** 530 Houston St. His small, sparsely furnished room is preserved, as are his plaid blanket and the velvet coat he wore everywhere. Downstairs in the Samoan Room are various Pacific artifacts and souvenirs – including a photo of Stevenson with Hawaii's King Kalakaua.

216

More closely associated with Monterey is John Steinbeck, who used the town as the backdrop for such novels as *Tortilla Flat, Sweet Thursday* and *Cannery Row*. Although Steinbeck today would hardly recognize the **Cannery Row** he knew – an old street lined with sardine canneries – a few of the places of which he wrote remain visible amid restaurants and kitschy souvenir shops. Look closely to spot the buildings that housed Doc Rickett's **Pacific Biological Laboratories**, 800 Cannery Row, and the **Wing Chong Market,** now the Old General Store. The true heart of Steinbeck country is 20 miles (32 km) inland in Salinas, the sleepy agricultural town where the author was born and raised. **Steinbeck House,** a gingerbread Victorian building at 132 Central Ave., was where he spent his boyhood. It is now a lunch restaurant, operated by a volunteer group called the Valley Guild, with some Steinbeck memorabilia on display.

Elsewhere in town is the **John Steinbeck Library,** where the author researched *East of Eden*, a novel set in Salinas. The library contains the Steinbeck Room, with photographs, first editions, and manuscripts on display. Tapes of interviews with people who knew Steinbeck are also available.

Not only was Salinas the birthplace of Steinbeck (1902-1968); it was his final resting place as well. His grave is beneath a large oak tree at the **Garden of Memories** cemetery, 768 Abbott St.

Carmel attracted many writers and artists in the early part of the 20th century. By far the most elaborate of their dwellings is **Tor House,** constructed by poet Robinson Jeffers in 1918 on a craggy knoll overlooking the Pacific at Scenic Road and Ocean View Avenue. The low-ceilinged rooms are filled with portraits, books and unusual art objects, including a white stone from the Great Pyramid of Egypt. Highlights of the small estate are Hawk Tower, a detached edifice set with stones from the Great Wall of China, and a Roman villa which served the poet's musician wife, Una, as a retreat.

CALIFORNIAN CUISINE

California is associated with things fresh and original. This also describes the Golden State's reputation when it comes to food and wine. From north to south, California is overflowing with fields of green, bearing everything from kiwifruit to avocados, broccoli to grapes. Food festivals celebrate the state's agricultural bonanza. In southern California, the famous **Ventura Strawberry Festival** brings people from around the state to sample the plumpest berries from the coastal fields, now concocted into cakes, pies, sauces and crepes.

Another favorite event is the **Gilroy Garlic Festival,** held every June in a town just south of San José. Epicureans can indulge in all manner of food bathed, dipped, dressed, sprinkled and baked in wonderfully aromatic garlic. Monterey County hosts several food fests, includ-

ing the **Castroville Artichoke Festival**, held every September for more than three decades. A newer food event is the **Great Monterey Squid Festival,** a culinary spectacular in which visitors can sample calamari cooked in more than 20 different ways. It is a three-day party with big-name entertainment.

One of the most unique California food experiences can be enjoyed every Thursday night in downtown San Luis Obispo. Here, visitors and locals alike come out in droves to revel at the Farmers Market. Recognized as one of the best open markets in the United States, the **San Luis Obispo Farmers Market** features a host of fresh local foods. In addition, area restaurants set up booths to serve delicious barbecued ribs and chicken.

A world-famous food district and market is San Francisco's **Fisherman's Wharf.** Visitors can sample fresh crab and lobster served with crusty sourdough bread. The taste of this sidewalk feast is unforgettable. A more formal dining is available at numerous bayfront restau-

Above: Chinese ducks in the window. Right: Gifts from the Pacific on Fisherman's Wharf.

rants at the wharf and nearby Pier 39. The city's Chinese cuisine is another gastronomical treat. For a new twist on Asian specialities, there is the **China Moon Café** on Post Street. At this small, informal cafe, chef Barbara Tropp prepares inventive versions of traditional specialties. Original Chinese food – in particular, Cantonese *dim sum*, which is served until midday – can be found at **Yank Sing's** in Battery Street and at **Tung Fong's** and the **Asia Garden** in Pacific Street, the atmosphere in the latter two making them particularly appealing places to dine.

California Cuisine

Be it from the earth or the sea, California's abundance of fresh, delicious harvests has given birth to a cuisine that celebrates food. Most food critics agree that the notion of California cuisine started with a self-taught chef, Alice Waters. She owns and operates Berkeley's favorite *haute cuisine* venue – **Chez Panisse.** She credits her success to her uncompromising passion for the freshest ingredients, the purest sauces, and an elegantly simple presentation. Chez Panisse is also famous for its warm, welcoming environment, where dinner conversations often spill over from table to table. A number of her chefs have learnt from her example and opened their own restaurants. The most interesting result of this has to be the new vegetarian restaurant **Green's** in Fort Mason, San Francisco, where the kitchen staff create the most innovative dishes with tofu and vegetables.

Southern California, too, knows California cuisine and celebrates it every night at **Michael's** in Santa Monica. Searching the globe for the best ingredients, Michael's presents many delectable originals like fresh Pacific oysters, deep-fried and served with zucchini flowers and salsa. The personable style of owner Michael McCarty sets the mood for this upbeat, relaxed-but-elegant restaurant that has been touted as serving California cuisine at its finest.

California cuisine would not be complete without mentioning **Spago's** in Los Angeles. It has been called overbearing, overcrowded and overdone, but no one can deny the cooking genius of chef and owner Wolfgang Puck. He is the ultimate improviser, yet he has absolute confidence in his concoctions. The results of his whimsy are fabulous pizzas with duck or lamb sausage, delicate pastas, and folk food that reintroduces mustard greens and sweetbreads.

No one should forget San Diego when it comes to fine dining or casual seaside nibbling. Seafood and Mexican cuisine come to mind first. **Anthony's Star of the Sea Room** is a dining tradition; more recently, the downtown **Pacific Grill** has been getting rave reviews. The Old Town is famous for its Mexican meals in hacienda-style restaurants or in quaint family-style cafés.

La Jolla offers great dining and atmosphere. **Top of the Cove** is acclaimed for its continental cuisine, and boasts one of the largest wine cellars in the area. **The Marine Room** is a La Jolla landmark: Waves literally crash upon the windows of this elegant restaurant.

Californians have always been ready for new trends in food. In recent years, the Golden State has welcomed Southwest cuisine, Thai food, Cajun and Creole cookery, and the rebirth of all-American food: the Fifties diner. The variety of ethnic and new-style cuisine makes dining an event to be savored throughout the state.

The Wineries

What better way to complement fabulous food than with world-class wine? California's vineyards produce wines that are famous around the world. From Mendocino to San Diego, the state is known

Right: An old–time bar in Columbia, near Sacramento.

for its wine production. Most wineries offer visitors' tours and tastings; the ideal time to visit is during the fall harvest.

Nowhere but the Napa and Sonoma valleys is wine touring so celebrated. The California winemaking tradition began in the Sonoma Valley when Franciscan fathers founded the Sonoma mission. Today, the valley is filled with historic landmarks, like the famous **Sebastiani Winery,** dating to the turn of the 20th century, and **Buena Vista Winery,** once the largest in the world.

Other Sonoma wineries worth a visit are the Benziger family's **Glen Ellen Winery,** south of Kenwood, and the **Chateau St. Jean,** north of Kenwood. After tasting premium white varieties in the Chateau's French Mediterranean mansion, visitors can enjoy a picnic dinner on the winery grounds while listing to a Mozart concert. At the south end of the Sonoma Valley, the **Gloria Ferrer Champagne Caves** offer underground tours: The Ferrer family is the world's largest producer of *methode champenoise* sparkling wines, the best known of which is Freixenet.

The Napa Valley is home to some of the largest wineries in California, including **Christian Brothers, Charles Krug** and **Robert Mondavi.** The valley's smaller wineries are equally impressive, however, and often allow more intimate looks at the winemaking process.

Stony Hill Vineyard is one of those small wineries. It is also known as one of the most prestigious wineries in the Napa Valley, and probably the hardest to reach – due to its dramatic location on a crest of the Mayacamas Mountains above St. Helena. The winery produces riesling, gewurztraminer and chardonnay wines, but in too small a quantity to permit tasting. Tours are offered by advance reservation only.

In Yountville, **Domaine Chandon** offers "stars from heaven". While this subsidiary of France's Moet-Hennessy

company is not permitted to call its sparkling wines "champagne," its bubbly is no less memorable. Visitors see all phases of the *methode champenoise.* The winery's restaurant is exceptional, and is open for lunch and dinner by reservation.

Speaking of food again, a Napa Valley tradition is **Mustards Grill,** a quick hop north of Yountville. Mustards' country-style exterior hints at the traditional earthiness of the cuisine. The emphasis is on freshness and the chef's home-smoked meats and fowl.

Grape-growing is not limited to the Napa and Sonoma valleys. Other "wine countries" can be found in the Sierra foothills, the mountains of Monterey County, and southern California's San Fernando and Temecula valleys.

More grapes are grown each year in Monterey County than in any other county in the United States, including Napa. The rolling hillsides of the Salinas Valley are home to seven wineries, all of them open to the public. Resembling a rambling ranch house, the **Jekel Vine-yard** in Greenfield is worth a detour to sample its award-winning wines.

Southern California's reputation for quality winemaking has steadily improved in recent years. Winemaking began in the 1840s in the scenic Temecula Valley, a short drive from San Diego; only now is it becoming well known.

Along Rancho California Road, visitors find a wide variety of Temecula wineries. **Filsinger Vineyard and Winery** makes several premium white wines, but is especially proud of its brut champagne, the latest rage. At **Callaway Vineyard and Winery,** guided tours include discussions on "South Coast cuisine" with menu suggestions for cooking with herbs, spices, fresh produce, and Temecula wines.

At the **Bernardo Winery** in Rancho Bernardo, visitors can sample and purchase homemade olive oil and fresh pasta. For a complete sit-down affair, the **John Culbertson Winery** in Temecula features California cuisine in its charming Champagne Café.

OCEAN SPORTS

Ever since the Beach Boys told the world about *Surfin' USA* in the early 1960s, and Frankie Avalon and Annette Funicello joined in with their *Beach Blanket Bingo* movies, California has been viewed as the world capital of sun and fun. The Golden State's Pacific coastline appeals to water sports enthusiasts of all kinds. From San Diego to the northern coast, there is always something exciting happening.

The most popular sport is swimming, and there are excellent beaches in protected bays all along the coast. The best part of the beaches are, of course, used for sunbathing, the aim being to produce the kind beautiful body that young Californians then show off in sporting activities. An even tan is as much a part of sport as it is of the Californian way of life. And

so it is that there are volleyball courts on many of the beaches, attracting players as well as spectators who flock to see the heroes and heroines of the game. If you want to swim, it is best to do so within view of a manned lifeguard station, as even excellent swimmers may be caught by unseen rip currents or undertows. Lifeguards patrol many public beaches year-round, but they are most active in summer. Manned lifeguard stations fly the American flag and post signs listing water, tide and weather conditions.

Many beaches permit both swimming and surfing, but in separate designated zones. Swimmers may swim free of potential collision with surfers in areas between two red flags, posted on shore.

Surfing

Surfers can be found riding the waves in San Diego, Orange and Los Angeles counties, as well as other locations up the coast to Santa Cruz and even as far north as San Francisco.

Above: Catching the wind at Hookipa Beach. Right: Candidates for muscle beach.

In the San Diego area, surfers favor **Tourmaline Surf Park, Windansea Beach** and **La Jolla Shores,** all in La Jolla. At **Moonlight State Beach** and **Swami's** in Encinitas, surfers may share the water with dolphins swimming close to the shore!

Hundreds of veteran body surfers challenge the waves at the world-famous **Wedge** in Newport Beach. Because of the treacherous shore break, no board surfing is allowed here.

Some of the state's best waves break farther north at **Huntington State Beach,** home of the International Surf Competition the first weekend in September.

In Los Angeles County, **Redondo Beach** is considered the second home (after Hawaii) of American surfing: The first crude 8-foot board was shaped from redwood in the 1920s by two young men who had seen the boardriders in Hawaii.

On the south central coast near Lompoc, good surf is found at **Tarantula Point** about one-half mile south of the remote Jalama Beach County Park. To reach the park from Highway 1, one must take a 15-mile (24-km) country road to the coast.

Surfing flourishes in northern California as well. In Santa Cruz, an area known as **Steamers Lane,** off Lighthouse Point, is surf heaven for hot doggers – but not for the inexperienced, as a wipeout here may toss one onto rocks.

Some beaches permit surfing all day, while others restrict the sport to morning and late-afternoon hours. An area marked by two red flags, posted on shore, indicates a swimming-only beach; surfers must then surf outside the two red flags. A yellow flag with a black ball in the center indicates "No surfing."

Sailboarding

Also known as Windsurfing, this growing sport – combining elements of surfing and sailing – is permitted at de-

signated areas along many beaches and bays. Most sailboarders ride the winds beyond the surf; however, at some beaches, sailboarders are allowed to ride the waves along with surfers. It is here, in the wild surf, that one can see some of the most spectacular sailboarding.

Near San Diego, some favorite sailboarding locations are **Mission Bay, Tourmaline Surf Park,** and **Glorietta Bay** near Coronado Beach. Sailboarders also throng to the **Seal Beach Municipal Pier** and **Long Beach Harbor** in the Los Angeles area. **Long Beach Windsurf Center** offers a six-hour course with all equipment provided.

Leo Carillo, Malibu, Santa Barbara and **Jalama Beach** are popular sailboarding locations further up the coast. And in San Francisco, sailboarders find ideal conditions at **China Beach** and off **Fort Mason Center,** in view of the Golden Gate Bridge and city skyline. Sailboard rentals and instruction are available from Sausalito Sailboards and Batten and Boards, both in Sausalito.

Boating

Visiting mariners find ample opportunities to explore California's coastal waters. Open-party boats, charters and rental boats are available at many small harbors and in the busiest pleasure-boating marinas.

In San Diego, sailing, power boating, water skiing and jet skiing can be enjoyed on the city's twin harbors of **San Diego Bay** and nearby **Mission Bay.** Rental boats, equipment and instruction are available from Mission Bay Sports Center, Seaforth Boat Rental, and Coronado Boat Rental.

Southern California pleasure-boating capital is **Newport Beach** in Orange County, where elegant homes with private docks line the harbor. Boats are available from Balboa Boat Rentals at Balboa Pavilion. On the upper bay, **Newport Dunes Aquatic Park** offers rentals of sea kayaks, water bicycles, ski boats and pedal boats.

Boaters on **Long Beach Harbor** cruise within view of the majestic *Queen Mary*. Power boats for fishing, water skiing, or pleasure cuising may be rented from Club Nautico. Long Beach Water Sports has a 3.5 hour course in sea kayaking. Just south of Long Beach, **Gondola Getaways** offers a one-hour cruise around Naples Island in Alamitos Bay, complete with a chilled bottle of California char donnay and a basket of French bread, cheese and salami.

Near Los Angeles, the well-developed **Marina del Rey** has sightseeing cruises, private charters, and boat rentals at Fisherman's Village. Rent-a-Sail offers sailboat rentals and instruction.

On the northern coast, sailors challenge the winds and sometimes tricky waters on **San Francisco Bay.** Spectators enjoy frequent regattas. Charters are available from A Day on the Bay, Rendezvous Charters, and Sail Tours of San Francisco.

Diving

Another colorful world, alive with ocean creatures and undersea flora, awaits snorkelers and scuba divers along California's varied coastline.

Some of the clearest waters may be at La Jolla Cove, at the southern end of the **San Diego-La Jolla Underwater Park.** The taking of sea life from this reserve is prohibited. But lobster and abalone, in season, may be taken from nearby coves, from manmade reefs off **Imperial Beach** and **Silver Strand State Beach,** and from reefs off **Sunset Cliffs.**

Many of the best diving locations around here are accessible only by boat. Dive-boat charters and instruction can be arranged from San Diego Divers Supply and the Diving Locker.

Off **Catalina Island,** divers explore the mysteries of underwater caves, cliffs and shipwrecks. **Catalina Underwater Park** off Casino Point offers excellent viewing for scuba divers or snorkelers; the adjacent game preserve is for snorkelers only. There are dozens of dive locations, many within 30 feet off shore.

Rocky coves in **Palos Verdes,** and offshore kelp beds, promise excellent viewing and opportunities for taking abalone, rockfish, and game fish in metropolitan Los Angeles.

Giant kelp forests create a rich marine habitat around the **Channel Islands,** off the Ventura County coast. Marine life here once nourished the Chumash Indians, who once inhabited the islands. Island Packers offer dive trips to the islands, now a national park.

Colder waters on the northern coast do not discourage wet-suited divers from exploring the plentiful kelp beds of **Monterey Bay.** Here, divers are likely to encounter playful sea otters, seals and sea

Right: Life seems to be pure fun on the golden beaches of California.

lions, as well as the usual game fish, lobster and abalone found further south. Charter boats take divers to the offshore reefs, but the Monterey Bay breakwater and **San Simeon Bay** are easily accessible and abundant in sea life.

Scuba divers are required by law to display a diver's down flag on a flotation device, to alert boaters of their whereabouts. They must stay within a 100-foot (30-m) parameter of the marker. A valid California fishing license is required for the taking of fish and shellfish.

Fishing

The California coast is home to more than 250 species of fish. Many public piers allow free unlicensed fishing day or night. Otherwise, there is surf fishing from shore, or sport-fishing from a chartered or rented boat. Visitors are advised to contact charter companies and tackle shops to find out what is biting.

Corbina, croaker, halibut and perch are the most common surf fish on the south-ern coast. Northern surf fish include cabezon, greenling, ling cod and rock-fish.

Southern California's deep-sea fish include barracuda, sea bass, bluefin and yellowtail tuna, albacore tuna (in summer), halibut, marlin and sailfish. In northern California, possibilities include rock cod, bass, albacore and king salmon.

Salmon may be caught during spring and fall in open waters from **Morro Bay** to **San Francisco Bay,** but the best salmon fishing is on the northern coast above **Fort Bragg.**

Everyone 16 years or older must obtain a California state license to fish. Most game fish and shellfish may be taken year-round, but there are restrictions on sizes, catch limits, and methods used. They are described in a Department of Fish and Game publication, available free of charge wherever fishing licenses are sold. The best fishing months are April to October in the south; January to October along the central coast; and February to September on the northern coast.

MOUNTAIN SPORTS

When people think of California, the "Golden State", it is often golden beaches that come to mind. But the state's incredible diversity also includes impressive mountain ranges.

The peaks above Los Angeles and Palm Springs reach to more than 11,500 feet (3,500 m). The California Coast Range runs the length of the state, with summits as high as 9,000 feet (2,750 m). Both sets of mountains offer a wide variety of hiking and mountain-biking trails, rock-climbing sites and even some skiing resorts.

The **Sierra Nevada**, one of North America's premier mountain ranges, is California's giant backbone. From Mount Whitney in the south, at 14,494 feet (4418m), to the enormous volcanoes of the north, the Sierra are a treasure trove of mountain scenery and recreation.

Above: A cliff hanger. Right: Gross-country skiing at Badger Pass.

Some of North America's best skiing and river rafting is here, and its most famous climbing location of all is in the Sierra.

The jewels of the Sierra are its national parks, each with a wide range of hiking trails, nature centers, and camping. **Sequoia National Park** and **Kings Canyon National Park** are characterized by their big trees, of course, and by deep river canyons slicing under snow-covered peaks. Most scenic areas in these parks can be reached by trail only.

In contrast, **Yosemite National Park,** California's most famous, is easily accessed by car, although vast regions remain a true wilderness reached only by foot. Most of the volcanic wonders at **Lassen National Park** in northern California are located just off the road.

Yosemite Valley, a picture-perfect canyon of granite cliffs and 2,300-foot (700-m) waterfalls, is America's cathedral of big wall climbing. In summer, climbers from around the world challenge famous routes like the sheer, 5,400-foot (1,650-m) **El Capitan.** Other faces, like **Half Dome** and **Sentinel Rock,** are equally attractive to climbers.

Yosemite is a great place to learn climbing. The Yosemite Mountaineering School runs summer classes from its base in the 8,000-foot (2,400-m) Tuolumne Meadows. Advanced climbers can rent equipment, including shoes, from the school. Other popular climbing locations include **Joshua Tree National Monument** in southern California, **Lover's Leap** at South Lake Tahoe, and **Castle Crags State Park** near Redding.

For mountaineers, California has a number of high peaks. Popular summits include 14,162-foot (4316-m) **Mount Shasta,** with 100-mile (160-km) views in all directions; **Mount Ritter** and **Mount Lyell,** on the eastern edge of Yosemite National Park; and **Mount Whitney,** reached from Whitney Portal off U.S. Highway 395.

Many of these peaks are reached by well-maintained trails, such as the state-long **Sierra Crest Trail,** part of the Pacific Crest Trail System. It is perhaps the backpacker's greatest challenge in North America, and there is a small brotherhood of trekkers who have completed the entire 2,600-mile (4,200-km) route from Mexico to Canada.

Whitney is just one of ten 4,000-meter peaks in the southern Sierra, a spectacular region labeled "The Range of Light" by naturalist John Muir. Their white granite wall rears up 10,000 feet (about 3,000 m) above Highway 395 and the Owens Valley. Just north is the equally picturesque **Mono Lake,** a unique volcanic region at the eastern, summer entrance to Yosemite park.

The high mountains of the Sierra spawn a number of excellent fishing rivers and streams, the best of them located on the eastern side. Stocked by government agencies, these rivers are famous for such tasty fish as the golden trout. In fall, the same areas boast excellent hunting, especially for deer.

The wild rivers that spill from the Sierra's western flank are known for a different kind of excitement: white-water. The **Kern River** in the south has long stretches of Class V rapids, regularly challenged by kayakers and commercial rafting companies. (A Class V river drops 60 feet per mile, or 11.3m per kilometer.) Heading north, the **Merced River, Tuolumne River, Stanislaus River, Carson River, American River** and **Yuba River** are all popular white-water locations for commercial rafting companies.

As these rivers fall into the foothills, they are contained in a series of lakes known for sailing, sailboarding, and water skiing. **Lake Isabella** in the south, and **Folsom Lake, Shasta Lake** and **Almanor Lake** in the north aré all popular recreation spots.

Tahoe's Playgrounds

California's most famous lake, however, is located on the Nevada border: **Lake Tahoe.** A giant expanse of water at an elevation of 6,279 feet (1,914 m), Tahoe can alternate quickly between perfect, glassy water-skiing conditions and big, ocean-like waves suitable for sailboards or large sailboats.

Tahoe is also California's winter recreation center – especially for skiing. California has more than 40 ski resorts, and 20 of them are centered around Lake Tahoe. **Squaw Valley** is famous as the site of the 1960 Winter Olympics, and is one of the most challenging ski resorts in North America. With a network of 32 lifts, including a 150-passenger cable car, the resort has an amazing uphill capacity of more than 47,000 skiers per hour. That allows management to guarantee a lift-like wait of no more than 10 minutes. Squaw spans 8,300 acres (3,360 hectares) on six mountains, all of them 8,000 to 9,000 feet (2,440 m to 2,710 m) high, and is surrounded by hotels, restaurants, and other full- service resort facilities.

Just south of Squaw Valley is the winter resort of **Alpine Meadows,** whose open bowls and modern snowmaking equipment help give it the longest ski season in the Sierra – from late November to late May. Catering to families, the 2,000-acre (800-hectare) resort boasts 13 lifts. Also on the north shore is **Northstar-at-Tahoe,** a newer alpine and nordic resort with 11 lifts and 1,700 acres (688 hectares) of skiing terrain.

Heavenly Valley, on Tahoe's south shore, offers incredible views over the lake. Everything here is superlatives: Spanning 20 square miles (54 sq km) along the California-Nevada border, it is North America's largest ski resort. Heavenly has Tahoe's highest elevation, 10,167-foot (3,099m) Monument Peak; the area's greatest vertical rise, 3,600 feet (1,100 m); its longest run, 5.5 miles (8.8 km); and the largest snowmaking capacity of any resort on the United States. The

24 lifts, including an aerial tramway, carry skiers to groomed open bowls or steep, unpacked powder runs.

Tahoe's other important area is **Kirkwood,** 30 miles (48 km) southwest of the lake off U.S. Highway 88. Along with Squaw the most challenging of area resorts, its 11 lifts serve 2,000 acres (800 hectares) of terrain. Its high elevation is 9,876-foot (3,010-m) **Thimble Peak**. Extensive nordic trails surround its base. Further south, along the Sierra's eastern slope, **Mammoth Mountain** is one of the continent's largest ski areas. It boasts 30 lifts and more than 150 trails, with a 3,300-foot (1-km) vertical drop.

While California's ski resorts are not as expansive as many European areas, they benefit from some of the world's best ski weather. Winter snowfall averages 33 feet (10 m), temperatures range from 23 °F to 41 °F (– 5 °C to + 5 °C), and four days out of every five are sunny. Storms that roll into the Sierra from the Pacific Ocean can be fierce, often leaving as much as 6 feet (2 m) of fresh snow. Southern California's ski resorts do not receive the same amount but they have the unique advantage of being only two hours' drive from the beach.

Cross-country skiing is also very popular in the Sierra, both in the back country and at established resorts. California has for long been a pioneer in nordic resorts; the best feature more than 190 miles (300 km) of groomed tracks, and extensive hut systems.

In most recreational areas, snowmobile rentals are also available. These motorized vehicles normally have their own areas, apart from the skiers.

With its series of excellent roads leading from low elevations to the "high country," the main attribute of California's mountain recreation land is accessibility. Californians may be beach people at heart, but they also have a deep appreciation of the spectacular peaks which tower so close at hand.

Right: The craggy solitude of Fletcher Peak.

HISPANIC SOCIETY

From music to art to magnificent Spanish missions, California is laced with Latino culture and society. Rich and vibrant, it has been a part of the state's character since the 17th century, when Spanish conquistadors and missionaries came from Mexico. Treaties, battles, trade, and business have integrated Hispanic culture into California.

Today, *La Raza,* as Latino society calls itself, is the youngest and fastest growing minority group in the state. A diverse mix of Mexican-Americans, Mexicans, Cubans, Puerto Ricans, and immigrants from Central America, they total 6.9 million people, or about 24 per cent of California's population. By 2030, population experts estimate, Latinos will be the largest ethnic group in the state, comprising some 38 per cent of the total population.

Largely urban and concentrated in *barrios*, or neighborhoods, Latino culture is alive. In San Francisco, the Mission District has been a vibrant and exciting Hispanic cultural center for centuries. East Los Angeles, with a population that is 90 per cent Latino, is the largest Hispanic community in the United States. In Fresno and other Central Valley cities, Latinos make up more than one-third of the population.

On cool summer nights, *mariachi* music plays in plazas and parks from Visalia to Los Angeles. Ballet Folklorico dance troupes perform traditional routines. Everywhere are emblems of the cultures and societies that comprise the rich fabric of Central America: the *rebozo* scarves of indigenous Mexicans, the brightly colored shawls of Guatemalan refugees, the delicious *papoosas,* filled tortillas, made by El Salvadoran chefs.

Right: Today, Hispanic culture has become an indelible feature of Californian art.

The mixture of old and new in Latino culture is most evident in the massive murals that decorate building walls in the *barrios.* Here, painted in brilliant colors, are exotic expressions of the Hispanic experience in California.

The Latino "establishment" is made up largely of families that have lived in California for generations. They own factories and businesses, serve in Congress, and are leaders and administrators in cities throughout the state.

But in many ways, this establishment is being eclipsed by waves of Hispanic immigrants and refugees crossing the U.S. border legally and illegally every day. These immigrants fuel California's economic engine, providing low-wage labor in fields, factories and service industries – in other words, doing jobs that most Californians would not take.

Despite the stereotypes of busboys, janitors, gardeners and maids, Hispanic immigrants are represented throughout the state's industries. They make parts for the U.S. Air Force's F-16 jet, stitch "Ocean Pacific" shirts, and even help mold artificial heart valves.

The immigrants renew the California dream with their vision of a better life. It is a dream shared by the first settlers, by Mexican immigrants following their revolution, by Depression-era refugees from America's Dust Bowl, by most everyone who has resettled in California.

The numerous immigrants that have crossed the border into the U.S. since the second decade of the 20th century also reinforced Mexican traditions in the Mexican-American communities. This renewed cultural impetus bore fruit in, among other things, the development of Mexican-American literature, particularly during the 1960's and 70's. Louis Valdez' *Teatro Campesino,* a Brechtian agitation-type of rural theatre, achieved renown internationally. This period saw the publication of several novels, like Richard Vásquez' *Chicano* (1970).

ASIAN SOCIETY

Along narrow streets, hawkers sell goods below flashing neon signs written in Chinese and Korean calligraphy. The frenetic energy, the shouts in foreign languages, the aroma of *dim sum* and other Oriental delicacies, suggest a scene some 5,000 miles distant.

But this is downtown San Francisco, Los Angeles, Sacramento, or many other Golden State cities. This is California as it enters the 21st century – what many are terming "the Pacific Century."

The state has long been known for its burgeoning Chinese American population. But in the last 20 years, California has experienced a population boom that has created a multi-ethnic Asian American society. Joining the Chinese are Japanese, Korean, Filipino, Vietnamese, Thai, Cambodian, Burmese, and other immigrants and refugees. The state was a major center for the relocation of Southeast Asian refugees in the 1970s. As a result, California's Asian American population nearly doubled from 1980 to 1990, to about 2.3 million. It is expected to increase another 50 per cent by the year 2000. By that time Asian Americans will account for about 11 per cent of the state's population.

Asian Americans are making their mark in the arts. Playwright David Henry Hwang, a Stanford University graduate, won the Tony Award for Broadway's best dramatic play of 1988 for *M. Butterfly*, and author Amy Tan, a San Francisco native, was honored with the 1989 National Book Award for *The Joy Luck Club*.

In virtually every California city, a plethora of ethnic Asian food is widely available. From Thai coconut curries to traditional Chinese dishes, the California palate is deliciously unique.

Despite their stereotype as the "model minority" in U.S. society, Asian Americans say they face real problems. Tremendous language barriers, a lack of social services, and anti-Asian racist sentiments are among the difficulties they face.

231

AGRICULTURE

From the rich alluvial soils of the Central Valley to the unique climate of the crucial coastal farmland, to the blooming desert of the Imperial and Coachella valleys, agriculture plays a major role in the life and times of Californians.

The state's agriculture also plays an important part in the worldwide food network, accounting for roughly 10 per cent of all types of food exported by the United States, including nearly all of its exported fruits and vegetables. Whether you live in London, Munich, New York or Los Angeles, there is a good chance that some of the produce in your refrigerator, or some of the grains in your cupboard, were grown in California.

The state's $13 billion agricultural industry is big business, and its power to produce is nothing less than awesome.

California farmers grow more than half of all U.S. fruits and vegetables, according to the California Department of Agriculture. They produce more than 250 different commodities, from almonds to cotton to kiwifruit. And they are America's producer of 48 of those commodities, the department reports.

Apricots, artichokes, asparagus, avocados, lemons, lettuce, navel oranges, peaches, rice, strawberries ... that is just a partial list of the products of which California farmers are the most prolific growers in the nation.

At least 500,000 people work on 80,000 farms throughout the whole of California, making it one of the state's leading employers. And according to a report by a leading California bank, agriculture's rippling effect on the rest of the state economy – from buying supplies to transporting crops – accounts for nearly $55 billion of California's $450 billion gross state product.

Right: Irrigation helps to increase productivity in the Central Valley.

A major part of this wealth has always been created by using cheap seasonal labor. When the missions started they domesticated Indians, later Chinese immigrants were used, and today there is a large reservoir of poor Mexicans waiting across the border to do almost anything for nearly nothing.

How big is California agriculture? Thirty-one million acres worth (12.5 million hectares), says the U.S. Soil Conservation Service. If all that farmland were brought together, it would create a nation larger than Czechoslovakia.

Though agriculture is big business, the relative size of a California farm is small: about 390 acres (158 hectares). Nearly all California farms are family-run.

But all is not peaches-and-cream on the farm. Four major resource problems confront the agriculture industry.

Looming largest is the rapid conversion of farmland to non-agricultural uses – about 44,000 acres (17,800 hectares) of cropland annually, according to estimates by the State Department of Water Resources.

Urbanization and the running wild leisure industry also soak up agriculture's dwindling water supply. In some areas, farmers may lose their water entirely, or find it priced exorbitantly high. But they themselves have used up enormous amounts of water on fields that used to be part of the desert before.

Erosion, though not as severe in California as in some other states, is affecting about 1.8 million of fertile cropland acres (730,000 hectares). Salinity problems, caused by minerals leaching into the earth, has cut soil production drastically, especially in the fertile Central Valley.

But groups such as The American Farmland Trust, a nonprofit agency dedicated to the conservation of productive agricultural land, have begun to mend the heart of California agriculture, so this most valuable of resources can continue to feed the world.

EARTHQUAKES

The sun rises over the Temblor Range, backlighting a twisted landscape of scarps and sags. In the low light and long shadows, the San Andreas Fault is clearly visible, rolling like a black highway through the desolate hills of the Carrizo Plains. It is an ironically beautiful sight.

Almost no one – neither residents nor visitors – actually views the fault. Yet nearly everyone has felt or heard about its devastating effects. The 1906 San Francisco earthquake and subsequent fire demolished the city. The 1971 Sylmar quake near Los Angeles did immense damage to hospitals, homes and freeways. And in 1989 northern California was again shaken by another deadly earthquake.

The fact is, most Californians share a shaky common ground. Coastal Californians, 80 per cent of the state's population, live on a landmass called the Pacific Plate, which like other continental plates is drifting on the surface of the globe. Geologists do not even consider it part of the continental United States.

The northbound Pacific Plate meets the North American Continental Plate at the San Andreas Fault. The two plates creep along past each other at an average of 2 inches (5 cm) a year – a rate which would situate Disneyland next to San Francisco's Fisherman's Wharf in 12 million years. But the creeping is not consistent.

Friction locks the Pacific Plate with the North American Plate at points near San Francisco and Los Angeles. But this does not prevent the plates from moving. Stress builds up, energy is released, and an earthquake results.

Following a quake, nervous Californians review their insurance policies, restock their shelves with emergency supplies, and make macabre jokes about the next Big One. The air waves and talk shows are full of complaints from civil servants and politicians that citizens ignore the threat of a big quake; citizens, for their part, insist that authorities are lax in enforcing building and safety codes.

233

After the shaking stops, following a few weeks of worry, most Californians relax and rationalize that the hurricanes, tornadoes, floods and blizzards that regularly plague other parts of North America are far worse than their occasional quake. After all, the chances of dying in an earthquake are very remote, indeed: More people are murdered in a one-year period in Los Angeles County than have been killed in all the California quakes put together.

"Where were you during the last earthquake?" is a question Californians often ask each other. It is a query almost guaranteed to unveil a glimpse of the impact of the San Andreas Fault on the California psyche.

The fault can actually be viewed in several places. Near Los Angeles, at the edge of the Mojave Desert, Devil's Punchbowl County Park is full of brown rocks that have been tilted in manifold

Above: He is just getting out the word on earthquake danger.

ways by the quaking crust. The somersaulted sandstone formations resemble pulled taffy.

Another great place to study the fault is Point Reyes National Seashore, just north of San Francisco. Wave-torn rocks of the craggy coast match rocks in southern California's mountain ranges, more than 300 miles (480 km) south.

Plates forming the earth's crust do not always creep quietly past each other. At Point Reyes, visitors can take the Earthquake Nature Trail and observe creeks and fences that were re-arranged by the 1906 quake. There is also a spot where, according to legend, an unfortunate cow was swallowed up by the heaving earth, leaving only her tail waving above the ground.

How and why Californians choose to live in this land, where a big quake might someday demolish everything they hold dear, is a question that puzzles visitors and residents alike. Perhaps Californians are essentially as restless as the ground beneath their feet.

ENVIRONMENTAL ISSUES

For most of the 20th century, Californians have been significantly more innovative than most other Americans in designing solutions to environmental problems. A love of the state's beauty and natural resources, coupled with a technological creativity, has helped California citizens to tackle questions of water quality, air pollution, coastline destruction, and disposal of toxic wastes.

Most of the state's environmental woes begin with the fact that there are just too many people who want to share the "good life" in California. Even with an increase in traffic congestion, pollution and crime, California still symbolizes a version of life that is hard to resist.

Both critics and boosters of California agree that the state is on the brink of a great destiny. California is becoming the communications and financial center of the Pacific Rim – a vast multinational and economic entity encircling Pacific Ocean from Alaska to Tierra del Fuego to Australia to China to Siberia.

By the year 2000, it is estimated that 60 per cent of the world's consumers will live in the Pacific Rim region, which already leads the world in new technologies and natural resources. If this is so, the face of California – and the faces in California – will soon change further.

Some of the environmental issues facing the state include:

Air Quality: Southern California has some of the worst smog in the nation. An unabated influx of people means more cars and trucks spewing out exhaust fumes, and more factories emitting smoke. As a result, Californians must attempt to reverse environmental damage without shutting down the factories that propel the state's economy.

California already has the strictest air-pollution laws in the United States. Automobiles sold in California must meet more stringent emissions requirements than those produced in other states. "Smokestack laws" on factories are much more restrictive in California than anywhere else in the world. Still, there is a strong feeling that more must be done.

Some economists argue that transforming southern California into a place of breathable air and wonderful views might actually stimulate the economy, by attracting that currently stay away to avoid the smog.

Water: The state has a vast water-supply system. Often, water travels several hundred miles through aqueducts, reservoirs and pipes before it gets to someone's home. Ecological battles often take place between northern Californians, who have the water, and southern Californians, who need it.

Another battle is raging between the huge agricultural corporations in the Central Valley and the growing urban areas on the coast. Agribusiness uses an enormous amount of water to grow such crops as cotton, which urban dwellers argue could easily be grown elsewhere. Farmers, with the use of large volumes of cheap water, heavily irrigate land that would otherwise be unfit for agriculture. The use of pesticides by large-scale farmers contaminates the water supply, and contamination is very costly to clean.

Growth: In communities across California, a "slow growth" movement is gathering steam. Liberal environmentalists are uniting with more conservative homeowners to pass laws that restrict commercial and residential building.

These movements reflect the concern of the average Californian with the environmental quality of his or her daily life. Even the most politically apathetic can be rallied for an environmental cause if it hits close to home.

Nature: It would seem, however, that many Californians are still not conscious enough of the active role they themselves and their life-style play in the destruction of the natural environment. The booming

leisure industry in the gold-sand-sunshine state of California is doing as much damage to the natural basis of life there as production industry.

Not only in Palm Springs, but all around the state, hundreds of golf courses are kept lush and green with the help of irrigation. Far removed from the natnatural environment, they document devastation at the hand of man – if they are looked at from this point of view.

Other leisure activities and sports cause similar damage. The unrestrained development of ski resorts is leading here, as elsewhere, to ecological catastrophe: Slopes are eroded and melting snow washes fertile upper layers of soil away into the valleys.

Ever sturdier cross-country vehicles mean that millions of people are now moving about over all kinds of "inhospitable" terrain. They destroy the habitat of plants and animals; oil and exhaust fumes

pollute the air and the ground; trash becomes a major problem. Even in the nature reserves and national parks most people get about in cars. Many never leave their vehicles at all, preferring to stay in the convoy of motorized "naturelovers" smoothly passing through dying forests.

Censure has to be mitigated somewhat due to the almost complete lack of a viable alternative in the shape of public transport. The basic assumption that freedom in California is best enjoyed with absence of state interference quite simply means that each individual is free to destroy the basis of life for one an all.

Most visitors to California also come to enjoy the immense recreational facilities the sunshine state has to offer, and so contribute to the ecological problems. If California is to survive as a vacation state, the trend of the nineties must be not only to think about more gentle forms of tourism but also to apply them. Even if this means doing away with the biggest absurdities of the leisure industry.

Above: Wind to watts, why not? Right: Motorbike culture is big in the state.

THE TREND-SETTERS

With a nickname like "LaLa Land", it is no wonder visitors have trouble taking Los Angeles seriously. Strangers have trouble seeing what makes Angelenos tick, let alone understanding how theirs can be a trend-setting city. For one thing, the tourists' perception depends upon which part of the metropolis they happen to see. And much the same is true of the San Francisco Bay Area.

Metropolises as spread out and as diverse as Los Angeles and San Francisco take time to get to know. Because public transportation is limited, especially in L. A., a car is essential. Angelenos who can afford it have one car per driver. They think nothing of driving an hour in any direction to go out for dinner. They often choose to drive rather than walk short distances, in spite of the city's perennially pleasant weather.

Southern California's sunny Mediterranean climate colors both the skin and the range of activities enjoyed year-round. To the casual observer, L. A. is the land of surfers, beautiful bodies and pretty faces. Why curl up with a good book, they ask, if the sun is shining, or if disco music sets your feet tapping? Even *The Los Angeles Times* has come up with a new "Quick Read" section, designed for the skimmer of the nineties.

California is still a frontier society, energetic, accepting and pioneering. Spanish *padres* built missions and called California home. Cattle ranchers settled in the San Fernando Valley and along the coast. Chinese came to build railroads and stayed to settle what are now two of the three largest Chinatowns in the United States. Japanese tended the fields; now they have a full-blown cultural center in Little Tokyo. Italians loved the warm California sun and planted grapes.

Scandinavians and Germans settled near the mountains in La Crescenta and Pasadena. Seafaring Yugoslavs and Portuguese sailed into the port of San Pedro and stayed. Hispanics came from Mexico, Central and South America. Re-

fugees from Vietnam and the Middle East enriched the mix. All added their own cultural and culinary spice.

This spicy mix is as important to California cooking as freshness and natural flavors. Trend-setting chefs – culinary pioneers – combine cuisines into individual melting pots: French-Vietnamese or Franco-Japanese, Thai-Italian, and Mexican-American.

At home in black tie or blue jeans, Californians adore their land of extremes. The glitz and opulence of Beverly Hills and Bel Air stand in strong contrast to the poverty of Watts and inner-city Oakland, and the rugged beauty of the Big Sur coast. L. A.'s Melrose Avenue is yet another world – some say it is more like outer space – bustling with a younger generation bent on making a life style statement. Oranges and avocados hang like exotic decorations on the trees of southern California.

Above: Classic cars attract a serious collectors' market – for those who can afford them.

Like the San Andreas Fault beneath it, Los Angeles and San Francisco have always been moving and shifting, creating something new. Change is the only constant. Living here is easy and exciting as if it were determined by the next eruption. Since the early days of the movies, California has set fads – often shallow, usually short-term. "Tinsel Town" (Hollywood) was looked to for idols. One decade it was Betty Grable and her shapely legs; the next, it was gravel-voiced John Wayne. Then came The Beach Boys, their songs praising California girls and reflecting the surfing cult. Soon, along came the hula hoop. Not surprisingly, the Los Angeles area leads the world as a center for creative sports toys, such as skateboards and roller blades.

But somewhere along the way, California came of age. During the 1980s, new sophistication brought the state to a position of setting trends with more substance. California is a leader in many fields because it is one of the few places on earth that dares to cross disciplines.

In other parts of the world, people may be easily compartmentalized. Californians draw on the resources of disciplines other than their own. Creativity is not reserved for artists alone; free thinking may also be the realm of scientists and businessmen.

Dr. Paul McCready is an example of a scientist who crosses disciplines. With a team of scientists, artists, engineers and athletes, he expanded his field of aerodynamics and physics by building a man-powered plane that could do figure-eights and fly across the English Channel. Gliders were not supposed to be able to do that. McCready's work with students from all over the world led him to feel that California students have a definite creative edge for thinking all around a problem in order to solve it.

In California, children are taught to be seen *and* heard, even though it may be hard on adults. This generation of free-thinkers and skeptics is now luring other creative people to California.

In the future, L. A. will continue to be a leader in the arts. Dorothy "Buffy" Chandler showed the way when she single-handedly set out to endow a music center for Los Angeles in the early 1960s. Peter Hemmings, director of the recently formed Los Angeles Music Center Opera, now predicts a 24-week opera season for the mid-nineties.

Look for Hollywood to remain in the seat of power for movie-making. With big business running the industry, the emphasis will continue to be on marketing rather than artistic excellence. But the graying of the United States will bring more movies with an adult story line, not just hype for the youth market.

More viewers will defect from network to cable television. Major stars will fight to make cable movies. Pay-per-view TV will replace movie theaters. Foreign-language programming and ethnic productions will increase. Going with this same trend, Peter Sellers, director of the L. A.

Festival, foresees ethnic and foreign art becoming more prevalent in California. Art collectors may donate money to museums, but they will only lend their art.

The pursuit of fitness is here to stay, featuring low-impact aerobics and a return to more traditional activities like walking and bicycling. Smaller families will look to do things together. Expect a return to nature, children dining with their parents at nice restaurants, and vacationing together. Long weekend getaways by car will become more popular.

Home entertainment, and informal dining with friends at neighborhood restaurants, will increase. Snobby, upscale restaurants will meet lean times as diners show a preference for comfortable local restaurants with excellent food. Iced tea will be the beverage of the nineties: no fat, no calories. Comfort foods and microwave ovens are in, along with Eastern Bloc-style peasant food. Fat substitutes will eliminate dessert eaters' guilt. Look for a return to simplicity in cooking – moderation but not deprivation.

Factory outlets will flourish, pinching department store sales. More people will work out of home offices, with facsimile (fax) transmission replacing mail service. Videophones might be commonplace.

The metropolitan area will continue to expand as a financial and banking center because of its orientation toward the Pacific Rim. There will be more foreign investment, both residential and commercial. Because of the high cost of living, it will be harder to attract mid-level professionals. Many areas will become bipolar as the middle class gets squeezed out. Los Angeles already is second in the nation in the number of renters versus home owners.

Entering the nineties, California is bursting with ideas and energy. A large segment of the population is well educated, dares to cross disciplines, has leisure time and money to spend. That adds up to a truly creative mix.

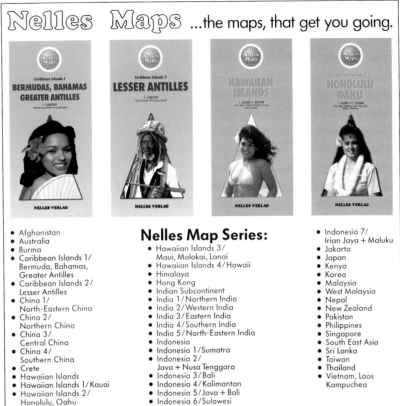

Nelles Maps ...the maps, that get you going.

Nelles Map Series:

- Afghanistan
- Australia
- Burma
- Caribbean Islands 1/ Bermuda, Bahamas, Greater Antilles
- Caribbean Islands 2/ Lesser Antilles
- China 1/ North-Eastern China
- China 2/ Northern China
- China 3/ Central China
- China 4/ Southern China
- Crete
- Hawaiian Islands
- Hawaiian Islands 1/Kauai
- Hawaiian Islands 2/ Honolulu, Oahu
- Hawaiian Islands 3/ Maui, Molokai, Lanai
- Hawaiian Islands 4/Hawaii
- Himalaya
- Hong Kong
- Indian Subcontinent
- India 1/Northern India
- India 2/Western India
- India 3/Eastern India
- India 4/Southern India
- India 5/North-Eastern India
- Indonesia
- Indonesia 1/Sumatra
- Indonesia 2/ Java + Nusa Tenggara
- Indonesia 3/Bali
- Indonesia 4/Kalimantan
- Indonesia 5/Java + Bali
- Indonesia 6/Sulawesi
- Indonesia 7/ Irian Jaya + Maluku
- Jakarta
- Japan
- Kenya
- Korea
- Malaysia
- West Malaysia
- Nepal
- New Zealand
- Pakistan
- Philippines
- Singapore
- South East Asia
- Sri Lanka
- Taiwan
- Thailand
- Vietnam, Laos Kampuchea

CALIFORNIA
©Nelles Verlag GmbH, München 45
All rights reserved
ISBN 3-88618-369-6

First Edition 1991
Co-publisher for U.K.:
Robertson McCarta, London
ISBN 1-85365-220-2 (for U.K.)

Publisher:	Günter Nelles	**DTP-Exposure:**	Printshop Schimann, Pfaffenhofen
Chief Editor:	Dr. Heinz Vestner		
Project Editor:	John Gottberg	**Color**	
Editor in charge:	F. J. Krücker	**Separation:**	Priegnitz, München
Cartography:	Nelles Verlag GmbH, Dipl. Ing. C.P. Waider Dipl. Ing. S. Stetter	**Printed by:**	Gorenjski Tisk, Kranj, Yugoslavia

- 01 -

TABLE OF CONTENTS

PREPARATION

Arrival Formalities

Customs and immigration formalities are completed at the first point of arrival in the United States, even though it may be only an intermediate stop en route. If, for example, a flight from London to Los Angeles stops in New York, customs and immigration procedures will take place in New York. Baggage will be put back on the plane and delivered in Los Angeles at domestic baggage carousels.

Immigration/Visas: A visitor visa and valid passport are required for entry into the United States. Consult the U.S. Embassy or Consulate nearest you for specific requirements from your country.

Customs: Visitors to the United States are allowed to bring with them duty-free: 300 cigarettes, 50 cigars, and one quart (0.946 liter) of wine or other alcoholic beverages. Remember that items such as cigars from Cuba are prohibited from entering the USA, even though some customs offficials don't seem to notice.

All produce, plant materials and wild animals are subject to border inspection by the State Department of Food and Agriculture, to determine their admissibility under quarantine laws. Fresh fruits and meats typically are forbidden entry. Dogs must have been certified as vaccinated against rabies within the previous year.

Climate

California's climate varies from dry and subtropical in the south, to wet and temperate along the northern coast, to subarctic in the high Sierra Nevada.

In Los Angeles, summer temperatures typically range in the mid 80s Fahrenheit (high 20s Celsius); January is the coldest month, with an average high of 65 ˚F (18 ˚C) and night-time lows in the mid 40s (5-10 ˚C). Light rainfall is most common from January to March; it rarely rains in summer, when the city's notorious smog is at its worst.

The same pattern prevails in San Diego and along the Central Coast, although sea breeze keeps summer temperatures a bit cooler. East of the Los Angeles basin, however, things really heat up – Death Valley has average July highs of 116 ˚F (47 ˚C), Palm Springs 108 ˚F (42 ˚C). Precipitation in the desert can be as low as 2 inches (50 mm) a year. The Central Valley is only a few degrees cooler, with only slightly more rainfall.

Nineteenth century author Mark Twain once deadpanned about the year's worth of weather he suffered in one week in San Francisco. Bay Area weather can indeed be very fickle, due in large part to the fogs that role through the Golden Gate on a regular if whimsical basis. Temperatures range in the 60s F (15-20 ˚C) most of the year, even mid summer. Winter chills stay close to 50 ˚F (10 ˚C). Rain can fall any time, though June through October is the driest period. San José, at the south end of the bay, avoids the fogs and gets notably warmer in summer, cooler in winter.

North of the Bay Area, in the redwood country of the far north coast, year-round temperatures remain in the 50-68 ˚F (10-20 ˚C) range of San Francisco – but rains may exceed 100 inches (2500 mm) annually. The High Sierra is used to warm summers and cold winters. Lake Tahoe, for instance, is typically 80 ˚F (27 ˚C) on a warm July day, but a mere 15 ˚F (– 9 ˚C) on a cold January night. Most of the precipitation falls in the form of voluminous winter snows.

Clothing

What you wear will depend upon where you plan to go, and what season you plan to travel. If your trip will keep you in Southern California in the summer, a pair of cotton slacks and a sweater (for evening wear) should be sufficient to accompany your shorts and T-shirts. If your travel plans include San Francisco, be prepared for any kind of weather:

Carry a jacket, and do not forget rain gear! If High Sierra adventures are a part of your itinerary, sturdy jeans and a warm coat are a must, even in summer. No matter where you are going, your number one priority should be a good pair of walking shoes. Limit your baggage to a single piece, if possible, to enjoy the freedom of traveling light.

Currency and Exchange

Most banks are open 10 a.m. to 3 p.m. Monday to Thursday, and 10 a.m. to 5:30 p.m. Friday.

Major banks and independent currency exchange bureaus will trade in major foreign currencies during banking hours. Los Angeles and San Francisco international airports have currency exchange offices in the international arrivals halls, with extended hours of operation to serve travelers.

Very few hotels or shops will accept foreign currency. Travelers checks in U.S. dollars offer the greatest convenience and safety for travelers. Plastic money, i.e. credit cards, are among the most common way of paying and are most respected. It is even possible to charge phone calls to your card, dial "0" for the operator.

A state sales tax of 6.5 per cent is added to the cost of many items, excluding grocery food. In addition, many cities and counties impose a tax of 6 per cent to 6.5 per cent on hotel rooms.

Health

There is no compulsory or government health plan in the United States. Therefore, travelers should purchase travel and health insurance to cover them in the event of any emergency.

Major hospitals all have 24-hour emergency rooms, and most cities have urgent care clinics that serve visitors as well as locals. Pharmacies often are open until 9 p.m. or later. In case of a medical emergency, phone 911 and request an ambu-lance. The water is safe to drink wherever you stay.

Hospitals and Medical Centers

San Francisco area: Children's, 3700 California (Tel. 386-0830); Pacific Medical Center, 2320 Sacramento (Tel. 563-4321); San Francisco General, 1001 Potrero (Tel. 431-2800).

Los Angeles: Highland General, 1411 East 31. St., Oakland (Tel. 534-8055); Mount Diablo, Bacon and East St., Concord (Tel. 682-8200); Stanford University Medical Center, Palo Alto (Tel. 497-2300); Valley Medical, 751 South Bascom, San José (Tel. 408-279-5100).

Other: Cedar-Sinai Medical Center, 8100 Beverly Blvd., (Tel. 855-5000); Hollywood Presbiterian Medical Center, 1300 N. Vermont Ave., (Tel. 660-3530); UCLA, 10833 Le Conte Ave., (Tel. 825-3901).

TRAVELING TO CALIFORNIA

Air: Many – perhaps most – of the world's major airlines arrive and depart from California's two huge international airports at Los Angeles and San Francisco. In addition the airports at San Diego and Oakland also handle some international flights. You will also be asked to declare money exceeding $ 10.000 in whatever form and currency.

Sea: San Pedro (Los Angeles harbor), San Diego, and San Francisco are ports of call for major cruise lines plying routes across the Pacific, around the world, and from the U.S. East Coast and Caribbean via the Panama Canal.

Land: The U.S. rail system, *Amtrak,* plies national east-west routes to Oakland (for San Francisco) and Los Angeles, and a north-south route from San Diego to Seattle. *Greyhound* and *Trailways* both have extensive bus routes linking California with the rest of the North American continent. Those who drive their own vehicles can reach the state via America's extensive system of interstate freeways.

TRAVELING IN CALIFORNIA

Domestic Air Travel

Numerous large suburban airports in the greater Los Angeles and San Francisco areas take some of the pressure off the international airports by handling many domestic flights. They include Burbank, Long Beach, Ontario, The Orange County, and Palm Beach in Southern California; Concord and San José in the Bay Area. The international airports in San Diego and Oakland serve domestic flights as well. Fresno, Monterey, Sacramento, and Stockton are also linked with California and North American cities by *US Air, America West Airlines, Alaska Airlines,* and other carriers.

Local Transport

Taxis: In urban areas, taxis can usually be hailed from the street or found waiting outside major hotels and attractions. Otherwise, it is usually necessary to call in advance for pickup. Hotels and restaurants can do this for you. Taxis are reasonably priced for distances up to a few miles, but expensive for longer distances. Then, it is best to take a bus or rent a car.

Buses: All cities have good public transportation systems. Those in San Francisco, Los Angeles, and San Diego are discussed in "Guideposts" following those chapters.

Car Rental: Agencies are easily found at airports or in city centers. Rates vary from $40 to $80 a day, with weekend rates somewhat lower. Most agencies require that drivers be 21 years old; some insist they be 25, for insurance purposes. Drivers require a license valid in any country signator to the 1949 Geneva Agreement. Drivers also should carry a major credit card or be able to post a cash deposit (sometimes $600 or more) in lieu of a credit card.

Unless otherwise posted, the speed limit on California highways is 55 miles per hour (88 km per hour).

PRACTICAL TIPS

Accommodation

California has a wide range of accommodations at all levels of price and quality. From world-class luxury hotels, found in cities and resorts throughout the state, to lower-priced hotels, motels, bed-and-breakfast inns, youth hostels and campgrounds, the state is well equipped for all types of travelers.

Especially in summer and holiday periods, as well as during the winter season at ski resorts, it is important to book accommodation well in advance.

Hotel prices are higher in metropolitan areas. Rooms at luxury accommodations in San Francisco, Los Angeles, and San Diego often run well over $150 a night, and even moderately priced rooms may cost close to $100. In smaller cities outside the metropolises, the finest hotels are rarely priced much above $100, and motel rooms can often be found in the $40 to $50 range.

Bed-and-breakfasts (B&Bs) are found in all corners of California, but especially in the northern part of the state, from city cores to isolated rural sites. Most charge between $50 and $100 per night, although several are higher priced, and a few are true budget lodgings. The most detailed listing can be found in a free booklet published by the **California Office of Tourism,** P.O. Box 9278-T99, Van Nuys, CA 91409. Also write to these addresses for free booklets, reservations and referrals: **Bed and Breakfast Innkeepers of Northern California,** P.O. Box 7150, Chico, CA 95927; **Bed and Breakfast Innkeepers of Southern California,** P.O. Box 15425, Los Angeles, CA 90015-0385.

There are more than two dozen youth hostels in California, including three each in Los Angeles and San Diego, and America's largest hostel in San Francisco. Rates typically are $10 or less a night, with discounts to members of the

International Youth Hostel Association. For locations or membership, write to **American Youth Hostels,** 1332 I St. N.W., Washington, D.C. 20005.

Campers can write to the following agencies for information and advance reservations: **California State Park System,** P.O. Box 942896, Sacramento, CA 94296 (tel. 916-445-6647); an official guide to the parks can be obtained by mail for payment of $2 plus overseas postage. Western Region Information Office, **National Park Service,** Fort Mason, Bldg. 201, San Francisco, CA 94123 (tel. 415-556-0560). **USDA Forest Service,** 630 Sansome St., San Francisco, CA 94111 (tel. 415-556-0122). **California Travel Parks Association,** P.O. Box 5648, Auburn, CA 95604 (tel. 916-885-1624); a directory of private campgrounds can be obtained by mail for $2 plus overseas postage.

Alcohol

The legal drinking age is 21, so don't forget your legal ID! Alcohol can be purchased by the package in any licensed store, or by the drink in any licensed restaurant or other establishment.

Electricity

Electric current in the United States is 110-115 volts, 60 AC. Most hotels do *not* have direct-current converters.

Festivals

January: *1,* New Year's Day Yacht Regatta, San Diego Bay; Tournament of Roses Parade and Rose Bowl Game, Pasadena. *Late,* Fiddlers Contest, Cloverdale.

February: Laguna Beach Winter Festival, Laguna Beach; World Championship Crab Races, Crescent City. *Early,* Chinese New Year, Chinatown, San Francisco and Los Angeles. *Mid,* Mardi Gras, Olvera Street, Los Angeles; National Date Festival, Indio. *Late-mid March,* Whale Festival, Dana Point.

March: Camelia Festival, Sacramento; Daffodil Festival, San Francisco; Easter Seal Western Festival, Sacramento; Kite Festival, Ocean Beach, San Diego. *Mid,* St. Patrick's Day Parade, San Francisco, Los Angeles, San Diego. *19,* St. Joseph's Day, San Juan Capistrano (swallows arrive). *Late, or early April,* Junior Grand National Rodeo, San Francisco.

April: Asparagus Festival, Stockton; Fisherman's Fantasy, Bodega Bay; Lilac Festival, Palmdale; Rhododendron Festival, Eureka; Strawberry Festival, Oxnard; Wildflower Show, Julian. *Mid,* Cherry Blossom Festival, Japantown, San Francisco. *Late,* Mule Days, Bishop. *Late-early May,* Ramona Pageant, Hemet. *Late-late May,* Renaissance Pleasure Faire, Paramount Ranch, Santa Monica Mountains.

May: Bay-to-Breakers Race, San Francisco; Calaveras County Jumping Frog Jubilee, Angels Camp; Festival of the Sea, San Francisco; Renaissance Pleasure Faire, Agoura Hills; UCLA's Mardi Gras and Sidewalk Art & Craft Show, Westwood, Los Angeles. *Early,* Cinco de Mayo, Los Angeles (Olvera Street) and San José; Firemen's Muster, Columbia. *Mid,* Fiesta de la Primavera, Old Town, San Diego; La Purisima Mission Fiesta Celebration, Lompoc; Wine Festival, Paso Robles. *Late,* Corpus Christi Fiesta, Mission San Antonio de Pala, San Diego.

June: Asian Cultural Festival, Los Angeles; Beethoven Festival, San Francisco; Craft Heritage Fair, Los Angeles; Elizabethan Faire, Ojai; Gay Pride Week, San Francisco; Shasta District Fair, Mount Shasta; Southern California Exposition, San Diego; Whale Festival, San Pedro. *Early,* Ox Roast, Sonoma. *Mid,* Livermore Rodeo, Livermore; San Francisco Birthday Celebration. *Late-early July,* Del Mar Fair, San Diego. *Through September,* Solvang Theater Festival, Solvang.

July: Alameda County Fair, Pleasanton; Gilroy Garlic Festival, Gilroy (the motto here is, of course, participate or keep your distance); Humboldt County Fair, Ferndale; International Surf Festival, beach communities, Los Angeles; Malibu Festival of Arts and Crafts, Malibu; Marin County Fair, San Rafael; Merced Fair, Merced; Napa County Fair, Calistoga; Old Miner Days, Big Bear Lake; Orange County Fair, Costa Mesa; San Francisco Fair and Exposition, San Francisco; San Mateo County Fair, San Mateo; Santa Barbara County Fair, Santa Barbara; Solano County Fair, Vallejo; Sonoma County Fair, Santa Rosa. *Early,* Tapestry in Talent, San Jose. *Mid,* Bach Festival, Carmel; California Rodeo, Salinas; Easter in July Lily Festival, Smith River; Festival of the Bells, Mission San Diego de Alcala, San Diego. *Early through August,* Hollywood Bowl Summer Festival, Los Angeles; *Mid through August,* Festival of Arts and Pageant of the Masters, Laguna Beach.

August: America's Finest City Week, San Diego; Castro Street Fair, San Francisco; Central Coast Wine Festival, San Luis Obispo; International Sea Festival, Long Beach; Nisei Week, Little Tokyo, Los Angeles; San Bernardino County Fair, Victorville; San Fernando Valley Fair, Northridge; San Luis Obispo County Mid-State Fair, Paso Robles; Steinbeck Festival, Salinas; Wine Country Music Festivals, Napa and Sonoma valleys. *Early,* Old Spanish Days Fiesta, Santa Barbara. *Mid,* Renaissance Pleasure Faire, Novato. *Late,* California State Exposition, Sacramento. Festival of Monterey County Wine and Food, Salinas.

September: Aki Matsuri (Japanese Fall Festival), San Francisco; The Big Fresno Fair, Fresno; Bowlful of Blues, Ojai; Festival of Art, Santa Catalina Island; Grape Festival and National Wine Show, Lodi; Hispanic Heritage Week, Los Angeles; Kern County Fair, Bakersfield; Los Angeles County Fair, Pomona; Mexican Fiesta, Ojai; Russian River Jazz Festival, Guerneville; Scottish Gathering and Games, Santa Rosa; Seafood Festival, Crescent City. *6,* Los Angeles City Birthday, Olvera Street, Los Angeles. *Early,* Begonia Festival, Capitola, Monterey Bay; Festival of the Saws, Santa Cruz; Labor Day Rodeo, Bishop; Steam Threshing Bee, Red Bluff. *Mid,* Danish Days, Solvang. *Late,* Cabrillo Festival, Cabrillo National Monument, San Diego; Oktoberfest, Big Bear Lake.

October: Blessing of the Fishing Fleet, San Francisco; Festival of the Californias, San Diego; Founders Day, San Diego Zoo; Golden Days, Azusa; Healdsburg Harvest Hoedown, Healdsburg; Pumpkin Festival, Half Moon Bay. *Mid,* California International Air Show, Salinas; Columbus Day Parade and Celebration, San Francisco; Fleet Week, San Francisco. *Late,* Exotic-Erotic Ball, San Francisco (in connection with Halloween). *Late-early November,* Grand National Rodeo, Horse Show and Livestock Exposition, San Francisco. **November:** Fiesta de la Cuadrilla, San Diego; Harvest Festival and Christmas Crafts Market, San Francisco; Kool Jazz Festival, San Francisco and Oakland. *Early,* Death Valley Encampment, Death Valley National Monument. *Mid,* Hannukah Celebration, Union Square, San Francisco. *Late,* Hollywood Christmas Parade, Los Angeles; Mother Goose Parade, El Cajon. *Through December,* Dickens Christmas Fair, Fort Mason, San Francisco.

December: Christmas at Pioneer Village, Bakersfield; Day at the Docks, San Diego. *Early,* Parade of Lights, Oxnard. *Mid to Late,* Christmas Light Boat Parade, San Diego; Christmas Tree Lane, Altadena; Las Posadas, El Pueblo de Los Angeles State Historic Park and Mission San Luis Rey, San Diego; Old Town Christmas Parade, San Diego.

Holidays

California observes all U.S. national holidays. Government offices and banks are closed on these days. If a holiday falls on a Saturday, the preceding Friday is a holiday. If a holiday falls on a Sunday, the following Monday is celebrated as a holiday. The exceptions are Independence Day, Christmas and New Year's Day, which are held on the actual holiday dates.

Official holidays in 1990:

Jan. 1	New Year's Day
Jan. 15	Martin Luther King's Birthday
Feb. 12	Abraham Lincoln's Birthday
Feb. 19	George Washington's Birthday
Apr. 13	Good Friday
Apr. 15	Easter
May 28	Memorial Day
July 4	Independence Day
Sept. 3	Labor Day
Oct. 8	Columbus Day
Nov. 11	Veterans Day
Nov. 22	Thanksgiving
Dec. 25	Christmas

Information

For visitor information in smaller towns, find the local chamber of commerce either in the telephone book or by asking at your hotel desk. Americans are generally friendly and willing to help, so you might get information in the street or at the local diner.

In San Francisco, try the Convention and Visitors' Bureau at Hallidie Plaza (open from Monday to Friday from 9 a.m. to 5 p.m., Saturdays from 10 p.m. to 2 p.m. and Sundays from 9 a.m. to 3 p.m.). The Bureau has a partner in Los Angeles on Sixth and Flower Street in the Atlantic Richfield Plaza (213) 628-3101 and in the Pacific Federal Building on Hollywood Boulevard, Tel. (213) 628-5857 (24 hrs.).

Newspapers and Periodicals

California's leading daily newspapers include the highly regarded *Los Angeles Times* (morning), *The Los Angeles Herald Examiner* (afternoon), *The San Francisco Chronicle* (morning), *The San Francisco Examiner* (afternoon), *The San Diego Union* (morning), *The San Diego Tribune* (afternoon), and *The Sacramento Bee* (morning).

California Magazine is a monthly that features the entire state. Each major city has its own monthly magazine, as well as weekly newspapers featuring local issues, politics and entertainment.

Photography

Photography is permitted almost everywhere but restricted areas of military installations and certain places of worship. When in doubt, ask. Film is readily available and reasonably priced.

Postal Services

Mail service is very reliable; your hotel desk may even sell stamps and be able to mail your letters and post cards for you. General delivery service (poste restante) is available at central city post offices.

Postage rates may rise in 1991, but in 1990, mail within the United States and to Mexico cost 25 cents per ounce; to Canada, 30 cents per ounce; to most destinations in Europe and Asia, 45 cents per half ounce. Post card rates are several cents less. Large numbers of books can be sent in book-bags at special surface rates, but it is wise to first pack the books in cardboard boxes leaving them open for inspection.

Restaurants

There is no shortage of places to eat – San Francisco, it is said, has the highest concentration of restaurants (per capita) of any city in the world, and Los Angeles must be approaching that rate.

Shopping

Most downtown stores and shops are open from 10:00 a.m. to 5:30 p.m. Mondays through Saturdays, but there are exceptions. Many stores, particularly department and apparel stores, are open one or more evenings a week (typically Friday, but check locally), and often on Sundays.

Statistics on California

Area: 158,706 sq mi (411,047 sq km); third largest in U.S.A. *Population:* (1989 estimate) 28,607,000; first in U.S.A. *Capital:* Sacramento, 340,483. *Other major cities:* Los Angeles, 3,402,342; San Diego, 1,073,466; San Francisco, 753,927; San José, 732,022; Long Beach, 413,670; Oakland, 367,782; Fresno, 294,695; Anaheim, 251,045; Santa Ana, 246,925. *Nickname:* The Golden State. *Highest point:* Mount Whitney, 14,494 feet (4418 m). *Lowest point:* Badwater, Death Valley, -282 feet (-86 m).

Time

California is in the Pacific Time Zone, eight hours earlier than Greenwich Meridien Time. When the time is 6 p.m. in London and 1 p.m. in New York, it is 10 a.m. in California.

Tipping

Tipping is an American custom so deeply ingrained in the modern hospitality industry that it is considered rude not to do so.

A minimum of 15 per cent of the bill, and up to 20 per cent if service warrants, is normally paid to restaurant waitpersons. Bartenders, taxi drivers, barbers, hair dressers, and other service industry people expect similar tips. Airport porters and hotel bellman should be paid at least 50 cents a bag; valets should get no less than $1 for retrieving your car from a parking lot. Chambermaids should be tipped $1 a day for housecleaning, if you stay more than a day at a hotel.

Tours

Dozens of tour operators serve California from its major cities. Leading operators with tours available in most major foreign languages include:

American Express, 222 Kearny St., Suite 608, San Francisco, CA 94108 (Tel. 415-981-6293); 900 Wilshire Blvd., Suite 1020, Los Angeles, CA 90017 (Tel. 213-488-1331).

Americantours International, 278 Post St., San Francisco, CA 94108 (Tel. 415-391-5209); 9800 Sepulveda Blvd., Los Angeles, CA 90045 (Tel. 213-641-9953).

Gray Line, 350 Eighth St., San Francisco, CA 94103 (Tel. 415-558- 7300); 6541 Hollywood Blvd., Suite 210, Los Angeles, CA 90028 (Tel. 213-481-2121); 1670 Kettner Blvd., San Diego, CA 92101 (Tel. 619-231-9922).

Weights and Measures

As with all of the United States, California has yet to convert to the metric system of measurement.
Thus:
1 inch = 2.54 centimeters
12 feet = 1 inch = 0.3048 meter
5,280 miles = 1 foot = 1.609 meters
3,560 acres = 1 sq ft = 0.4047 hectare
640 sq mi = 1 acre = 2.59 sq km
1 pint = 0.4732 liter
2 pints = 1 quart = 0.9463 liters
4 quarts = 1 gallon = 3.7853 liters
1 ounce = 28.3495 grams
16 ounces = 1 pound = 453.59 grams

Temperatures are measured in Fahrenheit. To get the Celsius value use the following formula: $°F - 32 \times 9{:}5 = °C$. Here is a chart to give you an approximate idea of the Celsius values:

$-4 °F = -20 °C$
$0 °F = -18 °C$
$15 °F = -10 °C$
$32 °F = 0 °C$
$50 °F = 10 °C$
$68 °F = 20 °C$
$75 °F = 23 °C$
$80 °F = 27 °C$
$90 °F = 32 °C$
$100 °F = 38 °C$

ADDRESSES

Foreign Consulates and Missions
(Telephone area codes are 213 for Los Angeles, 415 for San Francisco.)

Argentina. *LA:* 350 S. Figueroa St. (Tel. 687-8884). *SF:* 870 Market St. (Tel. 982-3050). **Australia.** *LA:* 3550 Wilshire Blvd. (Tel. 380-0980). *SF:* 256 Sutter St. (Tel. 986-4040). **Barbados.** *LA:* 3440 Wilshire Blvd. (Tel. 380-2198). **Belgium.** *LA:* 3921 Wilshire Blvd. (Tel. 385-8116). **Bolivia.** *SF:* 870 Market St. (Tel. 495-5173). **Brazil.** *LA:* 5900 Wilshire Blvd. (Tel. 937-4044). *SF:* 300 Montgomery St. (Tel. 981-8170). **Canada.** *LA:* 510 W. Sixth St. (Tel. 627-9511). *SF:* 1 Maritime Plaza (Tel. 981-2670). **Chile.** *LA:* 619 S. Olive St. (Tel. 624- 6357). *SF:* 870 Market St. (Tel. 982-7662). **China.** *SF:* 1450 Laguna St. (Tel. 563-4885). **Colombia.** *SF:* 870 Market St. (Tel. 362-0080). **Costa Rica.** *SF:* 870 Market St. (Tel. 392-8488). **Denmark.** *LA:* 3440 Wilshire Blvd. (Tel. 387-4277). *SF:* 1 Market Plaza (Tel. 781-1309). **Dominican Republic.** *LA:* 548 S. Spring St. (Tel. 627-3361). *SF:* 870 Market St. (Tel. 982-5144).

Ecuador. *LA:* 548 S. Spring St. (Tel. 628-3014). *SF:* 870 Market St. (Tel. 391-4148). **Egypt.** *SF:* 3001 Pacific Ave. (Tel. 346-9700). **El Salvador.** *LA:* 408 S. Spring St. (Tel. 680-4343). *SF:* 870 Market St. (Tel. 781-7924). **Finland.** *SF:* 120 Montgomery St. (Tel. 981-4656). **France.** *LA:* 9401 Wilshire Blvd., Beverly Hills (Tel. 272-2661). *SF:* 540 Bush St. (Tel. 397-4330). **Germany (West).** *LA:* 6435 Wilshire Blvd. (Tel. 852-0441). *SF:* 601 California St. (Tel. 981-4250). **Great Britain.** *LA:* 3701 Wilshire Blvd. (Tel. 385-7381). *SF:* 120 Montgomery St. (Tel. 981-3030). **Greece.** *LA:* 611 W. Sixth St. (Tel. 626-6696). *SF:* 2441 Gough St. (Tel. 775-2102). **Guatemala.** *SF:* 8870 Market St. (Tel. 781-0118). **Guyana.** *LA:* 2950 Los Feliz Blvd. (Tel. 666-3243). **Haiti.** *SF:*

430 Monterey Blvd. (Tel. 469-5629). **Honduras.** *LA:* 548 S. Spring St. (Tel. 623-2301). *SF:* 870 Market St. (Tel. 392-0076). **Hong Kong.** *LA:* 350 S. Figueroa St. (Tel. 622-3194). *SF:* 160 Sansome St. (Tel. 989-5005).

Iceland. *LA:* 6290 Sunset Blvd. (Tel. 981-6464). **India.** *SF:* 540 Arguello Blvd. (Tel. 668-0662). **Indonesia.** *LA:* 645 S. Mariposa Ave. (Tel. 383-5126). *SF:* 351 California St. (Tel. 982-8966). **Ireland.** *LA:* 1821 Wilshire Blvd. Santa Monica (Tel. 829-0081). *SF:* 681 Market St. (Tel. 392-4214). **Israel.** *LA:* 6380 Wilshire Blvd. (Tel. 651-5700). *SF:* 693 Sutter St. (Tel. 775-5535). **Italy.** *LA:* 1801 Avenue of the Stars (Tel. 879-0950). *SF:* 2590 Webster St. (Tel. 931-4924). **Japan.** *LA:* 250 E. First St. (Tel. 624-8305). *SF:* 1601 Post St. (Tel. 921-8000). **Jordan.** *LA:* 2049 Century Park East (Tel. 557-2243). **Kenya.** *LA:* 9100 Wilshire Blvd., Beverly Hills (Tel. 274-6635). **Korea (South).** *LA:* 5455 Wilshire Blvd. (Tel. 931-1331). *SF:* 3500 Clay St. (Tel. 921-2251). **Lebanon**. *LA:* 1680 Vine St. (Tel. 462-5384). **Liberia.** *LA:* 4757 S. Broadway (tel. 232-2535). **Luxembourg.** *LA:* 516 Avondale Ave. (Tel. 394-2532).

Malaysia. *LA:* 350 S. Figueroa St. (Tel. 617-1000). *SF:* 2 Embarcadero Center (Tel. 421-6570). **Malta.** *LA:* 5428 E. Beverly Blvd. (Tel. 685-6365). **Mexico.** *LA:* 125 Paseo de la Plaza (Tel. 624-3261). *SF:* 870 Market St. (Tel. 392-5554). **Monaco.** *SF:* 2209 Pacific Ave. (Tel. 362-5050). **Nepal.** *SF:* 3630 Jackson St. (Tel. 751- 3630). **Netherlands.** *LA:* 3460 Wilshire Blvd. (Tel. 380-3440). *SF:* 601 California St. (Tel. 981-6454). **New Zealand.** *LA:* 10960 Wilshire Blvd., Westwood (Tel. 477- 8241). *SF:* 1 Maritime Plaza (tel. 788-7430). **Nicaragua**. *LA:* 548 S. Spring St. (Tel. 629-4367). *SF:* 870 Market St. (Tel. 391-4738). **Nigeria.** *SF:* 369 Hayes St. (Tel. 864-8001). **Norway.** *LA:* 350 S. Figueroa St. (Tel. 626-0338). *SF:* 1 Embarcadero

Center (Tel. 986- 0766). **Panama.** *SF:* 1880 Wawona St. (Tel. 566-4144). **Paraguay.** *LA:* 4 Alegria St., Irvine (Tel. 714-731-7685). *SF:* 870 Market St. (Tel. 982-9424). **Peru.** *LA:* 1212 Wilshire Blvd. (Tel. 975-1152). *SF:* 870 Market St. (Tel. 362-7136). **Philippines.** *LA:* 2975 Wilshire Blvd. (Tel. 387- 5321). *SF:* 447 Sutter St. (Tel. 433-6666). **Portugal.** *SF:* 3298 Washington St. (Tel. 346-3400).

Romania. *LA:* 350 S. Figueroa St. (Tel. 614-1104). **Senegal.** *SF:* P.O. Box 850, Mill Valley (Tel. 383-8264). **Singapore**. *LA:* 350 S. Figueroa St. (Tel. 617-7358). *SF:* 251 Post St. (Tel. 391-8476). **South Africa.** *LA:* 9107 Wilshire Blvd., Beverly Hills (Tel. 858-0380). **Soviet Union.** *SF:* 2790 Green St. (Tel. 922-6642). **Spain.** *LA:* 5455 Wilshire Blvd. (Tel. 931-1284). *SF:* 2080 Jefferson St. (Tel. 922-2995). **Sweden.** *LA:* 10960 Wilshire Blvd., Westwood (Tel. 473-0901). *SF:* 1960 Jackson St. (Tel. 775-6104). **Switzerland.** *LA:* 3440 Wilshire Blvd. (Tel. 388- 4127). *SF:* 235 Montgomery St. (Tel. 788-2272). **Taiwan.** *LA:* 350 S. Figueroa St. (Tel. 628-8761). *SF:* 166 Geary St. (Tel. 989-8677). **Thailand.** *LA:* 3450 Wilshire Blvd. (Tel. 380-4400). **Tunisia.** *SF:* 3401 Sacramento St. (Tel. 922-9222). **Uruguay.** *SF:* 870 Market St. (Tel. 982- 3730). **Venezuela.** *LA:* 1052 W. Sixth St. (Tel. 977-0996). *SF:* 870 Market St. (Tel. 421-5172). **Western Samoa.** *LA:* 3422 Madera Ave. (Tel. 666-2154). **Yugoslavia.** *SF:* 1375 Sutter St. (Tel. 776-4941).

Tourist Offices

Inquiries on the state are fielded by the **California Office of Tourism,** 1121 L St., Suite 103, Sacramento, CA 95814 (Tel. 916- 322-1397). The office can provide a great deal of free information.

Cities have their own visitors bureaus, all of which are extremely helpful. Names, addresses and telephone numbers are listed in the "Guideposts" sections following each chapter.

CONTRIBUTORS

John Gottberg, editor, is a free-lance travel writer based in Seattle. He is the author of five travel books and co-author of another. An inveterate traveler, he has been door-to-door salesman in Australia, a carpenter in Sweden, honky-tonk piano player in New Zealand, and bartender in Amsterdam. He has also been a reporter for such newspapers as the *Seattle Post-Intelligencer* and *The Honolulu Advertiser,* and an academic fellow in Hawaii.

Robert Holmes, this book's principal photographer, is an internationally renowned cameraman and the 1990 Society of American Travel Writers photographer of the year. Originally an urban planner in Nottingham, England, Holmes first came to California in the 1970s. He now lives in Mill Valley, Marin County.

Fred Gebhart is a political science graduate of the University of California-Santa Barbara. He worked as a tax auditor for the Internal Revenue Service before serving as a Peace Corps volunteer in the West African nation of Senegal and fine-tuning his infatuation with scuba diving. He has lived in San Francisco as writer-photographer since 1981.

Elizabeth Hansen lives in La Jolla. In addition to her home town, Hansen focuses much of her writing on Australia and New Zealand. Her previous books are *The Woman's Travel Guide to New Zealand, Bed & Breakfast New Zealand,* and *Frommer's Australia.*

Gail Harrington is a managing editor of *Motor Home* magazine. She travels more comfortably than her ancestors, covering destinations in America and abroad.

Barbara Horngren is a former travel editor of *The Christian Science Monitor* whose work now appears in a wide variety of newspapers and magazines. She lives in Buena Park.

Mimi Kmet is the former editor of *Corporate Travel* magazine. A resident of

North Hollywood, she often writes on fitness and health subjects.

Maria Lenhart has covered many corners of California for Fondor's Guides and a variety of magazines and newspapers. She lives in Walnut Creek.

John McKinney is a Santa Barbara writer-editor active with the Sierra Club and other environmental organizations.

Shirley Miller is executive director of the Mexico West Travel Club in Bonita, Calif. She edits *Mexico West!*, a popular newsletter, and also writes and lectures extensively on Baja.

Chaco Mohler is a widely traveled outdoor writer-photographer, and a leading writer on skiing and windsurfing. A former graduate student at England's University of Kent, he is editor-in-chief of *Ski the Californias* magazine, a contributing editor to *Skiing* and *City Sports* magazines. He lives in Tahoe City.

Marty Olmstead is a staff writer for the *Marin Independent Journal* in Marin County, where he lives. A contributing editor to *San Francisco Focus*, he has co-authored two books on Florida and contributed to the *Gauklt Millau Guide to San Francisco*.

John Poimiroo is vice president of communications for the Yosemite Park and Curry Co. A widely published writer-photographer, Poimiroo is an outdoors addict who takes full advantage of his home in Yosemite National Park.

Cheri Rae is a native Californian who has lived in many parts of the state. Her most recent book is *East Mojave Desert: A Visitors Guide,* published in Santa Barbara, where she lives and works.

Peggy Rahn is a staff writer for the *Pasadena Star*. Rahn has traveled in North America and around the world to research stories on food and wine.

Morrison Shafroth is a free-lancer who came to San Francisco via the University of Vermont and newspapers in Montana, and Bangkok. Editor of *The Best of Marin* annual, he writes for *The San Francisco Examiner* and *San Francisco Business* magazine.

Yvonne Vollert writes for numerous gourmet and outdoor adverture magazines from her home in Agoura Hills.

Rick Browne, photographer, maintains his studio at his home in Scotts Valley, California.

PHOTOGRAPHERS